VISAS *for* Al Qaeda:

CIA HANDOUTS THAT ROCKED THE WORLD

J. Michael Springmann

AN INSIDER'S VIEW

Daena Publications LLC
Washington, DC

ISBN: 0990926206
ISBN 13: 9780990926207
Library of Congress Control Number: 2014919827
Daena Publications LLC, Washington DC

CONTENTS

"It is error alone which needs the support of government. Truth can stand by itself."

—Thomas Jefferson, *Notes on the State of Virginia.*

AUTHOR'S NOTE

J. Michael Resser's generosity and concern for principles made this work possible.

I wish to express my great appreciation for the example, encouragement, and assistance of Barbara Nimri Aziz, PhD; François Bringer; Habib; Andrew Kreig; Wayne Madsen; Richard Ray; Barrie Zwicker; and a retired European diplomat.

Additionally, I want to thank the Association of National Security Alumni, including Verne Lyon and David MacMichael, for giving me the opportunity to write something of my experiences for its magazine, *Unclassified*. Gratitude should also go to *Foreign Policy Journal*, *Global Outlook* (Canada), *Global Research* (Canada), *OpEdNews*, and *The Public Record*, for generously publishing several of my articles bearing on this publication's themes. I would like to acknowledge my pleasure at being able to express my views on the *Alex Jones Show*; BBC's *Newsnight*; CBC's Radio One program *Dispatches*; and James Corbett's *Corbett Report*. Giulietto Chiesa kindly had me interviewed for his movie *Zero*. Elizabeth Metz graciously let me speak at her 2010 Treason Conference in Valley Forge, Pennsylvania. If I've inadvertently omitted anyone who's given me the chance to raise these topics on their websites and radio shows, I apologize.

Dr. Aziz, David MacMichael, and Habib worked hard to help edit this book.

Also, of course, I wish to thank Joe Trento, the journalist, for alerting me to the Visas for Terrorists Program, the real link to al-Qaeda and the Arab-Afghan Legion.

DEDICATION

This opus is dedicated to the people of Afghanistan, Iraq, Libya, Russia, Syria, and Yugoslavia.

I offer it as a small commemoration to both the living and the dead of those unfortunate countries, particularly those who were murdered in their millions by the United States of America.

WHAT IS THIS ABOUT?

*A*l-*Qaeda* (Arabic for "The Base") grew out of and became identical with the Arab-Afghan Legion, those terrorists recruited by the United States of America, the Kingdom of Saudi Arabia, and the Islamic Republic of Pakistan. Originally sent to Afghanistan, they fought the USSR's army and air force following the Soviet Union's invasion of that country. Later, the Central Intelligence Agency (CIA, the Agency) directed them to cross the border and destabilize the Muslim republics of the Soviet Union. Still later, the American government moved them into the Balkans to destroy Yugoslavia, and then similarly to Iraq, followed by Libya and Syria.

They received visas to travel to the United States, usually from Saudi Arabia, for training, debriefing, and other purposes. In enabling their passage, American government officials violated the Immigration and Nationality Act as well as the State Department's regulations, codified in its Foreign Affairs Manual.

I *know*. I *was there*. I *issued* the visas, and I *objected* to gross violations of law and regulation. As a result, as happens to nearly all whistle-blowers, I was fired.

Since then, I have had inordinate problems with sending and receiving e-mails, being bombarded with more spam than Monty Python could handle, periodic difficulties with telephone service, mysterious computer crashes, and daily robocalls in violation of the FCC's Do Not Call List. And the Arab-Afghan Legion is still marching.

WHY DID I WRITE THIS BOOK?

Simple. It's past time to expose murder, war crimes, and human rights violations by the United States of America and its "intelligence" services. Using the dubious claim of "national security," the United States, through the Central Intelligence Agency and the National Security Agency (NSA), has engaged in and/or organized coups and other destabilization efforts around the world, most notably in the Middle East. From Libya to Iran, governments have been overthrown, politicians assassinated, and everyday citizens murdered—all with the knowledge of not only the president of the United States and the executive branch, but the legislative and judicial ones as well.

The "mainstream" news media will not report on these activities to expose them for what they are. In fact, TV, radio, and newspapers flat out support them. Instead of checking power, the media, print or electronic, commonly act as government agents, parroting the "company line" and attacking (or ignoring) reports and sources that expose injustice or illegal policies.

I know about unlawful government plots for a fact. As a career official with both the Commerce and State departments, I saw these plots close up during my nine years as a diplomat. First, I was an economic/commercial officer in Stuttgart (1977–1980), then a commercial attaché in New Delhi (1980–1982). Later I was a visa officer in Jeddah (1987–1989), a political/economic officer in Stuttgart (1989–1991), and, finally, an economic analyst at the State Department's Bureau of Intelligence and Research (1991).

For nearly a quarter of a century, I have been speaking Truth both to Power and the Public. Some people have read my articles, others have heard me speak. My published critiques on the Visas for Terrorists Program, my writings about the deliberate destruction of Iraq, and my speaking out in many venues about what amounts, in my opinion, to treason by many public officials have not made me invisible. Nonetheless, from what I've seen, many progressives, such as Stephen Zunes, Peter Kuznick, and Phyllis Bennis, have yet to come to grips with even part of the problem. Our past still remains obscure. That's one reason for writing this book.

Now, after more than twenty years of aggravation in dealing with the State Department's bumbling, stumbling Foreign Service officers, corrupt federal judges, and unethical US attorneys, I have decided it is finally time to tell the truth, the whole truth, and nothing but the truth about US government support for terrorism and relate it to the global picture.

I would like to give you, the Esteemed Reader, some background on this situation, particularly about the kind of people the US government hires to formulate and manage its imperialist foreign policy. I am providing my personal narrative to illustrate just how American foreign policy is really created and implemented, especially in terms of what I call the Arab-Afghan Legion, who are terrorists recruited and trained by the United States. This book will serve to illuminate the dark and ugly corners of the State Department and its handmaiden, the Central Intelligence Agency and will help you understand how they have destabilized a major portion of the world.

This tale is a sordid sketch of backstabbing, disloyalty, double crosses, faithlessness, falsity, perfidy, sellouts, treachery, and betrayal. All of this is in addition to the stupidity and incompetence normally manifested by the State Department and the intelligence services.

In the first half of the twentieth century, US foreign policy was already a record of disaster: grievous policy mistakes leading both to World War I and World War II and their aftermath, as well as our questionable intervention in, invasion of, and occupation of several countries in the Caribbean, Central America, and elsewhere. In the second half of that century, after the so-called "professionalization" of the Foreign Service and its merger with the Central Intelligence Agency (and its not-very-Clandestine Service), American foreign policy became a record of unmitigated disaster: Israel, Korea, Iran, Guatemala, Vietnam, Chile, and Argentina are but some of the catastrophes brought into the world by our government.

My story shows how things really work. Inept, degenerate government officials and career-obsessed idiots created the climate for what I call the Arab-Afghan Legion, and others know as "al-Qaeda," or "ISIS/ISIL." My story also shows why the quality of American government has gone from bad to worse. This opus demonstrates how and why the United States has so deeply embroiled itself in South and Southwest Asia, North Africa, and the Balkans.

Throughout this book, bear in mind the credo of the Association of National Security Alumni:

> ...covert actions are counterproductive and damaging to the national interest of the United States. They are inimical to the operation of an effective national intelligence system, corruptive of civil liberties,

including the functioning of the judiciary and a free press. More importantly, they contradict the principles of democracy, national self-determination and international law to which the United States is publicly committed.[1]

---

[1] Covert action is defined in US law as activity that is meant "to influence political, economic, or military conditions abroad, where it is intended that the role of the US Government will not be apparent or acknowledged publicly." 50 USC § 413(b)(e).

ENTER THE PATSY

The Beginning

Having just joined the "real" Foreign Service (after stints in the State-Commerce Exchange Program and the Foreign Commercial Service), I was assigned to Jeddah, the "Grandmother of Cities." (Eve, the grandmother of us all, is reputedly buried in it.) There, I learned that the Kingdom of Saudi Arabia was a mysterious and exotic place, but it was nowhere near as exotic and mysterious as the American consulate general on Palestine Road.

Upon arrival, I found, as a new visa officer, I was expected to winnow more than one hundred applications a day, separating them into "issuances," "refusals," and what turned out to be "free passes for CIA agents." However, none of the clean-cut young fellows at the consulate (or even any of the pudgy, "been around too many blocks" types) bothered to clue me in on this special class of applicants.

However.

One day, Eric Qualkenbush, the CIA Base Chief, stopped me while I was walking on the consulate's huge compound (which included a nine-hole golf course). He had a request. Could I issue a visa to one of his agents, an Iranian whose family owned an Oriental rug store? Eric said, "Mike, make it look good (wink, wink). We want him in Washington for consultations."

Flabbergasted, I said, "Sure." Up to that point, I had had almost a daily battle with Jay Freres, the Consul General, along with other CIA officials, who demanded visas for peculiar people, that is, people whom law and regulation required me to refuse. I also had running fights with visa applicants who told me to approve their paperwork or they would complain to Freres and have him overrule me.

Why, I wondered, did Qualkenbush clearly explain what was coming? And why didn't he tip me the wink about the others, instead of leaving me to fight continued violations of rule and directive all by myself?

I was even more flummoxed when Eric's agent appeared in line before me while I was on my stool behind the visa section's armored window. Secure in my industrial-strength cinderblock office, I went through the interview: Memo on company letterhead explaining trip and customers to be visited? *Check.* Properly filled out visa application form DS-156? *Check.* Clean passport with no hidden notations of previous travel refusals? *Check.* Coherent, comprehensive, clear account of travel purpose? *Check.* Previous US visa stamps? *Check.* Appropriate responses to my questions about proposed journey? *Check.*

I issued the visa and wished I had more applicants like him.

And yet...

I had heard in Washington about all sorts of abnormal problems tied to visas in Jeddah. None of it made sense at the time, but the office atmosphere after my arrival was increasingly poisonous as I invoked the Immigration and Nationality Act and the Foreign Affairs Manual in preventing scruffy types from apparently trying to emigrate to the United States. Despite my questioning people in the office, I began to suspect that something wasn't quite right. I knew it wasn't right when the State Department later fired me without explanation and then stonewalled my efforts to learn why.

The following story is what I learned about what was really happening in Jeddah, how I got there, and the dreadful consequences of what I learned to be American policy.

Here Are Two Key Points

First, the Consular Section's job was to secure visas for CIA agents, i.e., foreigners recruited by American case offfcers. The Department of State and the Central Intelligence Agency collaborated on sending ignorant pawns to Jeddah, a place that was handling about forty-five thousand visa applications annually. If they processed the paperwork like automatons and didn't ask awkward questions about the applicants, they kept their jobs. If they followed law and regulation and resisted illegal pressure to overlook the people who had no real reason for traveling to the United States, they "weren't with the program" and could easily be dismissed as incompetent.

Second, the Department of State already had a watchdog in place to prevent this type of problem: the Bureau of Diplomatic Security. According to its website:

> D[iplomatic]S[ecurity] works with the Bureau of Consular Affairs on cases involving allegations of corrupt American Embassy employees, fraudulent document vendors, and the use of visas by terrorists, and those smuggling and trafficking drugs and human beings.
>
> Passport and visa crimes are federal offenses punishable by up to 10 years in prison and a fine of $250,000. The maximum prison sentence is increased to 15 years

if the offense is connected to drug trafficking, and to 20 years if connected to terrorism.[2]

So who was committing these violations, and what were they doing? And why wasn't the watchdog watching? As I later learned to my dismay, the visa applicants were recruits for the war in Afghanistan against the Soviet Union's armed forces. Further, as time went by, the fighters, trained in the United States, went on to other battlefields: Yugoslavia, Iraq, Libya, and Syria. They worked with the American intelligence services and the State Department to destabilize governments the United States opposed. While it's no secret, most knowledgeable people still refuse to talk about this agenda.

The Magic Kingdom: Confusion to the Americans

Prelude

In 1986, A-100, the introductory class for new Foreign Service officers (FSOs), consisted of weeks of sitting through dreadfully boring and generally useless lectures (for which I was paid). At the graduation session, class members received their orders, along with a small flag of their country of assignment. Mine was the green flag of the Kingdom of Saudi Arabia. I was to be a consular officer in Jeddah on that country's west coast.

I was astonished. When I made discreet inquiry of John Tkacik as to how I ended up there, he replied that he thought I had bid on the assignment since I appeared so happy at the ceremony. I later contacted one of our lecturers in A-100 (whose name I've forgotten). My interlocutor told me that the State Department wanted someone a little older than the average junior officer (I was forty-one) for the

---

[2] http://www.state.gov/m/ds/investigat/

Jeddah position, and someone with my experience at the Commerce Department because Jeddah was a hub of mercantile activity. This rationale left me with more questions than answers.

In accordance with Foreign Service practice, I wrote to the American Ambassador, Walter Cutler, in Riyadh and told him of my delight in joining his official family. I sent a similar letter to Jay Philip Freres, the American Consul General in Jeddah at the time. I then went on to Arabic language class and engaged in regional and consular studies at the Foreign Service Institute (FSI), the educational arm of the State Department in Washington. Surprisingly, I got a call one day from a desk officer (essentially, those in Washington who follow political, economic, and social affairs in a country) for Saudi Arabia. Ambassador Cutler was in town for consultations about the kingdom with State Department officials, and he invited me to meet with him. I expected it to be a five-minute "hello and good-bye" session. Instead, Cutler kept me for about forty-five minutes, telling me the problems my predecessor as vice consul in Jeddah, Greta Holtz, had created for our embassy in Riyadh. Visas were being denied to servants of rich Saudi women who, after all, couldn't travel to the United States without their entourage of hairdressers, seamstresses, and other factotums. I sat there and listened and wondered at this report. Clearly, Cutler was conveying some message, but for the life of me, I could not puzzle it out. Afterward, I spoke to the desk officer, who had been there with me during the talk, asking what that meeting was really all about. His response was that he didn't know, saying that Cutler (who had previously been ambassador to Zaire and Tunisia) was "just a queer duck."

Years later, Cutler, then head of Meridian House, a nonprofit that promotes international understanding, flatly refused to talk to me about Jeddah. Despite his silence, he knew full well what had been going on. In a discussion about recruits for the Afghan war in Robert Dreyfuss's *Devil's Game*, Cutler is quoted as saying, "Where I was, nobody was looking ahead at what would happen to those unemployed freedom fighters."[3] (Contrary to what Cutler told me and, as I learned later, many of Jeddah's visa applicants were mujahideen recruits, alleged "freedom fighters", and not servants of rich Saudi women.)

Another letter went to John D. Moller, chief of the Consular Section. Unlike missives to Greta Holtz, I got an innocuous reply (although he remarked that State had not informed him of my assignment, and he knew nothing about it until my letter arrived). However, in June 1994, I tracked Moller down to Kings Colony Court in Palm Coast, Florida. In response to my letter about visa "issues," in part asking about a meeting with the Deputy Chief of Mission, Dave Dunford and Nick LaRoche, Counselor for Consular Affairs, and Jay Freres, he replied that he had taken early retirement rather than continually wrangle with Freres and others about questionable visas.

Things got stranger. I had a yellow Volkswagen convertible that the US government would ship to Jeddah for me. However, after I read in an official report on Saudi Arabia that yellow was a color reserved for taxicabs, so cars in that hue were not allowed into the country, I attempted to get advice on what to do. Paint the car? Get an exemption from the Saudi government if I promised not to moonlight as a cabbie? No one in Washington knew. Surprisingly, my cables on the subject to the Administrative Section at my new post were never answered. Given the seven-hour time difference between Washington and Jeddah, and my desire not to make waves, I elected not to telephone to ask why no one answered my messages. Yet I wondered what was going on.

Then, being "satiably curious," like Rudyard Kipling's Elephant Child, I began asking around about Cutler's odd remarks on visas in Jeddah. Heeding the advice of a consular officer that anything

---

[3] Robert Dreyfuss, *Devil's Game, How the U.S. Helped Unleash Fundamentalist Islam* (New York: Metropolitan Books/Henry Holt, 2005) 290.

out of the ordinary should be questioned as a source of potential trouble, I contacted Ellen Goff in the Executive Office for the Bureau of Near Eastern Affairs (NEA/EX), essentially a position handling administrative matters. She told me that, yes, she had heard stories about visa problems in Jeddah, but she had no details on the subject.

Still puzzled and confused, I went off to Jeddah in September 1987. I later learned that I had been assigned to a CIA post, another unpleasant surprise. [Most of the American officers and staff did not work for the State Department, but instead for the Agency (the CIA, or "Langley" for the location of the CIA in Virginia), or the National Security Agency (NSA).]

Arrival and Puzzlement

Welcomed with open arms by Jay Freres, the Consul General (identified by the German journalist Julius Mader as a CIA official), and Henry Ensher, the political officer, I was told I was an improvement over Greta Holtz, whom they alleged had had terrible problems at the consulate. [Years later, I began to realize that this was more a cover story than anything else, especially since my visa refusal rate was within five percentage points of hers. According to one biography, Holtz had had strong ties to the intelligence services, having previously worked at the Defense Intelligence Agency (DIA), later receiving the Christopher Award from the CIA (according to another biography].[4] For someone who created such problems for our embassy in Riyadh, Greta Holtz has done extremely

---

[4] Ostensibly from the State Department for sustained excellence and initiative in the substantive policy areas of the oceans, the environment, science; democracy, human rights, and labor; population, refugees, and migration; and international narcotics and crime. Greta Holtz, to my knowledge, never worked in any of these areas.

well for herself, moving steadily up the promotion ladder. Once Minister-Counselor for Provincial Affairs in Iraq, she became a Deputy Assistant Secretary of State. Then President Barack Obama named her Ambassador to Oman in September 2012. Her new official biography strangely omits her DIA service, saying just that she worked in the NATO policy office at the Defense Department. When in Washington, DC, she lives in a $2.4 million house in nearby Potomac, Maryland.)

My New Job as Consular Officer—Issuing Visas

Later on, during my service in Jeddah, I began getting referrals from Freres and Ensher (and others, such as Paul Arvid Tveit, a commercial officer listed in namebase.org as a CIA official). Initially, I was approached diffidently with the caveat that, while according to law and regulation, I had the final decision, they really wanted visas for their contacts. While no example springs to mind, the referrals, for the most part, were unremarkable. Later, after I had begun questioning the credentials of many applicants because they lacked ties to Saudi Arabia or their own country, the requests became demands. Then, they became threats.

Ghost Busters

While the Foreign Service is filled with people who do not work for the Department of State, Jeddah was my first experience with a majority-spook post. (Intelligence officers, in State Department slang, are spooks because they're invisible beings from another world.) According to both a former CIA station chief (head of undercover operations in a country) who asked not to be named, and Jay Hawley, now a retired FSO, the average percentage of intelligence officers to real diplomats at a given Foreign Service post is about one in three. My experience in Jeddah, Stuttgart, and New Delhi might place it higher—at least 50 percent, if not more. According to the *Anti-CIA Club of Diplomats: Spooks in U.S. Foreign Service* [sic], a twelve-page, 1983 Canadian publication (see namebase.org), the percentage is 60 percent. At Jeddah, to the best of my knowledge, out of some twenty US citizens assigned to the consulate, only three people, including myself, worked for the Department of State. The rest were CIA or NSA officials or their spouses. (NSA creates and breaks ciphers, listens to telephone calls, and reads e-mails. This allegedly makes US government communications more secure and those of American citizens and other nations less so. One of the languages it teaches its analysts is "Special Arabic"—that is, Hebrew, helping conceal Israel as being a target of NSA activity.)

Things rapidly went from bad to worse.

My name was on the visa plate that stamped applications to enter the United States, making me personally responsible for my actions. After opposing questionable demands for visas, I began to inquire about what was really going on. First, I asked Jean Bradford, the head of the Citizens' Services branch of the consular section. She told me that "Jay Freres (the source for most of the illegal visa pressure) just likes giving candy to babies." I then tried Justice (given name) Stevens, head of the consular section. He told me to keep quiet and do what Freres wanted. I later discussed the matter with Stephanie A. Smith (a former French citizen) who was Counselor for Consular Affairs in Riyadh, the capital. Another one of those listed as a CIA official in *Anti-CIA Club of Diplomats. Spooks in US Foreign Service*, she told me that Freres' and others' demands for illegal visas were "very bad." She later advised me to raise the issue with the Bureau of Consular Affairs on my next trip to Washington

Eric Qualkenbush[5], the CIA base chief at Jeddah, whose cover was head of the Political/Economic Section, came up with a new demand: he or his staff had to examine and approve all visas that my staff and I had issued before the stamped passports were returned to the applicants. I had to wonder if this practice originated from his experience as a Clandestine Service officer at the CIA station in New Delhi or as station chief in Sofia, Bulgaria, prior to Jeddah, where one European diplomat told me he served? (Eric's assignment after Jeddah was Bonn.) According to retired consular officers, this requirement was highly unusual. Another, who asked that I withhold his name, informed me that the CIA often trolled visa application files or sought specific information about visa-seekers.)

I myself became suspicious of Qualkenbush's nerve: amazingly, he once made an unnecessary point of having me issue a visa to one of his Iranian contacts, an Oriental rug merchant in Jeddah. Eric stopped me one day on the compound and told me he was sending me one of his agents (foreign nationals recruited and controlled by CIA case officers), asking me to make the visa interview "look good," because the CIA wanted the Iranian in Washington for consultations. Afterward, I thought, why was Eric doing making this request? The Iranian had a legitimate business, was going to the United States to meet real carpet buyers, and had been issued several visas before.

Exorcists Needed

In our spook-ridden Jeddah consulate, I sometimes found it was a daily battle to do my job. Here are just a few examples of what I discovered and how the laws of the United States were routinely

---

[5] Eric Qualkenbush's biography is available at http://www.tvworldwide.com/events/homelanddefense/040430/bush.cfm.

ignored. Little did I know that I was dealing with recruits for the Arab-Afghan Legion.

Two Pakistanis came to me for a visa. According to their story, they were traveling on a Commerce Department–organized trade mission to an automotive parts exhibition in the United States. However, they couldn't name the trade show or identify the city in which it would be held. I denied their visa request. Within sixty minutes, Paul Arvid Tveit (now retired and living in Virginia) called and demanded visas for these same Pakistanis. I explained the reasons for my refusal, citing § 214(b) of the Immigration and Nationality Act (a visa applicant is an intending immigrant unless and until he can prove otherwise) and the Foreign Affairs Manual (FAM, State's holy book that carries instructions for everything, including the requirement to refuse visas if there is any doubt as to the applicant's bona fides). Ignoring the law and regulation, Tveit went to Justice Stevens and the visas were issued.

Then, Karen Sasahara, the political officer and Henry Ensher's successor, demanded a visa for a Sudanese who was a refugee from his own country and unemployed in Saudi Arabia. Following the letter and the spirit of the law, I refused. Sasahara immediately went to Justice, and a visa was issued. When I later asked Justice why he authorized a visa to someone with no ties to the Sudan or the kingdom, he replied simply "national security," a phrase without legal definition.[6]

Besides staff going to Stevens (now retired and living in Switzerland), people from outside the consulate frequently went to Jay Freres to reverse my decisions. One individual, an expatriate company messenger with a stack of passports, appeared at the visa

---

[6] In "Our Man in Jeddah," an article written in July 2004 by Margie Burns for *onlinejournal.com*, Sasahara was linked to the CIA. Burns also noted Sasahara's undiplomatic behavior, yelling at a woman when she tried to get State's assistance in a parental kidnapping case. Sasahara's husband, Michael Ratner, is listed as consul general in Jerusalem at this writing.

window one day, telling me I could issue the visas then and there, or I could do it after he went to Freres. Per regulation, the only way a refusal could be overridden was by a senior FSO with a consular commission, which Freres lacked. Additionally, the senior officer had to have more information unavailable to the denying officer. Therefore, Freres acted without authority, also failing to make a required written report. (Cf. 9 FAM 41.121).

A Questionable Question

One question that I never addressed was, if a junior consular officer, such as myself, questioned the credentials of all the peculiar visa applicants, what were the far more experienced Immigration and Naturalization Service (INS) inspectors doing at the port of entry when these lowlifes entered the country? How is it that none of them were turned back? I well remember being told a story by Mike Carpenter, head of the consular section in Stuttgart in the 1970s. One of the applicants to whom he had given a visa had been sent home from New York. Although she had declared to the inspector that her US visit would be short, INS found a two-year supply of birth control pills in her handbag, thus indicating her fraudulent plans for a much longer stay.

Jay the Jailer

Jay Freres did more than help questionable people get visas. He helped the Saudi government put expatriates in jail. This seemed to be in keeping with his questionable past, such as his assignment to Kabul in 1979 when the American Ambassador, "Spike" Dubs, was kidnapped and killed. As the Afghan security forces blazed away at the people holding Dubs within Room 117 in the Kabul Hotel, somehow Freres, head of the Economic/Commercial Section, was situated outside the space. Dean Henderson, a writer, columnist, and blogger, asserts that Dubs was also CIA chief of station, unlikely in knowledgeable people's opinions. However, a European diplomat opined that Dubs, and likely Freres, were State Department officials co-opted by the Agency. Freres later became Political Counselor in Ankara in 1982. (Other than his service as consul general in Jeddah, these were his only assignments that I could find in the State Department's *Key Officers of Foreign Service Posts* booklet.)[7]

Not long after I arrived and began making contacts around town, consular officers from two European consulates took me to lunch. Over good food and "Saudi champagne" (sparkling water, apple juice, and citrus slices), they asked my help in identifying and publicizing the actions of a fellow of indeterminate nationality having multiple passports. They said this man possessed an arrangement with the Saudi government to import and sell liquor and drugs. According to my interlocutors, he would hold parties in alcohol-free Jeddah, generously supplying intoxicants, liquid and otherwise. As I understood it, he would then provide the names of his guests to the Saudi authorities who, on occasion, would raid the events, arresting as many attendees as they could catch. In return, he got to keep his profits (and stay out of jail). Subsequently, at one of the consulate's "pool parties," I happened to meet a man, an American citizen, who had been to one of the raided functions. Appearing to be in his fifties and far out of shape, he told me he ran out the back door as the police came in the front. Despite his age and physical condition, he said, he was up and over the wall at the rear of the house faster than a teenage athlete.

Learning about this scam, I felt I should post details of this mysterious dealer to warn American citizens in our consular district,

---

[7] This publication is now out of print and available only as a current issue online, thus forestalling any such tracking of individuals.

the Hejaz. A simple notice, mailed to those registered with the consulate, would be the easiest way to protect our citizens. When I suggested this to Freres, as head of the consulate, he refused. He said it would offend the Saudis, and he ordered me to keep silent.

While I didn't work in Citizens Services at the consulate, which deals with the welfare of US nationals and handles any imprisonments, I still thought it only prudent (and my duty) to quietly pass the word to people I knew about this subject, Freres be damned.

Pool Parties, the Marine House, and the Brass Eagle

Alcohol was a big deal in Saudi Arabia where, if you drank and were caught, you were (1) arrested, (2) flogged, (3) deported. Yet, despite our efforts to "conceal" alcohol use at the consulate (by crushing bottles and beer cans, for example), the Saudis knew all about what the Americans were doing. Saudi citizens and government officials attended receptions at my house where I served forbidden drinks. They also attended pool parties and functions at the Marine House[8] where alcohol was provided. Saudi citizens and government officials attended events at the Brass Eagle, several rooms that served as the consulate's private bar. And, if they didn't spill the beans about alcohol consumption, a movable Saudi "traffic" camera overlooked the compound with its parties, and provided a bird's-eye view of what went on there, including drinking and mixed-sex dancing.

Shortly after Lonnie Washington, the only State Department Communicator (who sent and received official messages) and I arrived, we learned about the Brass Eagle. Begun by former consular officer Brad Braford's wife, it was a remarkably dreary and sparsely attended place used mostly by CIA officials. We two, with

---

[8] The official residence for the consulate's Marine Security Guard.

our household effects still in transit, decided to invite official and unofficial contacts to this bar. Selling tickets for the local equivalent of ten dollars for five drinks, we filled the Brass Eagle to overflowing in no time and made a pretty good profit for the American Employees Family Support Association (AEFSA) (which may have been a CIA front). The Agency really didn't like that we brought non-Americans to the consulate. So, in retaliation, they put roadblocks into the otherwise smooth operation of our parties.

Later, after the CIA grasped what a good idea it was to ply expatriates with alcohol, it began organizing parties around the consulate swimming pool. The parties, with two hundred or more guests, generated about one million dollars per annum for said AEFSA, an alleged nonprofit organization.[9]

The Marine House was another watering hole. Invitations were highly prized, and guests tried to compensate for a booze-free week by drinking as much as they could in a few hours. Many departing guests staggered out onto Palestine Road, fronting the consulate, in various stages of drunkenness. (I had arrived in Jeddah too late to enjoy the Marine House's "Tarts and Vicars" party, where the female guests displayed abundant intoxicated skin as they left the grounds—a blatant violation of Saudi mores.) Sometime later in my tour, a Marine Corps inspection team arrived to question such consumption of alcohol and earnings from its sale.

Keep the Saudis Happy, Part One

Consul General Jay Freres's watchword at the consulate was, "Don't offend the Saudis." At the same time, he refused to hire a capable, American-educated Saudi female for a US Information

---

[9] The million dollar figure came from the author's conversation with Tim Hunter, a former consulate official.

Service position advising on academic study in the United States. (I learned the previous employee had been fired earlier because she had allegedly identified a CIA official at one of the pool parties.) Also, he allowed illuminated Christmas trees (regarded as religious symbols in Jeddah) to be displayed at the consulate and Christmas carols to be played over loudspeakers. (This might seem inoffensive, but the only religion permitted in the kingdom is Islam. Anyone caught openly practicing another faith suffers disproportionate consequences.)

Were Freres genuinely interested in not alienating the Saudis, he could have done more to keep liquor out of nondiplomatic hands on consular premises. Official receptions could have served fruit juice and soft drinks, and he could have stopped supplying liquor to the Mobil Oil Corporation's boat.

Keep the Saudis Happy, Part Two

Jay Freres and his "Don't Offend the Saudis" program had as many holes as a piece of Swiss cheese hit by a shotgun blast. Again, in Saudi Arabia, Islam is the only religion permitted. People of other faiths get their prayer books, hymnals, and other religious articles seized at the border, and if they act blatantly enough, can get themselves deported. Yet Freres, a Roman Catholic, had an undercover priest[10] say Mass at his official residence on Sundays for coreligionists from inside and outside the consulate. Protestant expatriates were allowed to hold services in the auditorium in the consulate's main building, something FSOs, such as myself, were ignorant of. After Freres retired, Tim Hunter, a devout Catholic, told me that he

---

[10] Roman Catholic priests operated in Saudi Arabia like they did in the time of Henry VIII in Britain. They concealed their identity and secretly provided religious services to the faithful. If discovered, then as now, they would be arrested and jailed.

(Hunter) had been ordered to discourage attendance at the Holy Church of the Consulate. When he objected, he was savaged by US government officials.

They're Like Termites...But Do More Damage

Besides direct confrontation and dubious "referrals," the spooks, the "Invisible Ones" were also assigned to the consular section for "diplomatic cover." Philip Agee, a former case officer, said to me that, in Mexico City, where he had been assigned, the CIA always had one of its Clandestine Service people occupying a consular position. From what I was told by people in Jeddah, Brad Braford, Andrew C. Weber's predecessor, had been assigned to the visa section as a "part-time" consular officer. (He went on to Dhahran as political/military officer.) Supposedly, he and Andy Weber had complained about Jay Freres's questionable visa issuances. (Without a consular commission, Freres had had a visa signature slug[11] made, and presumably, used.) Weber would occasionally sit at the visa window and say to me, "Mike, let me take this next guy in line, he's one of mine."[12]

CIA involvement in hanky-panky with visas, such as that in Jeddah, is common in almost every Foreign Service Post. If this behavior leaks out, it's quickly hushed up. Remember, it was a CIA "consular officer" at Khartoum in the Sudan who issued a tourist

---

[11] A slab of metal duplicating the consular officer's signature and authenticating the stamped visa.

[12] After assignments as an FSO to Bonn, Germany (with Eric Qualkenbush), Kazakhstan, and Hong Kong, Andy became Assistant Secretary of Defense for Nuclear, Chemical, and Biological Defense Programs. His official biography notably omits his assignment to Moscow as a bio-weapons inspector where he had been interviewed on-camera by former *New York Times* journalist Judith Miller for the PBS show *Bio-Terror.*

visa to Sheikh Omar Abdel Rahman, later linked to the World Trade Center bombing in 1993. The "blind" Sheikh had been on a State Department terrorist watch list when he was issued the visa, entering the United States by way of Saudi Arabia, Pakistan, and the Sudan in 1990. [I later wondered if this was the same fellow who had once sent an emissary to me in Jeddah with his passport and application. Since we required personal appearances for every nationality except Saudi (and sometimes even for them), I told the representative I needed to see the applicant, but I was told the man was "handicapped." Still, I thought, why could he not get on a bus in Mecca to travel to our consulate?][13]

Keep That Lid On (So the Whole Mess Doesn't Boil Over and Dirty the Stove)

I began to see Jeddah as a very strange place filled with people I really knew nothing about who conducted themselves in a remark-ably odd fashion. Questions got me nowhere. A plethora of contacts couldn't explain to me what really went on inside the consulate. European diplomats regularly asked about the number of spooks on Uncle Sam's payroll there, possibly because Agency staff didn't seem to care about their "cover." Unlike other American officers, they all drove identical, olive-drab Toyota Land Cruisers with orange-and-red lightning bolts painted on their sides—with buff Saudi,

---

[13] Joseph P. O'Neill was Deputy Chief of Mission (DCM) at Khartoum when Rahman got his visa. He says a spook issued the visa but blames a Foreign Service national (local hire), according to *The Association for Diplomatic Studies and Training; Foreign Affairs Oral History Project.* O'Neill added that there had been another CIA agent who was slipped a visa without any explanation or blame. He said he got his job in Khartoum through Frank G. Wisner, a member of a well-known CIA family.

instead of green Consular Corps license plates that real diplomats had on their cars.

As previously mentioned, before I left Washington for Jeddah, I wrote to Greta Holtz several times, asking about my job and what she wished she had known before she took up her post there. I never received a response. When I met her in person, during one of her visits to Jeddah from Yemen where she was next assigned, she told me she'd been "too upset" to give me a clear picture. Holtz called me in Washington, DC after I'd left the service and questioned me about the progress of my complaints about Jeddah, even though I'd never mentioned a word to her about the subject.

Then, the Inspectors came.

Periodically, Foreign Service Posts are examined for compliance with law and regulation, and a report is prepared. Nestor Martin, one of my close, well-connected contacts, a Cuban American with intimate ties to intelligence officials, had warned me to say nothing to the inspectors about problem areas. These included suspect visas, extremely profitable and voluminous liquor sales to expatriates, Muslim and otherwise, as well as the harassment of the Arab American language teacher, Salma Webber. If you do, he cautioned, you will be fired.

While serving in Jeddah, I was quizzed by Joseph P. O'Neill, one of the State Department's Inspection Team members.[14] O'Neill interviewed me and pressed me to confirm what he'd heard about visa problems and alcohol deals. He shared details new to me and repeatedly said anything I told him was and would remain confidential. When I repeated what Nestor had stated to me, O'Neill reassured me that nothing would happen to my career. After about an hour, I relented and, trusting my government, confirmed O'Neill's suspicions. Just a few days later, Jay Freres wrote a vicious efficiency

---

[14] The same O'Neill who had been DCM in Khartoum when Omar Abdel Rahman got his visa.

report on me that would virtually guarantee my dismissal from the Foreign Service.

During my conversation with O'Neill, I told him about the file of shady visas I had been keeping. Neglecting to make a copy or take the file with me, I later learned it had been mysteriously shredded (by a person or persons unknown), and O'Neill, I suspect, was the instigator of that. (He was the only American officer who knew about this file.) Subsequently, I wrote O'Neill a letter when he was consul general in Bermuda (and before he traveled to Afghanistan, the Ukraine, and Uzbekistan on several Foreign Service assignments as a retiree), asking about what really went on at Jeddah. No response. Perhaps this was a result of O'Neill's becoming an "off-the-books" liaison with the Arab-Afghans he seemed to be protecting. Or, possibly, it was his ties to the CIA, going back to 1979 when he was assigned to the American embassy in Tehran when irate students captured it.[15] (O'Neill wasn't listed in the 1979 Key Officers Booklet, and he wasn't listed as a hostage by the Jimmy Carter Presidential Library and Museum).[16]

Revelations on the Road to Unemployment

Like Saul of Tarsus on the road to Damascus, I was blinded by the "light of truth." In a chance meeting, Joe Trento, a journalist at the Public Education Center in Washington, DC, put all the hostility toward me into perspective. Joe revealed to me what had

---

[15] Obituary, *Washington Post,* July 6, 2014.

[16] Temporary Duty Tehran, January–March 1979. His position was unspecified. O'Neill criticized political officers who had been telephoning Washington to suggest evacuation. He also aided the escape of Israeli embassy staff. O'Neill had had his own problems with the Inspection Corps. His career summary shows a series of strange assignments for an FSO, including the one in Bosnia. *The Association for Diplomatic Studies and Training; Foreign Affairs Oral History Project;* Georgetown University, May 19, 1998.

been really going on with the CIA in Jeddah and what had been concealed from me. It wasn't garden variety visa fraud as I had once thought, but something much more serious: it was the Visas for Terrorists Program, set up to recruit and train (in the United States) murderers, war criminals, and human rights violators for combat in Afghanistan against the Soviet Union. These men became the founding members of al-Qaeda, the Arab-Afghan Legion. President Jimmy Carter (D-GA) and his National Security Advisor, Zbigniew Kazimierz Brzezinski, began the campaign to assemble these goons to engage in blowing things up and shooting things down, preferably with Soviet soldiers inside. To help them do that, Trento said, the Department of State and the Central Intelligence Agency sent patsies as visa officers to the Jeddah consulate, then handling about forty-five thousand visa applications annually. If they weren't bright enough to question what was going on, Trento noted, things would be fine. If they protested the spurious visa requests, as I would, and resisted illegal pressure to overlook them, they could easily be fired because, as he added, "they wouldn't get with the program" and there was "obviously" something wrong with them.

Supplementing Trento's remarks were similar statements made by a former US government employee at the Voice of America and another man connected with George Washington University in DC. I reached both by chance in the course of researching an article on the Middle East, and they told me that the CIA, ably assisted by asset Osama bin Laden and Saudi connections, had three recruiting offices in the kingdom: one was in Jeddah, one was in Riyadh, and one was somewhere in the eastern province of al-Sharqiah. However, the Saudis, once the Soviets had withdrawn from Afghanistan, they said, were not pleased with the saddle tramps[17] that they had helped recruit. In fact, the Saudis prevented those who'd been enlisted

---

[17] A term from America's Wild West for nomadic gunslingers who hired out to fight range wars.

21

within the kingdom, particularly the Palestinians, from returning. They feared they would use their newly acquired skills to promote "regime change" at home. Other nations in the region rejected these recruits as well, my contacts told me.

Many recruiting offices were located in the United States, too. According to background on Abdullah Azzam, one of the cofounders of the Services Office (an organization inter alia placing Arab volunteers with Afghan factions fighting the Soviets),

> The main aim of Sheikh Abdullah in creating the Jihad magazine (an Arabic publication providing information about the Afghan war, focusing on Arab efforts to help that struggle) was to inform the Arab world what is happening in Afghanistan; informing them, help funding, recruit people. [Eventually we printed] seventy thousand copies [an issue]. **Most of them go to the United States because we had fifty-two centers in the United States. The main office was in Brooklyn, [also] Phoenix, Boston, Chicago, Tucson, Minnesota, Washington DC, and Washington State.** [Emphasis added.] Every year [Abdullah Azzam] used to go to United States. The wealthy of the United States can help much more than Muslims who are living in poor countries or under dictatorship.[18]

When I contacted him by email and telephone in 2013, Sheikh Abdullah Anas, Azzam's son-in-law, somehow couldn't remember any of this. All he said was that there were only a handful of non-Afghan

---

[18] Peter L. Bergen, *The Osama bin Laden I Know*, (New York: Free Press, 2006) 25, 32, 33. NB: In an e-mail to me dated February 12, 2014, Bergen denied having any more information than the above.

fighters and that the CIA had no role in dealing with them. One cause of his faulty memory might be his gaining asylum in the United Kingdom. (The UK's Secret Intelligence Service was a participant in the Afghan war.) Another might be his rumored interest in moving to the United States and not wanting to offend the people who can make that happen.

Perhaps secret travel to the United States by members of the Services Office was another source of friction in Jeddah. While I was at the consulate, I proposed meeting with various Muslim organizations who had been sending me unqualified visa applicants. These interviewees were clerics ostensibly going to the United States to preach to congregations but couldn't explain why there were no qualified Muslim evangelists in America. I had wanted to describe to the groups what was needed for visa applications to reduce the time I spent with unfit candidates. Jay P. Freres forbade this.

In a subsequent conversation with Celerino Castillo, a former Drug Enforcement Agency official, I learned that the CIA's involvement in the visa process was a successful program of long-standing in Latin America and, I presume, a model for Saudi Arabia. South of the border, he said, the Agency would slip passports and applications from its contacts into packages sent to the local US consulate or embassy by travel agents. Sandwiched between legitimate applications, "Agency assets" would not be carefully examined by consular officers and would thus get a free ride to the United States.

The question, of course, is: Were these recruits selected in Washington, DC by CIA headquarters or locally by the base or station? (A "base" is a CIA office concealed in a consulate, while a "station" is a CIA office at an embassy and controlling all the intelligence activities in a country.) Former Agency official Marc Sageman, (one of only three people who managed the entire anti-Soviet war in Afghanistan), maintains that the stations and bases never dealt with

Washington. They didn't communicate with headquarters on enlisting fighters abroad, he asserted.[19] The three people "managing" the Afghan war were Sageman, Milt Bearden, and Gus Avrakotos ("Dr. Dirty," as he was called, the man in charge of arming the Afghans. He's now dead). In 2008, Sageman played up the threat of Muslims as dangerous because they were "self-recruited, without leadership, and globally connected through the Internet" and who "lack[ed] structure and organizing principles..." These were characteristics usually put forward to denigrate a risk.[20] Sageman ran "unilateral programs with the Afghan Mujahedin [sic] between 1987 and 1989 from Islamabad, and also was an advisor to the New York City Police for years. In 2008, he became its "scholar in residence."[21]

How Stupid Could They Be?

Very stupid.

If I had been informed of what the CIA, the State Department, and Osama bin Laden were doing in Jeddah, I may have been dumb enough at the time to have gone along with this policy. After all, I trusted my government. The CIA and the State Department would have saved themselves negative publicity, law suits, and twenty years of painful truth-telling from me.

Another example of gross incompetence at Jeddah was the inability of the CIA and NSA to learn about a real security issue: the delivery of Chinese Intermediate Range Ballistic Missiles (IRBMs) to Saudi Arabia. A major story in 1988, US spooks had no idea the things were actually being delivered. Until I told them.

---

[19] My conversation with Marc Sageman at his Rockville, Maryland, home, August 13, 2013; arranged by Matthew Hoh.

[20] Arun Kundnani, *The Muslims Are Coming* (New York: Verso, 2014), 75, 76.

[21] Ibid., 127. citing Elaine Sciolino and Eric Schmitt, "A Not Very Private Feud over Terrorism," *New York Times*, June 8, 2008.

After several of my European contacts came to my house for drinks before dinner out, I learned the IRBMs were being off-loaded from ships in the harbor. I was told that one of my sources had actually seen not only the missiles but also the Saudi attempts to conceal the missiles from prying eyes by blocking sight lines with shipping containers. The next morning, I surprised the Air Attaché with the story. He immediately worked to secure reconnaissance photos of the missiles. I managed to irritate Karen Sasahara and the CIA Base, along with the consul general's secretary, Jill Johnston, by demanding a classified cable be sent out to Washington immediately. (Married to the NSA chief, Johnston had told me she used to work for the CIA and was disgruntled at having to come to work on her day off.) I learned from a contact in the US embassy in Riyadh that my message had been included in the American president's daily intelligence briefing.

Aside from my scoop on the IRBMs, I did a goodly amount of reporting on political and economic issues, to the extent that Joe O'Neill, then one of the Inspectors, told me I had generated more analytical cables than the political officer or the Political/Economic Section. I had written about Saudi businesswomen (unheard of thirty years ago), my travels throughout our consular district, and the reasons why people came to America. I also visited American citizens imprisoned in Saudi jails and identified dead bodies (harder than it sounds when the passport picture is out of date and the corpse was three days dead before it was discovered).

I managed this despite wrangling daily with the intelligence officers who staffed and ran the consulate. These were the people who arranged for recruiting and training what were then the mujahideen, who later became al-Qaeda, who then transformed themselves into ISIS. I saw, but didn't recognize, their start at Jeddah. We've all seen their later development and what happens when the intelligence services control foreign policy and diplomacy: the people they assembled aided the breakup of Yugoslavia, the destruction of Iraq, the collapse of Libya, and the savaging of Syria.

How Did I End Up In The State Department?

In high school, after having read William J. Lederer and Eugene Burdick's book, *The Ugly American*, a damning account of American arrogance, incompetence, and corruption overseas, I became very interested in international affairs. This motivated me to attend Georgetown University's School of Foreign Service. In the 1960s, this was the only such undergraduate program in the country. Like most of my fellow graduates, I would enter the Department of State.

Coming from a working-class family, and despite having read Lederer and Burdick's book, I was really ignorant of the true nature of the Foreign Service and its respected members. I would later learn that most are an inbred, hidebound group of pseudo–upper class cookie-pushers more concerned with advancing their own careers than in formulating and carrying out an ideology-free, intelligent American foreign policy.

My 1967 oral interview for a post in the Foreign Service was conducted by three Foreign Service officers (FSOs), one of whom was Ellsworth Bunker (one-time ambassador to South Vietnam and a war hawk). While I had no problems with the history and geography questions, my answers to queries such as "Do you play bridge?" (No) or "Do you subscribe to the *New Yorker*?" (No) did not sit well with the three examiners: I was not of the elite. It got worse when, asked for an example of an American foreign policy problem, I replied "Vietnam." I added that I found it strange to learn that the US government was keeping information about its bombing attacks on Southeast Asia from the American people while the Thai, Cambodians, Laotians, and Vietnamese, who were being bombed, all knew what was going on. My interview went downhill from there. I thought I had walked into the 1955 Gary Cooper movie, *The Court-Martial of Billy Mitchell*, centered on the grilling of a nonconformist. My impression after that was, if I spoke my name, it would surely be challenged. Clearly, they didn't like me from the beginning and were looking for any excuse to get rid of me. How dare I question the basis for our disastrous war? Were I Jesus Christ on rollerskates, I would still have failed.

So I went to graduate school at Catholic University, again in international affairs, and joined the Commerce Department's International Trade Administration. In 1969, I again sat for the Foreign Service exam, once more passing the written but failing the oral, now set up to supposedly resemble a real day at the office. After another failure, I retook the test in 1984, emphasizing how much I wanted to work for the State Department and noting my work abroad in the Department of State–Department of Commerce Exchange Program, a way to provide Washington assignments for FSOs and overseas assignments for civil servants. This time, I passed.

Or, so I thought.

The medical office of the State Department decided that my admittedly lousy feet should disqualify me from of the Foreign Service. When I sued for discrimination, the Department fought back for two years, even though the law requires an employer to provide "reasonable accommodation" to an employee or job applicant with a disability. Although I needed no special accommodation for my feet, the Senior Deputy Assistant Secretary in Medical Services, Paul

A. Goff, MD, wrote that I shouldn't be hired because I couldn't run away from terrorists' bullets.

It ought to have been apparent to me right then that the State Department simply ignores laws it feels are inconvenient. I learned more about this later on when I was ordered to issue visas to terrorists.

A-100—Basic Training for FSOs

After two years of delay and litigation, the State Department finally offered me a choice of jobs I couldn't refuse. I could be a political officer, an economic officer, a consular officer, or an administrative officer. According to the Foreign Service's orientation program, called A-100, political and economic officers consort with presidents and kings, consular officers are social workers, and administrative officers fix broken toilets. Having an undergraduate minor in economics and having worked at the Commerce Department, I elected to become an economic officer.

As a reward for my persistence, I was sent to Saudi Arabia.

First placed in the thirty-fifth class of incoming FSOs, I got to interact with my fellow recruits, a remarkably disparate bunch, made up of several political appointees, some Congressional staffers, former Peace Corps members, along with others from State and local governments in the Southwest. There were former civil servants from the Internal Revenue Service, who routinely disparaged the taxpayer. And then there were a couple of CIA Clandestine Service case officers who were assigned there for diplomatic cover. Probably, their inexperience and naïveté gives an indication of how the Arab-Afghan Legion came to be raised and used.

Some class members had lived abroad, some were married to aliens, but most didn't appear to have a clue as to what the Foreign Service really did. To remedy this deficiency, A-100 provided seemingly eternal lectures on how the State Department and the rest of the federal government operated. There were visits to congressional offices and conservative think-tanks. There was a language aptitude test. There was the never-used Myers-Briggs personality test, which supposedly measures how people perceive the world and make decisions. Then there was John Tkacik, the moderator of the program. He once asked me, since I was older and presumably more stable than the others, if I knew which of my fellow A-100 colleagues, all with Top Secret security clearances, were using drugs.

During the program, we were all asked to bid on future assignments, using our interests, backgrounds, and language aptitude as qualifying factors. Since I had been there before, knew the country and its people well, and spoke the language fluently, I picked Germany as my priority and named several other countries worldwide. In its wisdom, the Foreign Service assigned me to Saudi Arabia, a state never on my bid list.

Be Careful What You Wish For

Maybe this is not a real Chinese phrase. Maybe this is an anonymous quote. Regardless, in reality, it certainly is a clear indication that there may be unforeseen and unpleasant consequences if you get what you really want.

I really wanted to be a Foreign Service officer. I really wanted to travel the world, formulating and conducting American foreign policy. I really wanted to belong to a Club of Gentlemen Adventurers who made their living through writing a weekly gossip column.

What I got was a world of trouble in Jeddah, followed by a sphere of strife in Stuttgart. All the while, I never grasped that I had gotten embroiled in a worldwide terrorist program. I thought I had been fighting simple corruption, not interfering with the recruitment of al-Qaeda.

Stuttgart, INR, and the Unemployment Line

Stuttgart

Happy to leave Jeddah in March 1989, I went on to Stuttgart, a city I knew and loved. Unfortunately, I found to my dismay that, in the intervening period, the consulate there had become infested with spooks who hadn't a clue about diplomacy. The alleged diplomats who really worked for State didn't either.

During my previous assignment in Stuttgart in the late 1970s, the only intelligence official I knew was the "Land (German State) Liaison Officer." He was a civilian working for the 66th Military Intelligence Group (MI 66) headquartered at the time in Munich. His task, as explained to me, was counterintelligence—looking for possible threats to the rear of the US armed forces in Baden-Württemberg, where the army's VII Corps was headquartered.

In 1989, it was another story. At that time, the Stuttgart consulate was a show of how the Foreign Service had fallen into ruin through providing cover to "intelligence" officers as well as hiring and promoting remarkably incapable individuals with serious mental problems.

In Stuttgart, I was reincarnated as political/economic officer (tagged a "CIA position" by M. Waltraut Enzmann, a longtime German employee at the consulate). Knowing that I, a real FSO, had been an Economic/Commercial officer in the past, Paul Warren-Smith, one of the locally hired staff, asked why I had been a consular officer in Jeddah and what I had been doing there. I jokingly said, "Selling visas for fun and profit." (The fun was relative; the profit was very real as visa fees paid for my salary and benefits as well as those of my three-man staff.)

When Jane Whitney, head of Stuttgart's consular section, overheard my remarks, she ran to the Consul General, Phil

Griffin, telling him I should be investigated for corruption. Griffin, who went on to become consul general at Jeddah in 1991, told me that he knew Whitney had mental problems and was a troublemaker, but he had to talk to me about what I did in Jeddah for form's sake. He then asked me if I had taken illegal payments for issuing visas to unqualified applicants. I told him the truth: I hadn't.[22]

Whitney wasn't the only corrupt FSO whom I had come across. While assigned to New Delhi in 1980 as part of the new Foreign Commercial Service (FCS), I had worked with Edward W. M. Bryant, Counselor for Commercial Affairs. Renowned for his insulting behavior, secretiveness, and petty feuds,[23] he had a remarkable inability to get along with US and other diplomats. Worse, I was told, he took bribes from Indian businessmen for recommending them to American companies as trade partners. According to the Defense Attaché's Office and the CIA station in New Delhi, one of these was Nand Khemka, a known Soviet agent and conduit for "black" money in India. More disturbingly, the counselor's wife, Bilha Mosheva Bryant, an Israeli, was believed to work for Israeli

---

[22] Griffin was right about Jane. According to my contacts, Whitney used to steal spoons from her staff and had taken paintings from the consulate. After Jane went to Perth, Australia, as consul general, retired FSO Fred Galanto told me what he had heard from Jim Gray, once in Jeddah, later one of the FSOs in Perth. Besides misappropriating $40,000 in government funds to decorate her office and residence, Gray said, Whitney had so outraged her staff, both American and Australian, that they wrote the ambassador, threatening to resign en masse unless he got rid of her. The State Department then let her retire on a full pension. When I tried to learn the specifics of the matter through a Freedom of Information Act request, State refused to provide any information because "it would violate Whitney's privacy."

[23] The Marine Security Guard told me Bryant placed classified documents on his secretary's desk after hours so that she would get a security violation. Enough violations and you lose the clearance and can't work. The secretary's name was Elizabeth Otey, a truly wonderful, helpful person.

intelligence. After their return to Washington, she took up a position in the State Department's Bureau of European Affairs. Like Whitney, what was widely known was never acted upon.

Phil Griffin, contrary to regulations, absolutely refused to write an interim efficiency report on me before he left Stuttgart for Jeddah in 1991. Griffin gave me no explanation for this omission, although I asked about his noncompliance with procedures. My thought then and now is that he had his instructions from the Central Intelligence Agency. After his retirement from the Department, Griffin represented the Saudi Bin Laden Group (SBG-USA) in Rockville, Maryland.[24]

There were other "problem" children in Stuttgart as well.

Leroy (Lee) Beal had been administrative officer there, before he was transferred to Jeddah, where I met him. In Saudi Arabia, he was totally ineffective, at one point flatly refusing to help me get my daughter a Saudi visa to visit me and later castigating me for questioning his racist evaluation of a Black man (Lonnie Washington) assigned to the Administrative Section. One German contact, Lisa Klemm, told me that Beal spent his days in Stuttgart folding and unfolding paper towels in his office. According to corridor talk, Beal had problems with alcohol, one of the two job hazards FSOs face. (The other is divorce.)

Beal's successor in Stuttgart was Donald S. Bryfogle, who did nothing that I knew of, and did it badly. The only good thing that

---

[24] Intelwire.com, citing a cable written by Albert Thibault, Deputy Chief of Mission, Riyadh. I had known Al as political officer in Delhi. Also, in Dec. 2013, in response to a letter to Griffin about Jeddah's visa issues, "Steve," a supposed son, called and harangued me for fifteen minutes about my questions. While Steve said he didn't know the facts, he insisted that Jeddah was a State Department consulate "with only a few" CIA employees. Steve asserted he was a GAO analyst and knew the State Department and Langley through travel with his parents. Steve also alleged that he had once applied to join the Agency but it did not accept him because his scores on the written test were not high enough.

Griffin's successor as consul general, Douglas H. Jones, did in his brief tenure there was to send Bryfogle back to Washington. Jones also wanted all my routine reports on Southwest Germany classified so that congressmen and others couldn't read them.[25]

Jones and his replacement, Day Olin Mount (formerly with the NSA in Bad Aibling, Bavaria), both had a curious career pattern: they had spent most of their working lives in Washington, DC, with brief excursion tours to Scotland and Greece, respectively, something totally out of character for a typical FSO. The Legal Advisor's Office at the State Department once called me and my editor, Verne Lyon, at *Unclassified*, telling us not to connect the two men to the CIA.

Mount was especially bad in that he was a poor manager and really didn't grasp how Germany was changing. He repeatedly blocked me from reaching out to less popular German politicians, such as Rolf Schlierer, the leader of the local Republikaner (the "Reps"), a farther right group. Olaf Grobel, once US Political Counselor at Bonn, wanted them investigated for Nazi ties. I tried unsuccessfully to get Schlierer sent to America in the US Information Agency's International Visitor Program. This would have gotten him meetings with local US politicians and immigration groups. (The Republikaner campaigned on immigration reform). But Mount held tight to the "old guard," the doddering, centrist, pro-US politicians and groups whose leadership had, essentially, ossified in the years since the 1950s.[26]

---

[25] Jones moved on to become Counselor for Political Affairs in Bonn and then to head the US Mission to Berlin. While there, in April 1994, he publicly criticized German domestic policy as being racist, earning a rebuke from Donald Kursch, *Chargé d'Affaires ad interim* [Acting Ambassador]. Jones didn't reply to my letter asking about his involvement in my termination.

[26] According to record-keepers, Schlierer and the "Reps" got fourteen seats and nearly 10 percent of the vote for the Baden-Württemberg parliament in March 1996. "Baden-Württemberg. Results of the Elections from 1964–2011." Statistisches Landesamt Baden-Württemberg.

Mount repeatedly defended his secretary, a former East German, Brigitte Shaw, who either had mental problems or was a "sleeper" agent for the German Democratic Republic's Stasi (secret police). (This latter possibility was alleged by Will Kramer, a former US Information Service official.) A one-time refugee from the East, she was unstable but remarkably adept at disrupting the smooth operation of the consulate. Besides watching to see who might come late to work or park an extra car in the building's lot (and then calling the offending individual's superior), Shaw would occasionally dump trash in my office. Mount thought so highly of Brigitte that he bought her a huge tropical fish tank to watch in the office—with taxpayer's money.

Another source of instability and bias in our office was Gabriele Pohlenz-Daniel, a German national and my Political Assistant. A staunch member of the center-right Christian Democratic Union (CDU), she always pressed its partisan views in official reporting and worked to suppress those of parties she opposed. These were usually the Free Democrats (a right-wing, business-oriented group) and the Republikaner. Despite my objections, Mount supported and promoted her.[27] Mount later became ambassador to Ireland (1996–1999).[28]

Then there was Kathy Hennessey, assigned to the consular section. When I met her in Washington, she was full of questions, not about what the consulate was like or about Stuttgart and its citizens, but rather about fashion trends. Later, I began hearing grumbles from Jane Whitney about how Kathy wasn't giving her the slightest idea when she would actually travel to the consulate and take up her posting. Telling Kathy that this could harm her career, I tried unsuccessfully to get her to take action.

---

[27] After Stuttgart's closure, she took a position with the American consulate in Munich.

[28] Mount did not reply to my letter about his efforts to ensure I became unemployed and stayed that way.

34

My next official dealing with Kathy came about through a problem she created for the consulate and the US government.

One day, I had a call from an officer at the US European Command (EUCOM) headquartered at Patch Barracks in a Stuttgart suburb. Kathy had refused to provide a tourist passport to an Air Force general traveling to Greece with his family within the next twenty-four hours. The general, who had only an official passport (neither military, diplomatic nor tourist), had learned he needed a Greek visa for the trip. This document would take time whereas a tourist passport didn't require a visa and could be issued quickly. For hours, I tried to negotiate with Miss Hennessey. She repeatedly refused, asserting she didn't do "walk-ins."

Using my very best diplomatic and political skills, I pointed out how her intransigence made the consulate look bad, needlessly antagonized a high government official, and might well spoil the vacation of an entire family. Additionally, I noted that gaining friends at Patch Barracks might shorten the inspection of consulate staff members' private cars when entering the base. (US military personnel, in their own vehicles, breezed right on through.) I was eventually successful: the passport was finally issued, although we kept a Foreign Service national (local hire) overtime.[29]

In Stuttgart, I also kept up my political and economic reporting, covering hot topics, such as Germans leaving the USSR where they had long been settled, the flow of East Germans across the inner German frontier after the Berlin Wall came down, and the Republikaner (whose questioning of the status quo nobody wanted to hear about). I even polled a series of "men in the street" about their mixed views of Mikhail Gorbachev, General Secretary of the USSR's Communist Party, during his Stuttgart visit.

---

[29] Miss Hennessey went on to become Counselor for Consular Affairs at the US Embassy in Madrid.

This reporting was familiar ground to me since I had done similar work fifteen years earlier as part of the State-Commerce Exchange Program when I was economic/commercial officer in Stuttgart. I covered nuclear power, then a divisive issue in the country, along with other energy issues, such as renewable forms of power. Besides carting moon rocks to Heidelberg's famous Max Planck Institute, I traveled to trade fairs around the country, promoting American business interests. Additionally, I met with German and American businessmen, and wrote about financial and industrial developments. I also summarized German newspaper reports on items of interest to Washington. To build on my contacts and improve my language skills, I hosted a weekly English/German conversational group in my residence. At one point, I was told that I had more official and unofficial contacts than any officer at the consulate save the consul general.

The Heats of India

Between my assignments to Germany (1977–1980; 1989–1991) and Saudi Arabia (1987–1989), I spent two years in New Delhi (1980–1982) as the FCS Commercial Attaché. In India, I had to contend with, as noted, Edward W. M. Bryant and his successor, Hallock Rutherford Lucius. The Economic Counselor tagged him "Luscious" Lucius, the "Loan Arranger," for unsuccessfully seeking high-profile credits for India. I traveled around Hindustan, meeting many local businessmen and writing reports on my contacts in the country. One, titled "Christmas Cheer," covered a luncheon at the home of a KGB officer, Boris Krylov. One of the Communicators, David Smith, told me that the account circulated to great merriment throughout the embassy. (I had humorously recounted the the tale of atheist Mr. Krylov's Christmas tree and other religious decorations. The report included his clumsy efforts to pour me full of Moldavian brandy to loosen my lips and reveal secrets I did not possess.)

The CIA was heavily represented in Delhi, with the "shadow" Economic Section larger than the real one. True to form, many of the spooks never declared themselves to the American diplomats they depended on for cover. One of the "Econ" officers drove a Padmini (an Indian Fiat) with Indian and not diplomatic license plates, occasioning many questions about her status.

Thanks to Nick Heflin, the Econ Counselor, I got to see how diplomacy was really done. A high-level Commerce Department trade mission had come to India, looking to conclude a mutually beneficial arrangement for both countries. While Indian government and US officials publicly sat at a table and wrangled about the terms of the agreement, Nick Heflin included me in a literal "back room" with an economic officer and several Indian government functionaries. There, we drafted the real pact that would be publicly signed later.

In contrast, "No Thanks" to Ambassador Harry G. Barnes Jr. and his Deputy Chief of Mission (deputy ambassador) Marion V. Creekmore. Through them, I learned how diplomacy was not to be done. For example, Barnes and Creekmore (the latter once associated with the questionable Southern Poverty Law Center[30]) were obsessed with selling big-ticket items to India, such as Lockheed C-130 cargo planes and General Electric jet-engine-powered generators. Either forbidden by American export control regulations or opposed by Indian government ideology, anyone could see that their pet projects were going nowhere. Meanwhile, the two men

---

[30] An organization seemingly obsessed with using fear of increasing but vaguely defined hate groups in America to generate greater donations for its work of monitoring "extremists." It has been said to equate anti-Zionism with "anti-Semitism." Muslim-American writers have tied the organization to the Jewish Anti-Defamation League, both of which have a record of spying on private citizens, and to the US Department of Homeland Security's "fusion centers" that collect personal data on Americans. Cf. *SourceWatch.org.*

flatly refused to help an American firm work with the Indians to bring solar-powered irrigation pumps to poor farmers beyond the electric grid. Expensive airplanes and oil field generating sets were sexy. Helping boost food production with bits of plastic, rubber, and a solar array apparently didn't enhance careers. Working with the US company, I myself set up an operating pump in a decorative pond in front of the embassy where Barnes and Creekmore would see it every day when they came to work. To no avail.

Bureau of Intelligence and Research (INR)

In 1991, transferred to Washington, DC from Stuttgart, I became INR's economic officer for all countries south of the Rio Grande along with the islands of the Caribbean. INR is the country's oldest intelligence organization, and I was not surprised to see Henry Ensher there. Up on the eighth floor, in my infrequently visited cubbyhole, I could smell them cooking pizza in the basement cafeteria. However, I spent most of my time in the Sensitive Compartmented Information Facility (SCIF), a glory hole that had no water fountains or toilets because spies could track messages through their pipes. To get into the SCIF, I needed a special badge (which also got me unescorted access to the CIA at Langley). To get this special badge, I had to wait until the special badge issuer returned from vacation. Then, I signed a paper saying I had read all the code words for the sources of all the information we would be consulting to write our reports. (These were words like "Keyhole," covering satellite photos called "overhead imagery." I've forgotten most of them, but they can be found in the 1989 novel *The War Birds*, by Richard Herman.)

INR was an information junkie's dream. Besides reading publications like the *New York Times*, the *Wall Street Journal*, the *Washington Post*, and wire service feeds from the Associated Press, United Press International, and Reuters, our staff had access to restricted diplomatic reporting, such as "NODIS," that is "No Distribution" beyond the addressee. We also saw NSA intercepts of telephone calls and encrypted communications. (While highly classified, these included an innocuous conversation between two Japanese businessmen in a Swiss hotel and the vice president of Panama talking on routine matters). Additionally, we got to see some, but not all, CIA messages. (The Agency has a tap on the State Department's circuits and can read every incoming and outgoing message.)

At the time of the questionable 1991 Russian coup attempt, I could compare what was reported in the newspapers with what State and the CIA were writing. It seemed the only difference between journalists' accounts and the highly classified versions were the specific names and other sources used in the government's messages. Either the press was very accomplished, or the intelligence services were not particularly proficient.

We were also treated to briefings at NSA (called the Puzzle Palace), based at Ft. Meade. According to experts there, if the NSA can't pluck messages out of the air, it can prevail on friends at the CIA to install listening devices at a target's location. Additionally, we visited the National Photographic Interpretation Center (NPIC), at the time located in Southeast Washington.[31]

The Unemployment Line

---

[31] We were shown what were called "happy snaps," unusually good overhead imagery (e.g., a photo of Dodger Stadium in Los Angeles, apparently taken at an altitude of several hundred feet and about half a mile's distance). In reality, it was from a satellite camera several hundred miles in space and three thousand miles away. Another picture was of men and women walking down the steps of the US Capitol building. Taken from hundreds of miles in the heavens, its detail could distinguish between the two sexes. I also saw photographs of a Brazilian military airfield on film a bit larger than the normal 2¼ x 2¼ format. The resolution was so good that I could almost count the rivets on the parked aircraft. Being an on-again, off-again photographer, I asked about image sharpness, something tied to the size of the film and camera. I was told that it wasn't an issue since the camera was the size of a railroad boxcar.

One day in late 1991, my career development officer called me into her office, and she told me that my appointment was being terminated. I asked if this was because I had scooped the CIA and NSA on the Chinese IRBMs or because I had done such extensive political and economic reporting in Jeddah and Stuttgart. Then again, was it because I had refused to issue visas to unqualified applicants?[32]

I never got a clear response to my question.

I decided then that I had nothing left to lose. I contacted the Government Accounting Office (GAO) branch at Main State, asking them to look into all the issues revolving around the suspicious visa program and my reports of questionable liquor sales at Jeddah. I approached the Inspector General's Office at State and filed a complaint on the same issues, and I met with the staff of the House Foreign Affairs Committee.

GAO's raison d'etre on its website is "to help improve the performance and ensure the accountability of the federal government for the benefit of the American people." Nonetheless, it sent me a "Thank you" but did nothing. The Inspector General's Office replied it could take no action because two years had elapsed and my boss, Freres, had retired. Besides, it said, visa issuance was a matter of "interpretation." The Diplomatic Security officer, Travis Moran, simply told me I had a "personality conflict" with Jay Freres.

To be sure, Diplomatic Security and the Department of State *sometimes* go after corrupt FSOs. The following are cases in point.

According to the *Washington Post*, government officials arrested Thomas P. Carroll at his parents' home in Chicago in March 2000.[33]

---

[32] In A-100, our orientation class, we had been told that only really bad apples were tossed out because the selection process was so stringent. The comment had been made by John Tkacik that the people whose appointments were terminated knew it well in advance because it was perfectly clear to them that they didn't measure up.

[33] William Claiborne, "Two Held in Visa Fraud Case," March 20, 2000.

Mr. Carroll, along with a Guyanese citizen, formed a conspiracy to sell visas to aliens. Carroll amassed a small fortune in the process: $1.3 million in cash and gold bars.

On February 6, 2003, the State Department announced that Alexander Meerovich had pled guilty to one count of visa fraud. According to State's press release, "We will continue to investigate all allegations of visa fraud vigorously and seek to prosecute and punish those people engaged in visa fraud to the fullest extent of the law." Really?

On August 1, 2013, David Seminara at the Center for Immigration Studies published an article, "Crooked FSOs Busted for Selling Visas." It recounted the stories of Michael Sestak, chief of the nonimmigrant visa section at Saigon, Vietnam, and Edy Zohar Rodriguez Duran of Georgetown, Guyana. Sestak had been arrested in May of that year for conspiracy to commit visa fraud and bribery while Duran was alleged to have sold visas for sex and money.

Considering these cases, why didn't they follow up on my charges? My guess is that they knew about the visa program for al-Qaeda.

Besides GAO and Diplomatic Security, I sought help from Congress, asking for intervention by the House Committee on Foreign Affairs. Astonishingly, during my Capitol Hill meeting with a committee staffer, he asked me, "Don't you think we need the CIA?" I don't recall my answer at the time, but I know what I would say now if I were asked the same question again: "Hell, no! The Agency is illegal." (It's principal division, the Clandestine Service, has no lawful basis for existence.)

When I was fired, State gave me no severance pay and DC's unemployment compensation (taxable thanks to Ronald Reagan) didn't go very far. In any case, I expected that speaking several languages and having lived and worked on three continents would get me a better paying and more interesting job than what I had had at the State Department. I was wrong. After hundreds of letters and telephone calls, none of which generated an interview, I thought,

"Am I being blackballed?" A reference-checking firm gave me a transcript of a conversation they had with Day O. Mount, former consul general in Stuttgart. In response to questions posed by a "prospective employer," his vague remarks appeared calculated to ensure that the "caller" wouldn't touch me.

This situation reinforced what I had seen earlier: efforts in Stuttgart to get me to fail, all of which were undoubtedly tied to the CIA and the visa incidents in Saudi Arabia.

While preparing this book, I found documents indicating some back-door communications (written, telephonic, and face-to-face) among Sally Lindover, then administrative officer; Samuel Shelton Westgate III, then director of Amerika Haus, the US Information Service facility in Stuttgart; and Day Mount. All were uniformly negative about my tenure in the Foreign Service. One report by Westgate to Lindover referred to papers that would reflect adversely upon my future in the Foreign Service. In that, he suggested she transmit them to Washington for inclusion in my personnel file.[34]

The Freedom of Information Act (FOIA)

I decided that I would try to get my job back. To do so, I needed information as to why I had been fired in the first place. (Remember that this was before I met the journalist, Joe Trento, who explained to me the incidents at Jeddah.) Depending on what I found, I could either be reemployed or obtain enough knowledge to sue the Department of State for wrongful dismissal.

In 1992, I decided to file under the FOIA to learn about my dismissal from State. I bought a copy of *Litigation Under The Federal Open Government Laws*. I also cadged free advice from the attorneys

---

[34] These records were never shared with me, then or since. Lindover never responded to my April 13, 2014 letter about the foregoing, nor did she return a May 12 telephone message about the correspondence.

who had earlier sued the government on my behalf for discrimination. If this project taught me anything, it is that the United States of America refuses to obey its own laws.

Passed in 1966, over the objections of the US Justice Department, the FOIA was strengthened in 1974 following the Watergate affair. President Lyndon B. Johnson (D-TX) at one point threatened to veto it. The object of the law is to provide people with access to material about the federal government or, for that matter, records that the government has about them. In practice, the executive branch and the courts do not treat the FOIA as the law of the land.

I saw exactly how this worked.

I filed a FOIA request with the Department of State in 1992. After delays, State sent me a few documents, which I already had, such as pay stubs and orders to travel to Saudi Arabia. I repeatedly challenged the department, stating explicitly what I was looking for. Exasperated, I filed suit in the US District Court for the District of Columbia. This action brought an excess of irrelevant paper: more pay stubs and copies of my travel orders and immaterial cable traffic that I had written or that had mentioned me in insignificant ways. I got nothing of substance relating to my dismissal. When I asked for records I knew I had created, such as my report about the Chinese IRBMs, or the classified attachment to the 1989 Inspection Report (an account of how well the consulate followed law and regulation), I was told that they couldn't be found. When I asked for reports about liquor sales at the consulate in Jeddah or the CIA's involvement in getting an American businessman fired and thrown out of Saudi Arabia, I was told that those matters were classified. The judge, Harold H. Greene (now deceased), could see those records, but I couldn't, even though I had been on the scene and knew what had been going on.

Eventually, the Justice Department prevailed on the judge to dismiss my case, after Justice and its client, the State Department, got the matter sealed as a threat to "national security." How could obtaining information about losing my job endanger "national security"?

In July 2010, I wrote State asking for what I should have requested twenty years earlier: copies of the visa application forms that I had denied and that Jay Freres and Justice Stevens subsequently approved. I also sought all records, cables, memoranda, notes, etc. that referenced them. I named the people involved in the creation of these documents and told State's Office of Information Programs and Services (OIPS), which manages the FOIA there, about their likely locations. For two years, I heard only that I was ineligible for expedited processing or a fee reduction for filing a FOIA request in the public interest.

When I sought advice and counsel from organizations supposedly having a stake in open government, such as the Electronic Privacy Information Center (EPIC), the Center for National Security Studies, Public Citizen, the Center for Constitutional Rights, as well as the Government Accountability Project, I got nowhere. They either didn't reply or, like Kate Martin, Director of the Center for National Security Studies, said they were too busy.[35]

The State Department's Position

State, through its representation at the office of the US Attorney for DC insisted that the judge assigned to my case, Reggie B. Walton, dismiss the matter because the Department (1) couldn't find any of the records I requested, and (2) it was State's policy to destroy documents according to a prescribed schedule. (Walton had been appointed to the court by George W. Bush. He was named to the

---

[35] Elizabeth Rindskopf Parker, former General Counsel at the CIA and NSA, once told me at an American Bar Association meeting that the intelligence services have a good relationship with Martin. Martin, in a class I attended at American University's Washington College of Law, told me that she believes the government's "theory" about September 11, 2001.

Foreign Intelligence Surveillance Court [FISA] by Chief Justice John G. Roberts, another Bush appointee.)

I rebutted State's remarks and I got virtually the same response each time. For example, I asked if they had contacted any of the people most directly involved in the Visas for Terrorists Program, listing their names and addresses. State's reply was that the agency didn't search officials' personal records, and it was under no obligation to contact people long retired for information. When I probed for confirmation of the records' destruction, I was told only that they no longer existed. When I pursued the dates of the alleged eradication and sought the names and titles of those who did the obliterating, I was only told that all was done according to the rules.

To rebut State's demand for the names on the visa applications I had sought, I filed an affidavit with the court, noting that, while in Jeddah, I had adjudicated about forty-five thousand visa requests per annum, an average of between one hundred and two hundred per day. During this period, I explained, the office held filing cabinets overflowing with very old visa requests, many dating back five to possibly ten or more years. Apparently, none of my predecessors in the position as Chief of the Nonimmigrant Visa Section had destroyed many or any visa applications during their tenure, even though State Department regulations required that this be done annually. During my time there, my small three-man staff and I could not destroy the ancient visa forms and still do our regular job. That involved handling the paperwork and background check procedures on the hundreds of people a day who applied for permission to visit the United States.

Conceivably, after twenty years, some records might finally have been shredded. However, what is impossible to grasp is that it was done without any record, however general, of that destruction taking place. Note the comment of Nick Pope, a former Deputy Director in the Directorate of Defence Security, British Ministry of Defence:

> ...It is certainly the case that in any large organization files and documents go missing or staffs, for whatever reasons, are unable to locate them. However, in government, the military, and the intelligence agencies document security and information management are generally taken extremely seriously, for obvious reasons, especially where classified and/or sensitive operations are concerned.[36]

However, Judge Walton ordered judgment in favor of the government, as most federal judges do in Freedom of Information matters dealing with subjects more substantive than the nesting sites of spotted owls.[37] He wrote that I had been claiming that the State Department had improperly withheld documents and said I had failed to exhaust my administrative remedies (an entirely incorrect assertion).[38] He also ruled that State had conducted an adequate search for the records I had sought (even though the Department repeatedly claimed it hadn't looked because it allegedly purges visa applications annually). In effect, Walton worked with the State Department's Office of Information Programs and Services (headed at the time by Margaret Grafeld, whom I believe

---

[36] Nick Pope with John Burroughs, USAF (ret.) and Jim Penniston USAF (ret.), *Encounter in Rendlesham Forest* (New York: Thomas Dunne Books, 2014), 226.

[37] Audubon Society v. U.S. Forest Service, 104 F.3d 1201 (10th Cir. 1997).

[38] There is a pattern to Walton's behavior on the bench. On September 26, 2014, the *Washington Post* carried an article written by Lisa Rein: "FDA whistleblowers' lawsuit over surveillance dismissed." Reggie B. Walton did not address the merits of the scientists' case, based on the government's spying on their official and personal e-mail accounts. Instead, Walton ruled that "the scientists failed to exhaust [their] administrative remedies."

to be a CIA official) to create a tenth exemption to the Freedom of Information Act: Nonexistent Records.

A similar story involves the Office of Information Programs, which has a declassification section staffed by former Foreign Service officers. One of them, Frank E. Schmelzer Jr., now deceased, told me that one declassification project he had been given had been sabotaged. Zionists at the State Department had "disappeared" records they didn't want to see the light of day. State, of course, took no action against anyone involved in that.

But What about FBI Help? Journalistic Help? High-Powered Political Help?

Ha!

After striking out with GAO and the House Committee, I called the Federal Bureau of Investigation and its parent, the Justice Department. No one wanted to talk with me. After the September 11, 2001, terrorist attacks, fifteen of whom, according to the *Los Angeles Times*, got their visas at Jeddah, I again called the FBI (at Joe Trento's suggestion).[39] After being passed from office to office, I was told to ring up their Washington Field Office. I did and was told "someone would get back to me." I'm still waiting. It's probably just as well, otherwise I would be at Guantanamo Bay or in a secret concentration camp somewhere else in the world. The Associated Press wasn't interested. I called Craig Whitlock at the *Washington*

---

[39] According to varied Internet sources, including *Linked-In, 9/11 Commission Documents, History Commons*, as well as Jon Gold, author and advocate for 9/11 Justice, Shayna Steinger issued most of these visas. Although she only had a master's degree, the State Department commissioned her as an FSO-4, a high rank for someone hired just out of Columbia University with no prior experience. The *Congressional Record* shows her name at her 1999 commissioning as Shayna Steinger *Singh*. Despite her issuing visas to terrorists and giving equivocal answers to the 9/11 Commission, Steinger is still an FSO.

Post and was ignored. I met with a journalist at the *Los Angeles Times'* Washington bureau, providing him with copies of all the information I had, including the denizens of the Jeddah CIA Base. Nothing came of that other than a lunch on their dime.

Over more than twenty years, I've written to the Chairmen of the Senate and House Intelligence Committees (John D. Rockefeller and Jane Harmon), the Democratic Leader of the House of Representatives (Nancy Pelosi), the Chairman of the House Government Operations Committee, and so on. I never received a response from any of them.

What Does This All Mean?

Like the September 11, 2001, attacks themselves (described by journalist Peter Lance as having become a cold case), the Visas for Terrorists Program, which helped recruit the "muj", later, al-Qaeda, later ISIS/ISIL, but what I call the Arab-Afghan Legion, is shrouded in secrecy, cover-ups, and deliberate government obfuscation. Just as Daniel Hopsicker recounted in detail in his book *Welcome to Terrorland, Mohammed Atta & the 9/11 Cover-Up in Florida*,[40] it's virtually impossible to penetrate the smokescreen generated by federal agencies. People refuse to talk, and people deny wrongdoing, while investigatory agencies, such as the FBI, either take no action or assert that there is no need to act. Essentially, as Hopsicker notes, "There is a demonstrable, provable, and *massive* federally supervised cover-up in place...But the real question, of course, is: *What* are they covering up? What's the *reason* for it?" [41] The reason, I believe, is this: murder, war crimes, human rights violations by government

---

[40] Daniel Hopsicker, *Welcome to Terrorland, Mohammed Atta & the 9/11 Cover-Up in Florida* (Venice, FL: The MadCow Press, 2004, 2007).
[41] Ibid., 253.

officials in support of al-Qaeda, and the creation of a cadre used to destabilize governments and countries on America's black list.

Throughout Hopsicker's investigation and during my experience and my inquiry into the visas issue, we were blocked—officially and unofficially. In my case, it was (1) the US Department of State, its Inspector General, and Diplomatic Security; (2) the Government Accounting/Accountability Office; (3) the Federal Bureau of Investigation and the US Justice Department; (4) individuals in the State Department and Central Intelligence Agency, both serving and retired; (5) the US District Court for the District of Columbia; (6) Congressmen and Congressional committee staff; (7) the *Washington Post*; the *Los Angeles Times*; the Associated Press. In a normal world, this might strain credibility, but, today, given the growth and reach of the National Security State, it does not.

This pattern of obfuscation has not gone unnoticed by others. In Peter Lance's preface to *Triple Cross*, in relation to unbelievable American governmental burial of evidence and failure to take action against attacks on the United States, he writes, "I believe that their motive was to sanitize the record and thus prevent the public from understanding the full depth of the FBI/DOJ [Department of Justice] *missteps*" [if, in fact, they were real missteps]. [42]

Too many people, and too many organizations with a watching brief for wrongdoing, ignored and continue to ignore clear evidence of questionable behavior linked to criminal activity. One or two or three individuals or institutions might disregard the evidence, arguing it being insubstantial or unauthoritative. However, when the roll is called, too many ignore too much. As we know, "national security" is a wonderful magic spell able to make malfeasance and misfeasance disappear, and corruption, fraud, mismanagement, and abuse of authority become invisible.

---

[42] Peter Lance, *Triple Cross* (New York: Harper Collins, 2006), xxiii.

Add to this situation those people who ought to know but profess no knowledge, and the soup gets mighty murky. Let me list three examples.

1) I spoke by telephone on April 15, 2013, with Andrew I. Kilgore, publisher of the *Washington Report on Middle East Affairs* and former US ambassador to Qatar (with a curiously-checkered State Department career pattern). In his soft Alabama drawl, he drew on his many years East of Suez to say that all the Arabs recruited for the war against the Soviet Union stayed in Afghanistan, rather than go home. In response to my question about their traveling to the Balkans to fight the Serbs or to Iraq to fight the Americans, he said that this was not so. He maintained that their whole purpose was to fight the communists (although, contradicting himself, he did say a few went to the Balkans).

2) Ali Ahmad Jalali, once a colonel in the Afghan army, a planner with the resistance there, a Minister of the Interior, and now a scholar at the National Defense University in Washington, DC simply doesn't answer phone calls, e-mails, or letters. (A retired European diplomat suggested that Jalali is still in the CIA's employ.)

3) Clovis Maksoud, a well-connected one-time Arab League ambassador and prolific writer and speaker on just about anything involving the Arab world, told me that he knew absolutely nothing of the Arab-Afghans.

This pattern is followed by other experts, such as Husain Haqqani, a journalist, diplomat, and adviser to four Pakistani Prime Ministers. Although a former Pakistani ambassador to Washington, now a Director of International Relations at Boston University, as well as a Senior Fellow and Director for South and Central Asia at the Hudson Institute, a policy research organization in Washington, DC, he does not respond to e-mails or letters about the itinerant gunslingers recruited by Jimmy Carter and Zbigniew Brzezinski. The same holds true for Simbal Khan, PhD, once Director for Afghanistan, and Central Asia at the Wilson International Center for Scholars in Washington, DC, and now CEO of Indus Global Initiative as well as a Senior Research Fellow at the Islamabad Policy Research Institute.

Silence in the face of twenty years of seeking answers to my not-very-complicated questions shows me that there are those in the US government who will never admit to folly. Some officials, judicial or executive, employed or retired, will forever hide illegal behavior, especially with the help of the Congress. Judge Harold H. Greene and Judge Reggie B. Walton were, and are, in my opinion, opposed to the public's right to know. Successive attorneys at the US Justice Department appear to be more loyal to their organization than to the federal Constitution, which they have sworn to "support and defend…against all enemies, foreign and domestic" (5 USC § 1331). They haven't, perhaps, considered the possibility that some individuals in the government are those enemies.

The same holds true for the officials of the CIA's "not-very-Clandestine" Service and the Foreign Service mentioned throughout this publication. Please take note of all the letters I had sent them and ask why no one, save Justice Stevens, ever responded. Similarly, Justice, in a telephone call, simply denied that any irregular visas were ever issued. Do these people really believe in what they were doing? Have they never questioned the results of their actions? Do they realize their lives served a lie? Do they fear retribution?

In my view, the answer is yes to all of the foregoing and more besides.

Tim Hunter, former US Army counterintelligence officer and administrative attaché in Jeddah commented as follows:

> The contradictions of US foreign policy are endless, traceable to the fact that few Americans care about foreign policy. Most Americans don't want a foreign

policy...period. Most, objectively speaking, are functioning isolationists. The intelligentsia has not created a foreign policy that has national support, only a series of ad hoc, periodic eruptions. Therefore, there is no consensus about foreign policy in America. Foreign policy in the United States is all about rip-offs by certain ethnic groups with power and major corporations with overseas interests.[43]

The Department of State, charged with formulating and administering American foreign policy, on occasion hires and promotes incompetents, drunkards, crooks, and human rights violators. Worse, that unfortunate organization then seeks to protect, to shield, and to defend them. Corrupt officials such as Jane Whitney and Ted Bryant, the Commercial Counselor in Delhi, are allowed to retire on fat pensions (averaging more than $5,000 a month), diagreeable and uncooperative applicants are hired and given tenure, while others, like my predecessor at Jeddah, obtain full careers in exchange for silence on the "Visas for Terrorists" Program (if, in fact, they even work for the Department of State).

Not even Adolf Hitler and the Nazis brought terrorists to Germany, trained them thoroughly, and then allowed them to operate against the German people. The United States did, though—and used its foreign ministry and intelligence services to help. And then covered it up. And still works very hard to keep the lid on.

Anyone who challenges the "official" view of American history is automatically labeled "conspiracy theorist," a carefully constructed term devised to divert attention away from dangerous reality and evidence demonstrating wrongdoing.

Yet...

---

[43] 2013 e-mail from Hunter to me.

Michael Parenti, political scientist and historian, put this all in perspective:

> Conspiracies do exist. If we define conspiracy as planning in secret for illicit purposes while misleading the public as to what is happening, then there have been conspiracies aplenty. There was the secretly planned Bay of Pigs invasion of Cuba, initially presented to the public as a purely Cuban émigré venture; the fabricated story about a North Vietnamese Tonkin Gulf attack against US destroyers, designed to induce Congress to support greater military involvement in Indochina; the CIA's clandestine operations to assassinate foreign leaders and overthrow governments; the FBI's COINTELPRO program to use illegal methods to disrupt dissenting organizations in the USA; the Watergate break-in and the Watergate cover-up; and above all, the Iran-Contra affair, involving the unlawful use of funds, secret bank accounts, the criminal destruction of government documents, the illegal financing of counterrevolutionaries in Nicaragua, the complicity of other nations, and a secret coterie of unsavory operatives all covered over with lies and misrepresentations served up by the president of the United States and other top policymakers. Not all conspiracies are fantasies.[44]

The foregoing personal account, Parenti's comment, the references to Peter Lance's *Triple Cross,* as well as Daniel Hopsicker's book *Welcome to Terrorland, Mohammed Atta & the 9/11 Cover-Up in*

---

[44] Michael Parenti, *The Sword And The Dollar, Imperialism, Revolution, and the Arms Race,* (New York: St. Martin's Press, 1989) 195.

Florida indicate deliberate government obfuscation, if not outright conspiracy.

Consider the following.

Former diplomat, university professor, and author Peter Dale Scott notes in *The Road to 9/11*[45] that, if the stories about Ali Mohamed being an FBI informant and CIA and army veteran are true, then:

1. A key planner of the 9/11 plot, and trainer in hijacking, was also an informant for the FBI.

2. This operative trained the members for all of the chief Islamist attacks inside the United States—the first World Trade Center bombing, the New York landmarks plot, and finally 9/11—as well as the attacks against Americans in Somalia and Kenya.

3. For four years, Mohamed, already named as an unindicted conspirator, was allowed to move in and out of the country.

In *Triple Cross*, Lance appears to solve this riddle: In Ali Mohamed's New York trial in 2000, he [Lance] commented, "Why did the Feds let Ali Mohamed sit out that trial? Why did they make a secret plea agreement with him; yet not force him to testify? Because Mohamed wasn't just the government's best witness to al-Qaeda's successes, he was also the best witness to the failures of the FBI and the CIA to stop bin Laden's terror campaign."[46]

Continuing, Peter Lance invokes the Spirit of Watergate, the vast Nixon "conspiracy": *What did the government know, and when did they know it?*

> There's little doubt that the CIA and DIA [Defense Intelligence Agency] ran interference for him from the mid-1980s at least until his army discharge in late 1989. Ali may have lost his official status as a

---

[45] *The Road to 9/11*. (Berkeley, CA: University of California Press, 2007) 154.
[46] *Triple Cross*, 6.

CIA asset in 1984, but it seems clear that some government agency helped him circumvent the Watch List, to secure his JFK Warfare Center posting, and to operate in the highly secure environment of Fort Bragg for years, despite compelling evidence of his loyalty to radical Islam.[47]

In one of the many instances in *Triple Cross* where there was clear evidence clearly ignored of untoward events that were to happen (or be permitted to happen), Lance states:

The FBI found that early warning of the 9/11 attacks on Ayyad's computer [Nidal Ayyad, one of Ali Mohamed's trainees] within one week of the Trade Center bombing in 1993. Why didn't they pick up on it? Why did senior FBI and Department of Justice (DOJ) officials continue to deny al-Qaeda's involvement and insist for years that the bombing was the result of a "loosely organized group" of Sunni extremists, a position that would persist right through the 9/11 Commission that endorsed the same conclusion?[48]

Lance's best description of the FBI is that it "was a dog asleep."[49] A dog "put to sleep" might be more apt, especially given the following incidents.

In *Triple Cross*, Lance continually brings in references to US government use of misinformation to cover-up (gover-up?) embarrassing knowledge of either its incompetence or corruption, or both. One instance demonstrating this situation was the sabotage of TWA

---

[47] Ibid., 68–69.
[48] Ibid., 116, citing *9/11 Commission Staff Statement*, 15.
[49] Ibid., 146.

Flight 800, a flight from New York to Paris and Rome in July 1996. In Chapter 23, "Bojinka Fulfilled," Lance dismisses the wild claim that an empty fuel tank exploded, causing the crash. His view is that a bomb on board did the job and provides persuasive information to support that outlook, such as the finding of explosives residue in the wreckage.[50]

In another instance, Lance notes in Chapter 24, "Crossing The Line," that "the Feds in the FBI's New York Office and the SDNY [Southern District of New York] had now begun to cross the line from negligence to intent in their disconnection of the dots [resulting from a series of investigations linking al-Qaeda and bin Laden and plotters in New York City]." In addition, he lambastes the carefully chosen ones, saying "the FBI and Justice Department had gone into containment mode [in later summer and early fall 1996], with key officials deciding to limit the evidence and affirmatively acting to disconnect certain dots...in others, the containment of intel was more subtle, designed to chill special agents who might otherwise have complained to their superiors about the disconnect."

Another example of Lance's belief that a "gover-up" was in place concerned the 9/11 Commission Report:

> I had developed a source on the commission staff, a former law enforcement officer [who] gave me an early warning that the commission had already begun to follow a predetermined "script" of events. Democrats and Republicans, he suggested, had gotten together and agreed up front to follow a limited investigation of the events...

---

[50] Ibid., 243, citing Matthew I. Wald, "Fate of Flight 800: The Overview: Jet's Landing Gear Is Said to Provide Evidence of a Bomb," *New York Times*, July 31, 1996. Don Van Natta Jr., "More Traces of Explosives in Flight 800," *New York Times*, August 31, 1996. Sylvia Adcock and Knut Royce, "Two Traces Found," *Newsday*, August 31, 1996.

The source insisted that evidence was being "cherry-picked" in order to fit their limited story the commission staff was prepared to tell...[51]

Transition

Having gotten this far, Esteemed Reader, you now have the background to understand the sordid history of US foreign policy. You've read the thumbnail sketches of State Department and intelligence service personnel. I hope you can see that there are failures to formulate a realistic, rational, ideology-free foreign policy based on tact and common sense, as well as universal human rights.

The visas issued in Jeddah for the mujahideen and, ultimately, al-Qaeda and ISIS/ISIL, were not a one-off program. My experience was only part of the picture. I was in at the beginning of a sordid, grim, and very dangerous shift in American foreign policy. Prior to the Afghan war against the Soviets, the United States destabilized or overthrew governments on an ad hoc basis. With the creation of the "muj," who morphed into "al-Qaeda," who then became "ISIS/ISIL," the American government developed a cadre of radicals. The government also did its best to get rid of anyone, like me, who came close to examining what was really happening.

Please bear this situation in mind throughout the following sections dealing with American involvement in other countries' internal affairs since 1945, which led to the Arab-Afghan Legion and its use in destabilizing governments and countries on Uncle Sam's "enemies list." My experience was not unique, but it helped lead to what the government was and is really doing.

---

[51] *Triple Cross*, 389.

INTRODUCTION

The US government has a long history of destabilizing or planning to destabilize countries and their rulers, not just in the Third World but in Europe and at home in the US. Here are but a few, truncated examples, providing a small taste of what was to come later.

Europe

In Italy, roughly one hundred people were blown up, first in Milan (in 1969) and then, Bologna (1980), ostensibly by anarchists but, in reality, by Italian military intelligence—at the behest of American covert organizations. General Vito Miceli, chief of Italian military intelligence, attested "that the [institution that did the bombings]…was formed under a secret agreement with the United States and within the framework of NATO." Paolo Taviani, one-time Italian defense minister, stated "that during his time in office [1955–1958] the Italian secret services were bossed and financed by 'the boys in Via Veneto'—that is, the CIA agents [sic] in the US Embassy in the heart of Rome." Years later, Italian secret service General Gianadelio Maletti said "that the CIA gave its tacit approval to a series of bombings in Italy in the 1970s to sow instability and keep communists from taking power...The CIA wanted, through the birth of an extreme nationalism and the contribution of the far right—to stop [Italy] sliding to the left.'"[52]

Italy was part of NATO, an "ally."

At Home

There was "Operation Northwoods."

This was a scheme devised by the American general staff to begin a war with Cuba. Likely growing from President Dwight Eisenhower's (R-KS) idea, the object was to put an end to Fidel Castro once and for all. "[T]he plan called for innocent people to be shot on American streets; for boats carrying refugees fleeing to be sunk on the high seas; for a wave of violent terrorism to be launched in Washington, DC, Miami, and elsewhere. People would be framed for bombings they did not commit; planes would be hijacked. Using phony evidence, all of it would be blamed on Castro, thus giving Lemnitzer [Lyman L. Lemnitzer, four-star general and Chairman of the Joint Chiefs of Staff] and his cabal the excuse as well as the public and international backing they needed to launch their war."[53]

"Operation Northwoods" looks like a blueprint for September 11, 2001.

---

[52] *Road to 9/11*, 180–181, citing Daniele Ganser, *NATO's Secret Armies: Operation Gladio and Terrorism in Western Europe* (London: Frank Cass Publishers, 2005), 63–83. Philip Willan, *Puppetmasters: The Political Use of Terrorism in Italy* (London: Constable and Company, 1991), 122–131, 160–167, 26. William Scobie, *Observer*, August 11, 1990. "Italian General Alleges CIA Link to Bombings," Reuters, August 4, 2000.

[53] James Bamford, *Body of Secrets* (New York: Doubleday, 2001), 82–83.

The Third World and Present-Day Troubles

Former professor of economics (University of Ottawa) Michel Chossudovsky, now President and Director of the Centre for Research on Globalization (CRG) and Editor of GlobalResearch.ca, linked a 2013 CNN video to an article on his website about former Secretary of State Hillary Clinton. In it she formally acknowledged that the United States created, trained, and paid the Afghan mujahideen, the same people she said American soldiers were fighting. Clinton admitted that President Ronald Reagan (R-CA), along with the Democratic leaders of Congress, thought it was a great idea to end Soviet attempts to control Central Asia. So, the American government worked, she said, with Pakistani Inter-Services Intelligence [ISI] and the Pakistani military to recruit Wahhabi fundamentalists from all over, including Saudi Arabia, to battle the USSR.[54]

This was the beginning of al-Qaeda. The "Base" formed the basis for the Arab-Afghan Legion, whose steady march to terror makes Xenophon's *Anabasis* (his account of Greeks trapped in Persia after helping a fifth century BC regime change) seem like a stroll in the park.

Chossudovsky added that Clinton neglected to mention that the United States had never, in the past thirty years, stopped supporting and financing al-Qaeda. America, in fact, used it as a means of wrecking free and independent states, violating the UN Charter and other treaties and international acts to which the US was signatory. As an example, he points out that the new Secretary of State, John Kerry, was in close contact with al-Nusra, an al-Qaeda-affiliated organization in Syria, a US-funded entity on the State Department's terrorist list.[55]

---

[54] Cf. http://www.globalresearch.ca/hillary-clinton-we-created-al-qaeda/5337222.

[55] Prof. Michel Chossudovsky, "Hillary Clinton: 'We Created Al Qaeda,'" *Global Research,* June 1, 2013.

Small beginnings? Unconnected events? Maybe. But, from tiny acorns, mighty oaks do, indeed, grow. For example, consider all those visas I was required to issue in Jeddah, the place where the September 11 hijackers got their papers to come to the United States. Are some really large buildings missing from New York's skyline?

VISAS FOR TERRORISTS

On September 11, 2001, alleged "terrorists" captured four airplanes. They flew two of them into the World Trade Center in New York City, and one into the Pentagon in Alexandria, Virginia. Another was reportedly retaken by the passengers on board, but later supposedly crashed. According to the *Los Angeles Times*, fifteen of the nineteen supposed hijackers obtained their visas to visit the United States from the American consulate general at Jeddah, Saudi Arabia. What the *LA Times* did not say was that the Jeddah consulate, like the American consulate at Benghazi, Libya, was an American intelligence operation in which close cooperation with terrorists was more important than diplomacy. Jeddah, in the 1990s, was the fifth-largest visa-issuing post in the Middle East. It had long been aiding the CIA and its then-asset Osama bin Laden in recruiting terrorists for training in the United States for use in the war against the Soviet Union in Afghanistan. Many had thought that, with the end of the USSR's occupation of Afghanistan, the American training program ceased. However, analysis of wars conducted by George W. Bush and Barack H. Obama in Afghanistan, Iran, Iraq, Libya, Pakistan, Syria, and Yemen seems to show that the Visas for Terrorists Program had never stopped and may well have been expanded, a view shared by journalist Joe Trento.[56] Further, it apparently had long been in operation elsewhere. I well remember speaking with a retired consular officer in the 1990s, telling him about the enormous pressure to issue illegal visas at Jeddah. His response was that it had happened before, was apparently happening again, and it was now time to get the CIA's Indians back onto the reservation.

---

[56] Communicated in a 2013 e-mail to the author.

HOW DID THIS START?

This Visas for Terrorists Program was set in motion by President James Earl Carter (D- GA) and his National Security Advisor, Zbigniew Kasimierz Brzezinski, upon the advice and counsel of the Central Intelligence Agency. However, this was not an ad hoc operation, conceived and carried out in response to a specific foreign policy issue. Rather, it was another of too many CIA efforts to destroy governments, countries, and politicians disfavored by the American "establishment" in its "bipartisan" approach to matters abroad. Whether it was opposing the imaginary evils of communism, the fictitious malevolence of Islam, or the invented wickedness of Iran, America and its intelligence services, brave defenders of "The City Upon A Hill"[57] sought out and created fear and loathing of peoples and countries essentially engaged in efforts to better their lives and improve their political world. Along the way, Agency-sponsored murders, war crimes, and human rights violations proved to be good business. Jobs for the Clandestine Service (people who recruit and run spies), sales of weapons and aircraft, as well as the myriad items needed to control banks, countries,

---

[57] "For we must consider that we shall be as a city upon a hill. The eyes of all people are upon us," John Winthrop, Governor, Massachusetts Bay Colony, 1630.

and peoples all provided income for and benefits to American companies.

The manner in which this was done helped create and shape a coast to coast consensus of support for the intelligence services and their actions. Kevin Robert Ryan, in *Another 19, Investigating Legitimate 9/11 Suspects,*[58] devotes chapter 11 to a discussion of originating and framing "the national conversation about terrorism," containing examples of terrorism propaganda and actions, including *Gladio*, devised by US government officials. *Gladio* was a NATO concept of stay-behind secret European armies to counter communist takeovers of countries at the ballot box. It engaged in subversive and criminal activities in several nations.

Discussing terrorism roles for L. Paul Bremer, head of the Coaliton Provisional Authority and Presidential Envoy to Iraq, and Brian Michael Jenkins, an alleged security expert, Ryan notes:

> ...it would not have been the first time that the American people were subject to the hard sell of a threat to national security only to discover that the threat was overblown or nonexistent. The Soviet military threat to the U.S. after World War II is now widely known to have been a fabrication that was hyped for political and financial gains.[59]

> The propaganda that drove the Cold War was effective in establishing government policy primarily because it was effective in framing the national conversation about what threats were important to consider and

---

[58] Kevin Robert Ryan, *Another 19, Investigating Legitimate 9/11 Suspects,* (Microbloom, 2013), 179–200.

[59] Ibid., 179, citing John Glaser, "CIA Documents Drastically Overestimated Soviet Capabilities," *Antiwar.com*, September 28, 2011.

in controlling the media. The same has been true for the propaganda driving the War on Terror.[60]

To improve our understanding of Langley and the US government's approach to foreign policy, let's focus on just a few American-engineered disasters as a means of gaining perspective on the Visas for Terrorists Program, run, in part, out of the CIA's Jeddah, Saudi Arabia, consulate. Aimed at getting the Soviets out of Afghanistan, that agenda drew on expertise acquired throughout the growth of the National Security State. Its first success in destroying governments was overthrowing the legitimate rule of Mohammed Mossadegh in Iran in 1953. The second success was in deposing Jacobo Arbenz Guzman, president of Guatemala, the following year. Thanks to the politicians in Washington, there were more and there will be more. America is, essentially, a failed state whose *raison d'etre* is global war to keep its economy "healthy."

Mohammad Mossadegh: First Victim of First CIA Coup d'Etat

In 1951, Mossadegh led the seizure of the Anglo-Iranian Oil Company (later, British Petroleum, now BP), with a near-unanimous vote in parliament where he piloted the National Front. After years of exploitation and fed up with British imperialism, including its invasion and occupation of the country during World Wars I and II, the Iranian government demanded damages and compensation for lost revenue. Britain retaliated with a boycott and an embargo on Iranian oil, designed to create economic problems there, not unlike US pressure on the country today. (Anglo-Iranian, 51 percent owned by the UK government, had kept 84 percent of Iranian oil revenues for itself, more than double the sum it gave Iran as

---

[60] Ibid.

royalties. In contrast, in a 1950 agreement, ARAMCO [Arabian American Oil Company] in Saudi Arabia gave its hosts 50 percent of profits derived from Saudi oil.) Mossadegh, on becoming prime minister, visited the United States in 1951, primarily to defend the nationalization of Anglo-Iranian. Despite a six-week tour of the United States, meeting President Harry Truman and addressing the UN's Security Council, the British and the new American government, led by yet another soldier (Dwight Eisenhower) and the Dulles brothers (Allen, Director of Central Intelligence; John Foster, Secretary of State) saw Mossadegh as a radical socialist with possible ties to the Soviet Union. All seemed to ignore British reality: that the UK government had nationalized coal, electricity, and railroads in the late 1940s. They also apparently ignored Mossadegh's foreign and domestic status of lawyer, anti-colonialist, and attendee at the Carthaginian Treaty of Versailles Conference in 1919. He was *Time* magazine's Man of the Year for 1951. The Anglo-Americans were undoubtedly concerned that his defiance of the colonialists thrilled the Arabs in the region. In Iran itself, Mossadegh had the support of nearly 100 percent of the population, according to the American ambassador in Tehran.[61]

The United States, working in concert with the United Kingdom, began to manipulate elections in Iran with a view toward removing Mossadegh's supporters through "free and fair" polls—and worse. Langley had been using its unlimited funds to buy the support of "Iranian journalists, preachers, army, and police officers, and members of parliament" to stir up opposition to the lawful government and to remove Mossadegh from power. Not unlike present-day events in the region, the Agency bought the help of the "Warriors of Islam" listed by that same

---

[61] Oliver Stone and Peter Kuznick; *The Untold History of the United States* (New York: Gallery Books, 2012), 258; citing *Foreign Relations of the United States, 1952-1954* Vol. 10, US Govt. Printing Office 1989, 80.

office as a "terrorist gang." [62] CIA official Kermit Roosevelt Jr., grandson of President Theodore Roosevelt (R-NY), organized the coup. Kermit set mobs loose in the capital and spread rumors that Mossadegh was "a Communist and a Jew." Roosevelt's "rent a thugs" (including Ayatollah Ruhollah Musavi Khomeini, a future leader), masqueraded as communists, attacked clerics, and wrecked a mosque.[63] At the same time, Roosevelt and his minions worked with the weak "Shah" Mohammad Reza Pahlavi to issue decrees removing Mossadegh from office. The Prime Minister retaliated by arresting the Shah's emissary and stating that the Shah could not remove him without consent of parliament. Fearing a backlash from Mossadegh's supporters, the Shah fled the country.

However, Roosevelt, the CIA, and Britain's Secret Intelligence Service (MI6), using mutinous soldiers and hired demonstrators, managed to get Mossadegh arrested and confined to his house for life. When the Shah flew back to Tehran from exile, CIA Chief Allen Dulles accompanied him. Mohammad Reza Pahlavi, becoming a staunch puppet of the United States to whom he owed everything, subsequently ran a brutally repressive government from 1953 to 1979. That year, he was overthrown by a popular revolt. In the meantime, the United States got access to a great supply of black gold. (Iran then pumped about 40 percent of Middle Eastern oil.)[64]

The CIA executed similar scenarios in Latin America. First, however, there was Guatemala.

---

[62] Ibid. 260, citing Tim Weiner, *Legacy of Ashes: The History of the CIA* (New York: Doubleday, 2007), 86.

[63] Ibid.

[64] Ibid., 259 and 260.

Guatemala

Dwight D. Eisenhower wanted to nullify the November 1950 free and fair election of Jacobo Arbenz Guzman as president of Guatemala. Arbenz, not unlike Hugo Chavez in Venezuela, sought a redistribution of wealth to benefit the poor, providing them freedom, health, and happiness. However, Arbenz had roused Dwight D.'s ire by speaking out against the 2 percent who had owned 60 percent of the land. He wanted to continue the revolution against the policies of the ruthless, US-backed dictator, Jorge Ubico, overthrown in 1944. America's "fawning corporate media" (to use ex-CIA officer Ray McGovern's term) went on the attack. The *New York Times* tagged the Arbenz government as a cancer and asserted that Communist influence was growing, calling the regime "a...front for Russian imperialism in Central America." The *Washington Post*, ever a tool of the US government, titled one article "Red Cell in Guatemala."[65]

Arbenz was undaunted. His first move was to target the United Fruit Company (UFC) holding five hundred fifty thousand acres, 20 percent of the country's arable land, with connections to railroads, ports, shipping companies, and banana plantations. He offered UFC $600,000, based on the company's own assessed value of the acreage. Unfortunately for Guatemala, the Dulles family and high officials at the State Department such as John Moors Cabot, Assistant Secretary of State for Inter-American Affairs; and Thomas Dudley Cabot, his brother, Director of International Security Affairs were large stockholders in and/or former board members of United Fruit. They would do whatever it took to preserve their personal interests. They could count on strong support in Congress, principally Senate

---

[65] Ibid., 262, 263, citing Piero Gleijeses, *Shattered Hope: The Guatemalan Revolution and the United States, 1944-1954* (Princeton, NJ: Princeton University Press, 1991), 150. "The Guatemalan Cancer," *New York Times*, June 8, 1951. "Red Cell in Guatemala," *Washington Post*, March 4, 1952.

Foreign Relations Committee member, Henry Cabot Lodge Jr. (R-MA), whose family had long profited from its United Fruit holdings.[66] (And whatever it took included using former US Ambassador to Greece, Jack Peurifoy as Ambassador to Guatemala. Tagged by his wife as "pistol packing Peurifoy," he was also known as "the butcher of Athens" for his direct, "undiplomatic" efforts on behalf of the right-wing, anti-communist government of Greece. Peurifoy, who could speak no Spanish, sent a long cable after an acrimonious dinner he had with Arbenz. He wrote, "I am definitely convinced that if the President is not a communist, he will certainly do until one comes along."[67]

In late summer 1953, following the Iran coup, the Eisenhower administration decided to use covert action in destroying the Arbenz government. Walter Bedell (Beetle) Smith, former CIA director and another military man took charge of wrecking the elected Arbenz regime using propaganda and disinformation. ("According to a United Fruit Company official, the Agency had help. 'United Fruit was involved at every level' in the planning and execution of the coup. [A] mercenary force was trained on one of the company's plantations in Honduras."[68] In a June 1954 armed attack, American warplanes supported CIA-trained hirelings from neighboring Honduras and Nicaragua. At first unsuccessful, the invasion was supplemented by additional US military aircraft. After Arbenz, seeing all was lost,

---

[66] Ibid., 262, 263, citing Stephen Kinzer, *Overthrow: America's Century of Regime Change* (New York: Times Books, 2006), 134–135.

[67] Ibid., 262–263, citing Peter Chapman, *Bananas*; Richard H. Immerman, *The CIA in Guatemala*; Stephen C. Schlesinger and Stephen Kinzer, *Bitter Fruit: The Untold Story of the American Coup in Guatemala*.

[68] Parenti, *Sword And The Dollar*, 198, citing Jeff McMahon, *Reagan and the World* (New York: Monthly Review Press, 1985), 13. Also Stephen Kinzer and Stephen Schlesinger, *Bitter Fruit: The Untold Story of the American Coup in Guatemala* (Garden City, NY: Doubleday, 1982).

handed the government over to a military junta, the CIA bombed the principal military base and the government's radio station.

Secretary of State, John Foster Dulles (for whom the Chantilly, Va. international airport is named), announced that democracy had triumphed over Communism in Guatemala. A British official noted otherwise, commenting "in places [that speech] it might almost be Molotov [then Russian foreign minister] speaking about... Czechoslovakia—or Hitler about Austria."[69]

Bill Blum related the American government's use of the news media (with CIA assistance) to isolate and bring down Guatemala's legitimate government. Misinformation spread by the US Information Service in Latin America, such as the distribution of one hundred thousand copies of the pamphlet "Chronology of Communism in Guatemala" along with twenty-seven thousand copies of "anti-Communist cartoons and posters" helped the coup succeed. The Americans even solicited the Roman Catholic Church's Francis Cardinal Spellman to help the CIA meet with churchmen in Guatemala and have them preach against the godless Communists.[70]

Esteemed Reader, that was then; this is almost now. Let's jump twenty-five years to Afghanistan, "the Graveyard of Empires."

---

[69] Stone and Kuznick, 263–265, citing Weiner, *Legacy of Ashes*, 461; Young, "Great Britain's Latin America Dilemma," 588.

[70] William Blum, *Killing Hope, U.S. Military and CIA Interventions Since World War II* (Monroe, Maine: Common Courage Press, 2004), 77.

ASLEEP AT THE SWITCH? OR
WAS THAT TRAIN WRECK LONG
PLANNED?

Afghanistan

In 1979, a popular, student-led revolt drove the brutally repressive Shah of Iran, a longtime American lapdog, from power. Consequently, US intelligence agencies lost access to Iranian-based message interception posts targeting the Soviet Union, at the time extending its influence in Afghanistan. To replace these posts, American officials suggested that Pakistan take over. Simultaneously, the Central Intelligence Agency advocated secret American backing for Afghans resisting the Soviet-supported Communist government in Kabul. To avoid directly antagonizing the Soviets, the CIA would pass money and weapons through the Pakistanis, who already had been providing aid to the rebels using Saudi money.

US President Carter (D-GA) and his National Security Advisor, Zbigniew Brzezinski bought this idea, although Carter did not accept it at first. The selling point was that it would oppose Soviet policy in Afghanistan. Additionally, it would divert Muslim energy (buoyed up by their success in overthrowing the Shah) away from the United States. The intent was to channel it toward the Russians. Carter set the train wreck in motion on July 3, 1979, when he signed an intelligence "finding" allowing $500,000 in nonlethal Agency aid to Afghan insurgents. That day, Brzezinski asserted, he wrote a note to the president saying that this assistance would likely "result in military intervention by the Soviets."[71]

Zbig's crystal ball had the right wavelength. On December 24, 1979, the Red Army marched into Afghanistan. Apparently, the initial purpose was to replace an unmanageable but pro-USSR government with a more flexible one. Zbig and "official" Washington saw it otherwise, as a Soviet drive toward the Indian Ocean, the greatest of Britain's fears in the nineteenth century.

Pakistan's military government (with its interest in atomic bombs) was no longer an odorous polecat. It was an ally. It needed America's support and protection, no matter its questionable policy toward human rights or support for attacks on the US embassy in Islamabad. Brzezinski wanted to make the Soviets pay. In a secret memo to Carter on December 26, 1979, he wrote that the invasion gave the United States a chance to "sow shit in [the Soviets'] backyard." According to Trento, America "would pay for the shit, the Pakistanis would deliver it, and the Afghans would do the actual sowing. Years later, the blowback from the operation would result in a worldwide shit storm."[72]

As Senator Everett McKinley Dirksen (R-IL) is often misquoted as saying, "A million here and a million there, pretty soon, you're talking real money." Carter and Brzezinski's war in Afghanistan proved the phrase to be right on the mark. Carter's State Department first offered Pakistan $150 million in aid and credits. Then, Secretary of State Cyrus Vance upped it to $400 million. After Pakistan deemed

---

[71] D. Armstrong and J. Trento, *America and the Islamic Bomb* (Hanover, NH: Steerforth Press, 2007), chapter 5.
[72] Ibid., 90.

this insufficient, Warren Christopher, Deputy Secretary of State, and Brzezinski proposed $500 million in economic aid over two years. This was also unacceptable. As finally configured, the dollars for dynamite program began with a piddling $20 million for weapons in 1980, and $30 million in 1981, but then jumped substantially through that decade, reaching $630 million in military aid per annum by 1987. During the '80s, more than $3 billion moved out of the taxpayer's pockets and into the CIA, which passed the funds on to Pakistan's Inter-Services Intelligence (ISI) and then to the Afghan terrorists.

The United States and its supposed "intelligence" service directed that $3 billion to the Afghan "insurgents," the mujahideen, through Pakistan's president, Muhammad Zia Ul Haq. He then guided the funds (and weapons purchased with them) to the most extreme faction there, led by Gulbuddin Hekmatyar.[73] Former State Department official Stephen Cohen noted: "The people we did support were the nastier, more fanatic types of mujahideen." Oliver Stone, film director, screenwriter, and producer and Peter Kuznick, history professor at American University in Washington, DC, add that "The CIA even provided between 2,000 and 2,500 U.S.-made Stinger missiles, some of which Wikileaks revealed were used to down NATO helicopters three decades later."[74]

---

[73] "A man of legendary cruelty," he "was known...to patrol the bazaars of Kabul with vials of acid, which he would throw in the face of any woman who dared to walk outdoors without a full burka covering her face." He was also remembered for skinning prisoners alive. See following note.

[74] Stone and Kuznick, 459, citing James J. F. Forest, ed., *Countering Terrorism and Insurgency in the 21ˢᵗ Century; International Perspectives,* vol. 2 (Westport, CT: Greenwood Publishing Group), 468. Robert Dreyfuss, *Devil's Game: How the United States Helped Unleash Fundamentalist Islam* (New York: Henry Holt, 2005), 267. Stephen Buttry and Jake Thompson, "UNO's Connection to Taliban Centers on Education, UNO Program," *Omaha World Herald,* September 16, 2001, 1.

According to *Washington's Blog*,[75] Brzezinski said of and to the mujahideen, "We know of their deep belief in God—that they're confident that their struggle will succeed. 'That land over there is yours, and you'll go back to it someday because your fight will prevail, and you'll have your homes, your mosques, back again because your cause is right, and God is on your side.'" Citing a variety of sources and the Maktab al-Khidamat (Services Office, which supported the Arab-Afghans), www.globalsecurity.org wrote:

> Many Muslims from other countries assisted the various mujahideen groups in Afghanistan. Some groups of these veterans have been significant factors in more recent conflicts in and around the Muslim world. Osama bin Laden, originally from a wealthy family in Saudi Arabia, was a prominent organizer and financier of an all-Arab Islamist group of foreign volunteers; his Maktab al-Khidamat[76] funneled money, arms, and Muslim fighters from around the Muslim world into Afghanistan, with the assistance and support of the Saudi and Pakistani governments. These foreign fighters became known as "Afghan Arabs" and their efforts were coordinated by Abdullah Yusuf Azzam. (A highly influential Palestinian Sunni Islamic scholar and theologian, who preached in favor of both defensive jihad and offensive jihad by Muslims to help the Afghan mujahideen against the Soviet invaders and became a leader of al-Qaeda.)[77]

---

[75] "Sleeping With The Devil," *www.globalresearch.ca*, September 5, 2012.

[76] A front organization—*Washington's blog*, citing MSNBC, 1998.

[77] Bill Moyers, "A Brief History of Al Qaeda," *PBS.com*, July 27, 2007.

As *Washington's Blog* observed (and as my experience in Jeddah confirmed), Osama bin Laden partnered with the CIA to recruit Arabs from countries all over the Middle East, including Egypt, Lebanon, Syria, as well as from Palestinian refugee camps. Non-Arab militants from Pakistan were also enlisted. The Agency, it was said, felt that Arabs were easier to deal with than Afghans. Prof. Michel Chossudovsky's article "Who Is Osama Bin Laden" [78] recounted the numbers of those Arab-Afghans marching towards global war. Cheered on by the CIA and Pakistan's ISI, roughly thirty-five thousand Muslim radicals hailing from forty countries fought in Afghanistan from 1982 to 1992. Tens of thousands more studied in Pakistani religious schools. In all, one hundred thousand Arab-Afghans "were directly influenced by the...jihad." [79] Part of the funds for this came from the drug trade. [80] CIA affiliates boosted drug production and use in South Asia and beyond astronomically. [81]

Despite (or, perhaps, because of) the decision to send a considerable amount of modern weapons and a bonanza in covert funds, the people involved still support that policy. As *Washington's Blog* noted, Senator Orrin Hatch (R-UT), then on the Senate Select Committee on Intelligence where he remained until 2011, asserted in the 1990s he would still support Osama bin Laden's fighters. Even knowing what they might do subsequently, "It was worth it," he said. (Hatch serves now on the Senate Subcommittee for Crime and Terrorism.) In 1998, Brzezinski, asked by *Le Nouvel Observateur* if he regretted "having given arms and advice to future terrorists," responded "No." As *Washington's Blog* recounts it, Brzezinski went on to say, "What is most important to the history of the world? The Taliban or the

---

[78] *Global Research*, September 12, 2001.

[79] Ahmed Rashid, "The Taliban: Exporting Extremism," *Foreign Affairs*, November–December 1999.

[80] Alfred McCoy, "Drug Fallout: the CIA's Forty Year Complicity in the Narcotics Trade," *The Progressive*, August 1, 1997.

[81] cf. Gary Webb, *Dark Alliance* (New York: Seven Stories Press, 1998).

collapse of the Soviet empire? Some stirred-up Muslims or the liberation of Central Europe and the end of the Cold War?"

Brzezinski, who later became foreign policy advisor to Barack Obama, left out something a bit more substantive in his "clarification" of his actions. According to Peter Dale Scott in *The Road to 9/11*, Carter's National Security Advisor[82] set up a Nationalities Working Group to exploit Muslim dissatisfaction within the USSR. [83] At the center of this group were the disciples of a Russian count, Alexandre Benigsen, who viewed fundamentalist Islam in Central Asia as a great threat to the Soviet Union.[84] The group worked with the Saudi intelligence service to contact Soviet Muslims visiting Mecca for the Hajj.[85] [86]

What's more, Brzezinski said that Carter, as early as 1978, had approved his (Brzezinski's) proposals to undertake "a comprehensive, covert action program designed to help the non-Russian nations in the Soviet Union more actively pursue their desire for independence—a program in effect to destabilize the Soviet Union."[87] The CIA distributed written materials to different ethnic regions, especially in the Ukraine[88]and worked with ISI, Saudi Arabia, and the International Islamic Relief Organization (IIRO)

---

[82] Son of a toffee-nosed Polish aristocrat displaced by the Communists

[83] *The Road to 9/11*, 70–71.

[84] Ibid., citing Alexandre Benigsen and Marie Broxup, his daughter, *The Islamic Threat to the Soviet State* (New York: St. Martin's Press, 1983).

[85] A ritual pilgrimage required of all Muslims at least once in their lifetime, if they are able.

[86] *Road to 9/11*, citing Robert Dreyfuss, *Devil's Game, How the United States Helped Unleash Fundamentalist Islam* (New York: Metropolitan Books/Henry Holt, 2005), 254.

[87] Ibid., 72, citing National Security Archive Interview with Dr. Zbigniew Brzezinski, June 13, 1997.

[88] Ibid., citing Robert Gates, *From the Shadows: The Ultimate Insider's Story of Five Presidents and How They Won the Cold War* (New York: Simon and Schuster, 1996), 91–92.

to distribute Wahhabi-oriented Qurans in the USSR.[89] (Wahhabis are extremely purist Muslims who dominate religious life, politics, and society in Saudi Arabia.)

It wasn't just money, propaganda, and influence that Brzezinski was peddling. In January 1980, the Polish national security advisor traveled to Egypt to drum up support for jihad in Afghanistan. He persuaded Anwar Sadat, then president of Egypt, to allow the US air force to fly Soviet-made Egyptian weapons to recruited fighters in Afghanistan. Sadat, who despised the Muslim Brotherhood, worked with the Americans to recruit, train, and arm groups of Brotherhood members, who were later called the mujahideen.[90] Just like Obama and Syria today,[91] US military trainers were sent to the "Gift of the Nile" to instruct Egyptian volunteers for jihad.[92]

It wasn't just in Egypt or elsewhere that the mujahideen were trained. Beginning in 1980, thousands were brought to America and made competent in terrorism by Green Berets and SEALS at US government East Coast facilities.[93] According to *Jane's Defence Weekly*, quoted in *The War on Truth*,[94] "Over ten thousand mujahideen were 'trained in guerilla warfare and armed with sophisticated weapons.'"

---

[89] Ibid., 127. Interesting. Unlike the Christian Bible, there is only one Quran.

[90] *Devil's Game*, 274.

[91] After all, Brzezinski was reportedly one of Obama's professors or advisors at Columbia.

[92] *Devil's Game*, 275, citing John Cooley, *Unholy Wars* (London: Pluto Press, 1999), 32; and also Andrew Kreig, *Presidential Puppetry, Obama, Romney, and Their Masters* (Washington, DC: Eagle View Books, 2013), 28.

[93] Ibid., 277.

[94] Nafeez Mosaddeq Ahmed, *The War On Truth* (Northampton, MA: Olive Branch Press, 2005), 11, citing Bedi, Rahul, "Why? An Attempt to Explain the Unexplainable," *Jane's Defence Weekly*, September 14, 2001.

Are Turkeys Smarter Than American Government Officials?

Not unsurprisingly, Brzezinski's turkeys, after 1993, came home to roost. Several men who were convicted of blowing up the World Trade Center in 1993 "had trained or fought with or raised money for Brzezinski's "agitated Muslims."[95] Peter Dale Scott concluded that the CIA-supported opposition to the Soviets in Afghanistan was the "worst conceived" covert operation in US history. Some of the "disastrous details" were "to sponsor an 'Arab-Afghan legion' and then expand the resistance campaign into an international jihadi movement."[96] Scott further notes that "Casey [CIA Director William J. Casey] began to use the outside—the Saudis, the Pakistanis, BCCI[97]to run what they couldn't get through Congress."[98] Scott explains "Thus BCCI enabled Casey to conduct foreign policy without the constraints imposed by the public democratic state. Our archival and mainstream histories have not yet acknowledged this." [99]

Washington's Blog goes on to quote journalist Robert Dreyfuss as writing:

> In the decades before 9/11, hard-core activists and organizations among Muslim fundamentalists on the far right were often viewed as allies for two reasons because they were seen as fierce anti-communists and because they opposed secular nationalists such

---

[95] *Road to 9/11*, 74–75, citing Tim Weiner, "Blowback From the Afghan Battlefield," *New York Times*, March 13, 1994.

[96] Ibid., 114, 115.

[97] Bank of Credit and Commerce International, eventually shuttered for money laundering and other financial crimes. It worked closely with Langley to arm and finance the "Arab-Afghan Legion." See following note.

[98] *Road to 9/11.*, 116, citing Peter Truell and Larry Gurwin, *False Prophets: The Inside Story of BCCI* (Boston: Houghton Mifflin, 1992); 133–134.

[99] Ibid., 116–117.

as Egypt's Gamal Abdel Nasser, Iran's Mohammed Mossadegh…Choosing Saudi Arabia over Nasser's Egypt was probably the single biggest mistake the United States has ever made in the Middle East.

According to *Washington's Blog*, Dreyfuss allowed that another great error was the wild idea that Islam would penetrate the USSR and unknit the Soviet Union's Asian regions. He added that the US alliance with the Afghans long predated the Soviet invasion in 1979. It was really rooted in CIA actions there back in the 1960s and 1970s, and it progressed to the jihadists' civil war in the 1980s, giving rise to the Taliban and al-Qaeda. In his book, *Devil's Game*, Dreyfuss shows that the diplomats and analysts at the US Department of State were clueless as to what was occurring in Iran and other countries, and that they had little knowledge of Islam, something my own short experience at State confirmed.

Perez Hoodbhoy, Pakistani nuclear scientist and peace activist, was quoted in the *Blog* as writing: "Officials like Richard Perle, Assistant Secretary of Defense [1981–1987], immediately saw Afghanistan not as the locale of a harsh and dangerous conflict to be ended but as a place to teach the Russians a lesson."[100]

Washington's Blog noted that the Saudis readily embraced the Afghan war, if only as a means of providing an outlet for their disaffected subjects who questioned the kingdom's corruption and repression, and its alliance with the United States. CIA-funded ads appeared in publications all over the world, seeking recruits for the Great Jihad against the Soviets. The US Agency for International Development (USAID) gave $50 million to the University of Nebraska to print textbooks urging Afghan children to "pluck out the eyes

---

[100] Perle was among those who helped bring about the destruction of Iraq in 2003, a state whose five thousand years of history included inventing the wheel and creating the written word.

of the Soviet enemy and cut off his legs." They glorified Islamic militancy and sought to neutralize Marxism. As examples, fifth-grade Afghan refugees once learned the Pashto language from characters named Maqbool and Basheer in a story book. Maqbool tells Basheer they should help the rebel fighters ready their machine guns. Basheer concurs. Soon they are meeting with a mujahideen commander. "We want you to help clean the weapons and fight the Russians in jihad," he tells Maqbool and Basheer. Additionally, boys learned arithmetic by counting pictures of soldiers, tanks, guns, and land mines.[101] [102]

The Thinking (?) behind This "Policy"

RAND Corporation (Reseach and Anylsis Corporation) Analyst Cheryl Benard, wife of the ethnic Afghan Zalmay Khalilzad who was successively US Ambassador to Afghanistan, Iraq, and the United Nations (2003–2009), said:

> We made a deliberate choice. At first, everyone thought, there's no way to beat the Soviets. So what we have to do is throw the worst crazies against them that we can find, and there was a lot of collateral damage. We knew exactly who these people were, and what their organizations were like, and we didn't care. Then we allowed them to get rid of, just kill all the

---

[101] Cf. Martin Schram, "The unintended unmaking of Afghan hearts and minds," *Washington Post*, March 23, 2002.

[102] An academic at the University of Nebraska, Thomas Gouttiere, director of its Center for Afghanistan Studies, took the money, which really came from the CIA, and produced the propaganda. A Taliban delegation to the United States was so taken with his efforts that they went out of their way to meet him in 1997. *Devil's Game*, 328.

moderate leaders. The reason we don't have moderate leaders in Afghanistan today is because we let the nuts kill them all. They killed the leftists, the moderates, the middle-of-the-roaders. They were just eliminated during the 1980s and afterwards.[103]

Esteemed Reader, please go over the foregoing quote again. The United States of America, deliberately, with malice aforethought, sought out, hired, and turned loose murderous, crazed fanatics to engage in Mongol-style barbarism. No thought, apparently, was given to the results, other than to destroy the Soviet Union's forces in Afghanistan. The United States ignored the effects and ignored the future activities of those creating such effects. If you hire terrorists, are you not a terrorist yourself?

Stone and Kuznick noted: "Casey [Director of Central Intelligence William J. Casey] ignored repeated warnings that the religious fanaticism he was helping unleash would eventually pose a threat to US interests. He instead persisted in his view that the unholy partnership between Christianity and Islam would endure and could be used to bludgeon the Soviets throughout the region. In fact, in mid-decade [the 1980s], Casey unleashed mujahideen raids across the border into the Soviet Union [with half the world's arsenal of nuclear weapons] in the hope of inciting Islamist uprisings by Soviet Muslims."[104]

Training for Destruction—Turkeys Roost Anywhere They Want

US helicopters, after the American invasion and occupation of Iraq, were targeted by freedom fighters there. This "was a typical

---

[103] Stone and Kuznick, 461, citing Dreyfuss, *Devil's Game*, 290.
[104] Ibid., 461.

example of how the aid supplied by the CIA to Islamist terrorists in the 1980s contributed to the escalation and spread of terrorism in the world." The 'copters have been downed by hitting the stabilizing tail rotor with a rocket-propelled grenade (RPG), a tactic similar to shooting down Blackhawk machines later on in Somalia in 1993. This stratagem had been taught to Arab-Afghans fighting the Soviets, who had then taught it to the Somalis and Iraqis.[105] Besides educating Arab-Afghans in helicopter destruction, George Crile, *CBS News* producer and correspondent, noted that their CIA training also included "urban terror with instruction in car bombings, camel bombings, and assassination."[106] One of the instructors was Ali Mohamed, chief al-Qaeda terrorist teacher as well as an FBI informant. He was also a US Army and CIA veteran. He recruited and trained Arabs at the al-Khifah Center in Brooklyn, New York. (The Center, founded by Abdullah Azzam, Osama bin Laden's mentor, was part of the Maktab al-Khidamat [Services Office]). Located on Atlantic Avenue in Brooklyn, al-Khifah inducted Arab immigrants and Arab Americans into the fight in Afghanistan and, later, Bosnia. Al-Khifah was a channel for funds supporting these operations and had close ties to the CIA.)[107] A second branch of al-Khifah was located at 2824 Kennedy Boulevard in Jersey City, N.J.[108]

Scott's summary of this is excellent: "…small cliques of policymakers, acting at the highest levels of secrecy, are able to make ill-considered decisions…that will have long-term and tragic effects worldwide. This system also preserves itself by cover-up." The establishment view of US ties to Afghanistan and al-Qaeda makes

---

[105] Ibid., 117–118, citing M. Bowden, *Black Hawk Down* (New York: Atlantic Monthly Press, 1999), 110.

[106] Ibid., p. 118, citing George Crile, *Charlie Wilson's War*, New York: Atlantic Monthly Press 2003; p. 335.

[107] Ibid., citing *Triple Cross*, 141–43, and L. Williams and E. T. McCormick, "Al Qaeda Terrorist Worked with FBI," *San Francisco Chronicle*, November 4, 2001.

[108] *Triple Cross*, 19.

"no mention of Ali Mohamed, the al-Khifah training camp, or Springman's [sic] statements about CIA visas for Islamists and jihadis."[109] [This quote is from a television program with clips from investigative journalists Greg Palast, Joe Trento, several others, and the author. The gist of my remarks was: *What I was protesting was, in reality, an effort to bring recruits, rounded up by Osama Bin Laden, to the United States for terrorist training by the CIA. They would then be returned to Afghanistan to fight against the then-Soviets.*] It wasn't just Peter Dale Scott's picking up on this point. Craig Unger did as well, in his book *House of Bush, House of Saud, The Secret Relationship Between the World's Two Most Powerful Families.*[110] He quoted me as saying "I complained there [Jeddah]. I complained here in Washington to Main State, to the Inspector General, and to Diplomatic Security, and I was ignored."

Journalist Joe Trento covered this situation in more detail in his book, *Prelude to Terror.*[111] Basically, I "repeatedly confronted [my] bosses about their approval of questionable visa applications. Springman [sic] pushed so hard for answers that he was eventually warned to do just what he was told…As Springman [sic] kept pushing for an explanation, his fitness evaluations became more critical of him and he was eventually dismissed."

In addition to Trento's publication, in his two books, *The War On Freedom* and *The War On Truth*, Nafeez Mosaddeq Ahmed, Executive Director of the Britain-based Institute for Policy Research and Development, published excerpts from my interviews with the BBC

---

[109] *Road to 9/11*, 118–119, citing "Has Someone Been Sitting On The FBI," BBC Newsnight, November 6, 2001.

[110] Craig Unger, *House of Bush, House of Saud, The Secret Relationship Between the World's Two Most Powerful Families* (New York: Scribner, 2004), 109–110; citing M. Springmann, BBC interview as reported in the *Sydney Morning Herald*, November 7, 2001.

[111] Joe Trento, *Prelude to Terror* (New York: Carroll & Graf, 2005), and citing interviews with me between 1993 and 2004, 342–344.

and the Canadian Broadcasting Corporation (CBC).[112] This started a new and still continuing debate.

Citing an interview with Frank Anderson, CIA Near East Operations Chief, Unger wrote "This was blowback. 'Afghanistan provided a place where these guys could hang out in a subculture for people who wanted to be warriors...It built up the craft of giving money to people like this that undoubtedly continued past when it should have.'"[113]

Unger continued: "The forces opposing the United States in the wake of the Afghan war are almost entirely of its own making."[114] Furthermore, the Arab-Afghans have never been completely disbanded.[115][116]

As noted elsewhere in this book, "Under the encouragement of CIA Chief William Casey, the United States then participated in the decision to deploy these Muslims outside of Afghanistan..." In 1981, Casey, Saudi Prince Turki bin Faisal (1968 graduate of Georgetown University's Foreign Service School; Director General of Saudi Arabia's General Intelligence Directorate, 1979–2001; Saudi Ambassador to the United States, 2005–2006) and ISI began working to create a foreign legion of jihadi Muslims, that is, Arab-Afghans.[117]

According to John Pilger, Australian journalist:

---

[112] *The War On Freedom* (Joshua Tree, CA: Tree of Life Publications, 2002), 104–106. *War On Truth*, 218–22.

[113] *House of Bush*, 110.

[114] *Road to 9/11*, 119.

[115] Ibid., 120, citing Jason Burke, *Al Qaeda* (London: I. B. Tauris, 2004), 72–86.

[116] As related in this publication, the Arab-Afghans have marched from Afghanistan to Syria, by way of Bosnia, Iraq, and Libya. Not organized in a hierarchical sense, nevertheless, they are cohesive enough to be used as a cadre to destabilize governments the United States opposes.

[117] *Road to 9/11*, 122.

[In 1986] CIA director William Casey had given his backing to a plan put forward by Pakistan's intelligence agency, the ISI, to recruit people from around the world to join the Afghan jihad. More than 100,000 Islamic militants were trained in Pakistan between 1986 and 1992 [the Soviets left Afghanistan in February 1989], in camps overseen by CIA and MI6 [the UK Secret Intelligence Service, its external spy agency], with the SAS [Special Air Service, UK Special Forces, soldiers undertaking "unconventional" missions] training future al-Qaida and Taliban fighters in bomb making and other black arts. Their leaders were trained at a CIA camp in Virginia [Camp Peary, or "The Farm," near Williamsburg]. This was called Operation Cyclone and continued long after the Soviets had withdrawn in 1989.[118]

This, in essence, was the origin of the Arab-Afghan Legion. It takes no great logic to infer that it would be used wherever best it might be employed as a cadre to destabilize governments disliked by Washington. It's clear that continuing Operation Cyclone, even after the Soviets left Afghanistan, showed that the operation would continue as long as the intelligence services wanted and as long as it proved useful for their designs.

Scott wrote "Casey startled his Pakistani hosts by proposing that they take the Afghan war into enemy territory—into the Soviet Union itself...Pakistani intelligence officials—partly inspired by Casey—began independently to train Afghans and funnel CIA supplies for scattered strikes against military installations,

---

[118] Ibid., 123, citing John Pilger, "What Good Friends Left Behind," *Guardian*, September 20, 2003.

factories, and storage tanks within Soviet territory..."[119] [The architect for this plan was Graham Fuller, a former CIA official whose daughter, Samantha, married Ruslan Tsarnaev, uncle of alleged Boston Marathon bombers Dzhokhar A. Tsarnaev and Tamerlan Tsarnaev].[120]

As Peter Dale Scott continues:

> Unquestionably...MAK centers [Makhtab al-Khidamat, Services Offices] in America, such as the al-Khifah Center in Brooklyn, were in the 1980s a major source of both recruitment and finance for the MAK, if only because the United States was one of the few countries in which recruitment and financing were tolerated and even protected. "Millions of dollars each year" are said to have been raised for the MAK in Brooklyn alone.[121]

To continue the links between the parts of the Arab-Afghan Legion and its masters at Langley, the journalist John Cooley, in *Unholy Wars: Afghanistan, America, and International Terrorism*[122] characterized Sheikh Omar Abdel Rahman (involved with the 1993 World Trade Center Bombing and now jailed at the Buttner Federal Correctional Institution in North Carolina) as "helpmate to the CIA in recruiting young zealots, especially among Arab Americans in the United States for the 'jihad in Afghanistan.'"[123] Rahman, commonly called the Blind Sheikh, had worked with

---

[119] *Road to 9/11*, 136, citing Steve Coll, "Anatomy of a Victory: CIA's Covert Afghan War," *Washington Post*, July 19, 1992.

[120] J. Michael Springmann, "Boston Baked BS: It Goes So Good With Turkeys When They've Come Home To Roost," *Foreign Policy Journal*, May 19, 2013.

[121] *Road to 9/11*, 123, citing Lance, *1,000 Years For Revenge*, 41–42.

[122] John Cooley, *Unholy Wars: Afghanistan, America, and International Terrorism* (London: Pluto Press, 1999), 41.

[123] *Road to 9/11*, 123.

Abdullah Azzam, creator of the Maktab, and Osama bin Laden in Afghanistan. Yet, the CIA had brought him to the United States with a tourist visa. Once here, he had preached (and helped recruit mujahideen) in Brooklyn at the al-Farooq Mosque, part of the al-Khifah center on Atlantic Avenue. The Overlords of Langley either didn't know, didn't want to know, or didn't care what would happen once their tool, the Sheikh, had finished his work. Or, is it, perhaps, that the spooks hoped that the uproar generated by Omar Abdel Rahman's actions and his arrest would direct the public's attention away from their next move in their Game of Life and Death?

Pakistani journalist and author, Ahmed Rashid, recounted:

> In 1986, the secret services of the United States, Great Britain, and Pakistan agreed on a plan to launch guerrilla attacks into Tajikistan and Uzbekistan. Afghan Mujahideen units crossed the Amu Darya River in March 1987 and launched rocket attacks against villages in Tajikistan. Meanwhile, hundreds of Uzbek and Tajik Muslims clandestinely traveled to Pakistan and Saudi Arabia to study in madrassahs (religious schools) or to train as guerrilla fighters so that they could join the Mujahideen. This was part of a wider U.S., Pakistani, and Saudi plan to recruit radical Muslims from around the world to fight with the Afghans. Between 1982 and 1992, thirty-five thousand Muslim radicals from forty-three Islamic countries fought for the Mujahideen."[124] Yet, the Soviet Union formally dissolved on December 25, 1991.

---

[124] Ibid., 126, citing Ahmed Rashid, *Jihad: The Rise of Militant Islam in Central Asia* (New Haven: Yale University Press, 2002), 43–44.

Can anyone believe the lies that the US government and those of its "allies" put out about being attacked by "terrorists"? The United States and the United Kingdom created the problem they use to justify repression at home and endless war abroad.

Although there is no clear date when the United States decided to employ these fighters all around the world, it is most likely that the decision to do so was taken during the Afghan war against the Soviets. However, as Peter Dale Scott says (and history shows),

Jihadi Muslims connected to al-Qaeda continued to be used for Western causes throughout the 1990s. In Azerbaijan in 1993, former KGB strongman Heydar Aliyev seized control of the country with Agency help. His backing came from hundreds of jihadis recruited by Gulbuddin Hekmatyar and shipped to Azerbaijan. To aid Aliyev as quickly as possible, they flew on an airline set up by CIA veteran Ed Dearborn. Funds for this allegedly came in part from Western oil companies who paid to collect the jihadis. In 2003, the US State Department designated Hekmatyar, a Pushtun rebel commander, as a "terrorist".

Jihadis also took part in two Balkan campaigns in the 1990s, on the same side as the United States and NATO. Scott adds, "In Bosnia, in the mid-1990s, NATO and al-Qaeda were on the same side..."[125]

The efforts to destabilize and destroy the Soviet Union were practiced and perfected in the Balkans and Iraq. Additionally, the propaganda used to cover US actions was fine-tuned during those conflicts.

First, the USSR was a nation of many different ethnicities, religions, and tensions. The CIA managed to exploit them, causing upheavals in Chechnya, Dagestan, Kazakhstan, Tajikistan, etc. Langley

---

[125] *Road to 9/11*, 131, citing Peter Dale Scott, *Drugs, Oil, and War: The United States in Afghanistan, Colombia, and Indochina* (Lanham, MD: Rowman and Littlefield, 2003), 7. Thomas Goltz, *Azerbaijan Diary* (Armonk, NY: M. E. Sharpe, 1999), 274–275. Mark Irkali, Tengiz Kodarian, and Cali Ruchala, "God Save The Shah: American Guns, Spies, and Oil in Azerbaijan," *Sobaka*, May 22, 2003.

used its influence with the American news media and politicians in the United States to depict the crises the CIA had created as homegrown, the result of problems inherent in a totalitarian state. As Peter Bergen explains in his book *Holy War, Inc.*:

> But then:…there have been at least two decades of collaboration by the United States and CIA with Islamist elements who made no secret of their hostility toward America. It is striking that this collaboration continued even after bin Laden in 1996 issued the first of his fatwas [legal opinions or rulings issued by an Islamic scholar] declaring the United States to be an enemy. It came long after the identification of the 1993 World Trade Center bombers Ramzi Yousef and Mahmud Abouhalima, who had trained in Afghanistan.[126]

Scott adds:

> What is slowly emerging from the revelations of al-Qaeda's activities in Central Asia throughout the 1990s is the extent to which the group acted in the interests of both American oil companies and the US government. In one way or another, a few Americans in the 1990s cooperated with al-Qaeda terrorists in Afghanistan, Azerbaijan, Kosovo, and possibly Bosnia. In other countries—notably Georgia, Kyrgyzstan, and Uzbekistan—al Qaeda terrorists have provided pretexts or opportunities for a US military commitment and even troops to follow.[127]

---

[126] Ibid., 131, citing Peter Bergen, *Holy War, Inc.: Inside the Secret World of Osama bin Laden*, (New York: Free Press, 2001), 136–137.
[127] Ibid., 161.

Americans Richard Secord, Harry "Heinie" Aderholt, and Ed Dearborn, were all career air force officers with ties to Langley. Veterans of US activities in Laos and Oliver North's Iran-Contra operations, they materialized in 1991 in Baku, the capital and largest city of Azerbaijan. The company they allegedly worked for, MEGA Oil, never found any black gold, but the firm's activities substantially aided in the removal of Azerbaijan from post-USSR influence. These men, although not officially on Langley's payroll, were, on occasion, loaned out as CIA detailees, according to Thomas Goltz in his book, *Azerbaijan Diary*.[128] "Over the course of the next two years, the company they worked with [MEGA Oil] procured thousands of dollars' worth of weapons and recruited at least two thousand Afghan mercenaries [read: Arab-Afghans] for Azerbaijan—the first mujahideen to fight on the territory of the former Communist Bloc."[129]

Brief History Lesson

At this point, readers should carefully consider some American history, particularly the penchant of the federal government to provoke war while giving the appearance of being the victim of an armed attack.

Mexico

Just before the US war against Mexico in 1846, President James Knox Polk (D-NC) ordered soldiers to occupy disputed territory between the Nueces and Rio Grande rivers. When the Mexicans defended against this incursion, Polk used this reaction as a *casus belli*, eventually seizing half of Mexico in 1848.

---

[128] Ibid., 163, citing Goltz, *Azerbaijan Diary*, 272–275.
[129] Ibid., citing Irkali, Kodarian, and Ruchala, "God Save The Shah."

The South

In April of 1861, US President Abraham Lincoln (R-IL), knew that abandoning Fort Sumter in Charleston, South Carolina's harbor would give legitimacy to the Southern secessionist movement. He used warships to resupply the federal garrison with supplies that may have not been needed. The ships also carried reinforcements for the garrison. The timing is clearly suspect. Lincoln did this shortly after negotiations to head off the war had taken place in March and early April in Washington. When the Confederate commander, P. G. T. Beauregard, saw the federal ships, he opened fire on the fort, giving Lincoln his war, one that killed more Americans than in all previous and subsequent conflicts combined.

World War II

Prior to December 1941, "Peace President for Life" Franklin Roosevelt (D-NY) evidently wanted war with Germany. When his unrestricted antisubmarine warfare against German U-Boats west of the twenty-sixth meridian failed to goad Hitler into war, Roosevelt turned his attention to Germany's ally, Japan. He hoped to provoke a clash with that partner, one that would drag the Nazis into conflict with the United States. While hectoring Japan for its actions in China and Southeast Asia, Roosevelt, in July 1940, cut off all exports to it, including vital raw materials, such as oil. The same month, he also ended all imports from Japan and froze that country's assets. The former US president Herbert Hoover characterized this action as "sticking pins in a rattlesnake."

Vietnam

Then there was the Gulf of Tonkin incident, which President Lyndon B. Johnson (D-TX) used to gull an ignorant Congress into authorizing virtually all-out warfare against North Vietnam on August 7, 1964. To quote John Prados from the National Security Archive in Washington, DC: "[T]he United States at the time was carrying out a program of covert naval commando attacks against North Vietnam and had been engaged in this effort since its approval by Johnson in January 1964."[130] Johnson and the US government asserted that, on August 4, 1964, there had been a night attack on two American destroyers, USS *Maddox* and USS *C. Turner Joy*, by North Vietnamese forces. Unfortunately for the American politicians, the drafted citizenry, and the Vietnamese people, "there was absolutely no gunfire except our own, no PT boat wakes, not a candle light let alone a burning ship. None could have been there and not have been seen on such a black night," wrote Commander James B. Stockdale in his memoirs.[131]

Yet the American program of causing unrest continued, with combatants sent to Kashmir in Northern India and Chechnya in the USSR. The ISI sent "Islamist fighters to Central Asia and the Caucasus...When Kazakhstan, Kyrgyzstan, Tajikistan, and Uzbekistan became independent of Moscow in 1991, the ISI played a pivotal role in supporting Islamist armed insurgencies, which destabilized them."[132]

Saddle Tramps

Like America's decades-long war in Indochina, the war in Afghanistan, which could be considered illegal and unconstitutional,

---

[130] John Prados, "Essay: 40th Anniversary of the Gulf of Tonkin Incident," Posted August 4, 2004, http://www2.gwu.edu/~nsarchiv/NSAEBB/NSAEBB1 32/essay.htm.

[131] Ibid.

[132] *Road to 9/11*, 148, citing Loretta Napoletani, *Terra Incognita: Tracing the Dollars Behind the Terror Networks*, (New York: Seven Stories Press, 2005), 89.

produced well-trained experts in death and destruction. Whether US government officials thought beyond the moment in Afghanistan, or whether they gradually came to the realization that the lowlifes they had organized, trained, and sent off to war could be used as a cadre of destabilizing agents elsewhere, won't be known until someone is brave enough to talk. Further, given the American penchant for covering up murder, war crimes, and human rights violations to protect careers and pensions, that will likely be never.

As is not generally known, many countries the United States worked with to produce "jihadists" for the war in Afghanistan against the Soviets simply emptied their prisons and sent the inmates to the "Front." [133]

Finally, what is more remarkable, is that "progressives," including people supposedly conversant with international affairs and ostensibly opposed to America's imperialist, capitalist, and terrorist foreign policy, still toe the government's line on the Arab-Afghans.

I spoke briefly with Phyllis Bennis, a Fellow from the Institute for Policy Studies and a writer, analyst, and activist on Middle East affairs in Washington, DC. I had met her by chance on Saturday, June 15, 2013, at the American-Arab Anti-Discrimination Committee (ADC) annual convention at Washington's Marriott Wardman Park Hotel. In response to my questions about the Arab-Afghans and their worldwide jihad, she denied that they had ever existed and said, even if they once did, they no longer were in operation. (According to one source, Bennis has no idea of what constitutes "Imperialism.") Also at the convention, I met Houeida Saad, once ADC Legal Director when I was an intern there. She denied the existence of anything called "Arab-Afghans." However, before going to law school and joining the ADC, she told me that she had been a registered nurse in South Asia treating wounded mujahideen. Since, to the best of my knowledge, she speaks only English and Arabic, I doubt that she

---

[133] *Devil's Game*, 275, citing an unnamed CIA source.

ministered to many Afghans. Saad is now General Counsel, Renown Health Care, Reno, Nevada, and has been an adjunct professor of law at American University's Washington College of Law.

Summary

The US government has a long history of destabilizing or planning to destabilize countries and their rulers, not just in the Third World but also in Europe and, most surprisingly, at home.

The CIA worked with, inter alia, Italy to ensure that the dreaded Communists would never gain control. To do that, Langley organized bombings, "false flag" events that killed one hundred people, ostensibly by the "Commies" in 1969 and 1980.

At home, America's General Staff planned a series of "false flag" attacks against Cuba in the eaerly 1960s. Assassins were to kill US citizens on the street, vessels carrying Cuban refugees were to be sunk, planes were to be hijacked, and a wave of violent terrorism was to be launched in Washington, DC, Miami, Florida, and elsewhere. (These actions appear to parallel September 11, 2001, along with events in the Balkans, Libya, Iraq, and Syria.)

Misdirection is an old American tradition. James Knox Polk used it to dismember Mexico, Lincoln to attack the South, and Lyndon Johnson to escalate the destruction of Indochina.

Building on past "clandestine" successes, such as the overthrow of Mohammed Mossadegh, lawfully elected prime minister of Iran, and Jacobo Arbenz Guzman, constitutionally elected president of Guatemala, the American president, James Earl Carter (D-GA) and his National Security Advisor, Zbigniew Brzezinski, set about to use Afghanistan to shatter the Soviet Union. Of course, they only planned to kick out the "Commies," while splintering the Muslim republics of the USSR. But in doing so, they created al-Qaeda, which, to all intents and purposes, is the Arab-Afghan Legion. It's now operating in Syria (after past successes in the Balkans, Iraq, and Libya). Carter, Brzezinski, and their underlings recruited, trained, and armed fanatics from all over the Islamic world, using the intelligence services and money from Saudi Arabia and Pakistan to do so. Their object was "plausible deniability."

The result was a reliable, not-too-well organized cadre of "saddle tramps" who could be used anywhere, anytime, for anything (as long as there were "enemies" of the United States to be found). America used carefully chosen leaders, such as those of the al-Farooq Mosque in Brooklyn, the Blind Sheikh Omar Abdel Rahman, and Osama bin Laden to create and coordinate the arms of the octopus.

Yet, despite this sordid part of the history of the United States, alleged progressives, including people supposedly conversant with international affairs and ostensibly opposed to America's imperialist, capitalist, and terrorist foreign policy, still toe their government's line on the Arab-Afghans.

THE BALKANS

On the Road to Elsewhere

Scott notes that America, following the Soviet withdrawal from Afghanistan, ended up with a "disposal problem." What happens to "the well-trained militants if their long-established channels of support were suddenly broken off"? To avoid justified anger and redirect their attention elsewhere, "an easy solution was to divert its Arab-Afghans to Bosnia." A writer for the *Independent* (a British newspaper), Andrew Marshall, penned, "In December 1992, a US Army official met one of the Afghan veterans from Al-Khifah [in Brooklyn] and offered help with a covert operation to support the Muslims in Bosnia, funded with Saudi money, according to one of those jailed for assisting with the New York bombings."[134]

Stone adds that "many of the US-backed jihadis who had fought against the Soviets in Afghanistan joined the Islamist cause in Chechnya, Bosnia, Algeria, Iraq, the Philippines, Saudi Arabia, Kashmir, and elsewhere."[135] What is also known is that they were

---

[134] *Road to 9/11*, 149, citing Andrew Marshall, "Terror 'Blowback' Burns CIA," *Independent*, November 1, 1998.
[135] Stone and Kuznick, 468.

likely initially used in Bosnia, in the first "war of humanitarian aggression." That self-contradictory phrase aptly described the idea of President William J. Clinton (D-AK) to justify attacking Serbia. He grounded this on questionable claims of genocide and "ethnic cleansing" (something Israel has been engaged in for decades).

Breaking Up Is Easier to Do

In the former Yugoslavia, another country of varying religions, ethnicities, and regional hatreds, US policy was to capitalize on internal tensions, helping pit Croats and Slovenians against Serbs, Roman Catholics and Orthodox against Muslims, and Slavs against non-Slavs (modern Albanians). All the while imported fighters from the Legion were wreaking havoc, the Americans were insisting something had to be done "to protect" the various groups being exploited. As tensions rose, the different states of Yugoslavia declared (or were encouraged to declare) their independence. Germany, a US client state, hastened, if not directly caused, the breakup of the country through its 1991 recognition of the most economically developed states of the Yugoslav Federation, Slovenia and Croatia. The Americans, for their part, wanted to control the other parts of the confederation in order to command routes to Caspian Sea oil resources.[136]

American propaganda, flooding the media, was particularly effective, initially convincing long-term observers of the international scene, such as myself, that something had to be done about murderers, war criminals, and human rights violators in what was once Yugoslavia. However, the lies, half-truths, and distortions of

---

[136] Michael Parenti, "The Rational Destruction of Yugoslavia," www.michaelparenti.org. Michel Chossudovsky, "Dismantling Former Yugoslavia, Recolonizing Bosnia-Herzegovina," *globalresearch.ca*, February 19, 2002.

fact used to support US policy soon became glaringly evident and increasingly out of touch with reality.

As in past actions against the USSR, the United States and Germany trained fighters, supplied arms, and provided financial aid to rebels seeking overthrow of their government. Economic sanctions were applied to Yugoslavia, hastening the country's collapse. Furthermore:

> *The Kosovo Liberation Army* [note that the word "Liberation," like the word "Free" in "Free Syrian Army," has connotations for Americans, who, as Ali Mohamed noted, see what they want to see and hear what they want to hear]...directly supported and politically empowered by NATO in 1998, had, in the same year been listed by the US State Department as a terrorist organization supported in part...[by] loans from Islamic individuals, among them allegedly Osama bin Laden...Ramush Haradinaj, a former K[osovo] L[iberation] A[rmy] commander...today an indicted war criminal, was the key US military and intelligence asset in Kosovo during the civil war and the NATO bombing campaign that followed. The London *Sunday Times* reported that "American intelligence agents have admitted they helped to train the Kosovo Liberation Army before NATO's bombing of Yugoslavia.[137]

---

[137] *Road to 9/11*, 131, citing Ralf Mutschke, Assistant Director, Criminal Intelligence Directorate, Interpol, "Threat Posed By the Convergence of Organized Crime, Drugs Trafficking, and Terrorism," before a hearing of the US House of Representative's Committee on the Judiciary, Subcommittee on Crime; December 13, 2000. Scott, "Oil, Drugs, and War," *Halifax Herald*, October 29, 2001.

Here Comes al-Qaeda

According to Yossef Bodansky (an Israeli American who served as Director of the Congressional Task Force on Terrorism and Unconventional Warfare for the US House of Representatives from 1988 to 2004): "Bin Laden's 'Arab-Afghans' also have assumed a dominant role in training the Kosovo Liberation Army."[138]

Kosovo was an area where US and al-Qaeda interests crossed and supported each other. In fact, freelance journalist Tim Judah noted that Kosovo Liberation Army (KLA) representatives met with American, British, and Swiss intelligence officers in 1996 and, possibly, even earlier. US "private" firms dealing with the military, such as MPRI (known only by its initials and headquartered in Alexandria, VA) may have handled these links. MPRI's Richard Griffiths (Maj. Gen. USA, ret.) had a long-term relationship with KLA commander Agim Çeku. Together they planned "Operation Storm," an attack by Croatia against Serbia.[139]

The former Canadian Ambassador to Yugoslavia, James Bissett, once stated: "Many members of the Kosovo Liberation Army were sent for training in terrorist camps in Afghanistan...Milosevic is right. There is no question of their [Al Qaeda's] participation in conflicts in the Balkans. It is very well documented."[140]

---

[138] Ibid., 334, citing Yossef Bodansky, *Bin Laden: The Man Who Declared War on America* (Roseville, Calif.: Prima, 2001), 298.

[139] Ibid., 167–168, citing Tim Judah, *Kosovo: War and Revenge* (New Haven: Yale University Press, 2002), 120; and Michel Chossudovsky, "Macedonia: Washington's Military-Intelligence Ploy," Transnational Foundation for Peace and Future Research.

[140] Ibid., 168, citing Isabel Vincent, "U.S. Supported al-Qaeda Cells During Balkan Wars," *National Post*, March 15, 2002.

Oh Joy! Bin Laden's Still Our Boy!

John R. Schindler, professor of strategy at the US Naval War College, prominent Neocon, and former NSA intelligence analyst and counterintelligence officer, was cited in *Washington's Blog* on the Legion. Schindler, in his book *Unholy Terror: Bosnia, Al-Qa'ida, and the Rise of Global Jihad*,[141] asserted that the United States backed Osama bin Laden and al-Qaeda members in the Bosnia conflict, 1992–1995.

Specifically, Schindler stated that interventionists seeking the destruction of Serbia controlled the US State Department, but the George H.W. Bush administration would not back them. However, Bill Clinton, with "scant interest in foreign and defense policy" became president. Clinton sought to bomb the Serbs to help the Muslims, following "the lead of progressive opinion on Bosnia."[142] Schindler amplified his remarks, writing that

> Thousands of Muslims, mainly, but not exclusively Arabs, emerged from the Afghan crucible with invaluable combat experience, the largest contingent, like Osama bin Laden himself, were Saudis, some 5,000 in all, followed by 3,000 Yemenis, 2,800 Algerians, 2,000 Egyptians, Tunisians, 370 Iraqis, 200 Libyans, dozens of Jordanians, plus a fair number of Pakistanis, and small contingents from Indonesia to Bosnia.[143]

Unable or unwilling to return home, they were looking for work. (Egypt and Algeria, for example, were not hospitable, having a

---

[141] John R. Schindler, *Unholy Terror: Bosnia, Al-Qa'ida, and the Rise of Global Jihad* (St. Paul: Zenith Press, 2007).

[142] *Unholy Terror*, 110.

[143] Ibid., 118, citing James Bruce, "Arab Veterans of the Afghan War," *Jane's Intelligence Review*, April 1995.

decidedly unfriendly political climate.) The Maktab al-Khidamat (MAK), Services Office, set up by Osama bin Laden, Abdullah Azzam, and Abdullah Anas to manage recruitment, training, and weapons for Afghanistan, handled the Arab-Afghans' transfer to Bosnia. Al-Qaeda led most of the four-thousand-odd Arab-Afghans who were bin Laden's boys. The rest was comprised of mujahideen from other countries, such as Egypt's Islamic Group and Algeria's Armed Islamic Group. Fighters and instructors came also from Turkey and Lebanon, including some from Hezbollah. It was not easy getting these groups to the Balkans, owing to the siege of Bosnia's capital, Sarajevo, and a dearth of secure ways in. Thus Zagreb, capital of Croatia, became the center of MAK'S operations (and that of nineteen other organizations).[144]

The "muj" used "an intricate support web that spread across countries and continents to keep the holy war going." One of the most important pieces, left over from the Afghan war's recruitment, was the al-Khifah mosque in Brooklyn.[145]

Bin Laden's deputy, Ayman al-Zawahiri, was often in Bosnia, as was bin Laden himself, the latter using a Bosnian passport. Renate Flottau, the German newsmagazine *Der Spiegel's* Balkan correspondent, saw bin Laden there in 1994 with the mujahideen, who claimed they were "humanitarian aid workers."[146]

You Can't Tell the Players Even with a Scorecard

During the Bosnian war of 1992–1995, some foreign Muslims came to Bosnia as mujahideen. The war had been depicted in the international press as an attack on Muslims by Serb forces that

---

[144] Ibid., 119.
[145] Ibid., 121.
[146] Ibid., 123, 124.

struck Bosniak (Bosnian Muslim) communities indiscriminately and committed significant atrocities against the Bosniak population. This moved Muslims who shared mujahideen beliefs to come to the aid of oppressed coreligionists, and presented an opportunity to strike at "infidels." The number of foreign Muslim volunteers in Bosnia was estimated at about 4,000 in contemporary newspaper reports,[147] and much like fighters sent to Afghanistan, they came from places such as Saudi Arabia, Pakistan, Afghanistan, Jordan, Egypt, Iraq, and the Palestinian Territories, to quote the summary of the International Criminal Tribunal for the former Yugoslavia judgment.[148] John Schindler estimated their numbers as being between five thousand and six thousand.[149]

The evidence shows that foreign volunteers arrived in central Bosnia in the second half of 1992 with the aim of helping Muslims against the Serbian "aggressors." Mostly they came from North Africa, the Near East, and the Middle East. The foreign volunteers differed considerably from the local population, not only because of their physical appearance and the language they spoke, but also because of their fighting methods.

The *Independent* noted that a large number of Britons traveled to Bosnia for the war. On February 10, 1993, Steve Boggan wrote that "Thousands of Britons, including ex-servicemen, boy adventurers, and 'untrained idiots and psychopaths' may be fighting in the former Yugoslavia, according to Whitehall sources and the editor of a specialist magazine."[150] As reported by former army officer David Lord, editor of *Combat and Survival*, the British Foreign Office

---

[147] "Bosnia Seen as Hospitable Base and Sanctuary for Terrorists," Nettime. org.

[148] ICTY: Summary of the judgment for Enver Hadihasanovic' and Amir Kubura.

[149] *Unholy Terror*, 162, citing *Vecernji List* [*Evening Gazette*], Zagreb, April 10, 1996.

[150] "Britons flock to fight in Bosnia," *The Independent*.

underestimated the number of UK citizens acting as combatants in the Balkans. An "astonishing amount of mail" from British men fighting there came to his magazine, Lord said. Additionally, he noted, his estimate of "thousands" battling in the former Yugoslavia came from numerous soldiers seen wearing UK Royal Marine and Parachute Regiment berets. Soldiers of the British Territorial Army (the Reserves) also were engaged in combat in Bosnia. Particularly valued, the article said, were British soldiers with experience in Northern Ireland. Bosnian officers, as one of the British mercenaries stated, were asking him, and presumably others, to help recruit groups of former servicemen for the war.

In April 2000, the official Yugoslav news agency *Tanjug* published a story from Priština, Kosovo, about Osama bin Laden and Abu Hassan being there. Their intent was to "carry out terrorist acts in Kosovo". The AFP [*Agence France Presse*] wire service picked up and carried the story.[151]

What *Tanjug* did not publish was the information that the Blind Sheikh, Omar Abdel Rahman, had been involved in bringing "al-Qaeda/Arab-Afghan" fighters to the region. Here's what Nafeez Mosaddeq Ahmed had to say:

> It was the blind sheik's status as a CIA asset vis-à-vis the Bosnian conflict that appears to be the primary reason he was granted effective immunity by US intelligence agencies despite being implicated in criminal acts and terrorist plots. His involvement in a covert US operation to transfer al-Qaeda militants to the Balkans in order to escalate the destabilization of Yugoslavia granted him free reign [sic] to pursue criminal and terrorist activities within the US, to the point that even after the bombing, high-level elements

---

[151] "Bin Laden in Kosovo," *The Tribune* (India), AFP, April 27, 2000.

of the US government were extremely reluctant to prosecute him—perhaps for fear of revealing the extent of post–Cold War US co-optation of al-Qaeda. [Maryland attorney] Jack Blum, investigator for the Senate Foreign Relations Subcommittee, complained that: "One of the big problems here is that many suspects in the World Trade Center bombing were associated with the Mujahadeen [sic]. And there are components of our government that are absolutely disinterested in following that path because it leads back to people we supported in the Afghan war"—and crucially, to people whom the government continued to support in the Bosnian war.[152]

Back to the Future

Since the Muslim fighters in the former Yugoslavia didn't walk or swim to the Balkans, it would seem that someone or some entity paid their travel costs, outfitted them, and provided them with weapons. Perhaps it was the same someones and same entities that assisted Osama bin Laden and others to attack the USSR in Afghanistan?

Yes, indeed.

The Americans created a covert conduit involving Iran, Turkey, Saudi Arabia, and the Bosnian Muslims "to fly in al-Qaeda mujihadeen [sic] forces connected to Osama bin Laden from Afghanistan, Algeria, Chechnya, Yemen, Sudan, and elsewhere."[153]

John Schindler notes that Richard Holbrooke, Assistant Secretary of State for European Affairs (1994–1996), had believed that secret

---

[152] *War On Truth*, 39, citing Richard Labévière, *Dollars for Terror: The United States and Islam* (New York: Algora Publishing, 2000) and David Weiner, "Tangled History Set Up Arab 'Blowback,'" *Progressive Populist*, December 2002.

[153] Ibid., 33.

American support for the Afghans was an ideal pattern for sending arms to Bosnia through Saudi Arabia, Turkey, and Pakistan.[154]

The American ambassador to Croatia, per orders from Washington, DC, contacted leaders in Croatia and Bosnia about supplying them with arms, with the help of Iranian Boeing 747s as transport. Providing the president of Croatia with a check for $1 million, the Iranians then followed up with three flights a week carrying arms and ammunition. President Bill Clinton's National Security Council oversaw this operation, without informing Congress, reminiscent of Ronald Reagan's Iran-Contra operation.[155] In July 1994, Assistant Secretary of State Alexander Vershbow allegedly told Dutch government officials that the United States knew of the weapons supply line and that the American government backed it.[156]

The not-so-secret arms drops antagonized many people, especially officials of NATO governments that had soldiers in Bosnia. One British general flatly stated, "They were American arms deliveries. No doubt about that." While US officials denied that the flights took place, Europeans knew that the American Airborne Warning and Control System aircraft (AWACS) had to have seen the clandestine, coordinated activity. Despite all this, the Director of Central Intelligence, R. James Woolsey, asserted that the CIA was not moving weapons to Bosnia. (This was not unlike Milt Bearden's and Marc Sageman's statements on Afghanistan.) Schindler wrote "Britain's Defence Intelligence Staff investigated the reports and concluded that the operations involved three countries and were directed by Clinton's NSC."[157]

"Front companies" (ostensibly real businesses that mask intelligence operations) could well have been doing Washington's bidding.

---

[154] *Unholy Terror*, 181.

[155] Ibid., 182, 183.

[156] Ibid., 183, citing Cees Wiebes, *Intelligence and the War in Bosnia 1992–1995* (Muenster: LIT Verlag, 2003), 169.

[157] Ibid., 184, citing Wiebes, 173–174, 192, 197.

Cees Wiebes, a Dutch scholar who has researched the topic with thoroughness and balance, and enjoyed access to classified NATO records, concluded that although there is "no hard evidence" that the Clinton administration was behind the mystery flights, Washington's involvement appears beyond question. Given US control of Bosnian airspace during the conflict, no sustained air supply program could have operated without American awareness and backing, according to most of those who looked into the matter.[158]

Not unlike present-day actions in Syria and Iraq, there was a massacre at a market in Sarajevo designed to show that the opponents of "regime change" were responsible. When an explosion killed sixty-eight civilians, wounding over one hundred, unlike today, the intelligence services of Canada, Britain, Denmark, Sweden, Belgium, and Holland independently concluded that the Muslims had blown those people up to put the Serbs in a "bad light."[159]

Yet, years later, no one acknowledged that it had been US policy to allow al-Qaeda into the Balkans and to provide unofficial American diplomatic and military support. How Osama bin Laden's boys got to the region "were questions no one in Washington seemed eager to ask or have answered."[160]

"Coincidentally," one of those entities involved, the United States, forcefully opposed the Serbs and their government, savagely bombing them in 1995 and 1999, under the guise of NATO (an alliance formed in 1949 to oppose the Soviet Union). The American government and its NATO partners, just as they later did in Iraq and elsewhere, targeted bridges, factories, power stations, telecommunications facilities, and refugees. The more refugees that could be created, the better. The aim was, essentially, to dehouse, deculturalize, destabilize, and destroy the civilian population. That had been

---

[158] Ibid, 185, citing Wiebes, 193–197.

[159] Ibid., 186.

[160] Ibid., 274.

the North's goal in the American South during the War Between the States and the United States' aim against Germany and Japan in World War II.[161] After all, nothing succeeds like success.

Al-Khifah and the Big Green Machine

In 1993, the al-Khifah mosque of New York set up a Bosnian office in Zagreb, Croatia, apparently in close correspondence with Brooklyn. "The Deputy Director of the Zagreb office, Hassan Hakim, admitted to receiving all orders and funding directly from the main US office of Al-Khifah on Atlantic Avenue controlled by Shaykh Omar Abdel Rahman." Bosnian Jihad handbills were also disbursed by al-Khifah's Boston branch.[162] But it wasn't just people "unofficially" recruited off the streets for the Arab-Afghan Legion. The US Army helped provide fighters to destroy Washington's "enemies" in the Balkans. Before his conviction for his part in a plan to blow up public structures, government offices, and other locations following the 1993 World Trade Center bombing, Clement Rodney Hampton-El related a chilling tale. Hampton-El, a convert to Islam and a fighter wounded in the Afghan war, was called to Washington by

---

[161] The phrase comes from A. C. Grayling's *Among The Dead* Cities (New York: Walker & Co., 2006). Prof. Grayling makes an excellent case that the American and British bombing of civilians constituted "war crimes." The *New Georgia Encyclopedia* termed Sherman's 1864 March to the Sea, the most destructive campaign against a civilian population during the War Between the States. According to the US Army Logistics University, in 1864, Maj. Gen. Philip H. Sheridan began a systematic destruction of the Shenandoah Valley's bounty using a cavalry force of nearly ten thousand men. They burned the Valley from end to end.

[162] *Road to 9/11*, 149, citing Evan F. Kohlmann, *Al-Qaida's Jihad in Europe: The Afghan-Bosnian Network* (Oxford: Berg Publishers, 2004), 39, 40, 41; citing Steve Coll and Steve LeVine, "Global Network Provides Money, Haven," *Washington Post*, August 3, 1993. Ramzi Yousef, lead World Trade Center bomber, had placed many calls to Yugoslavia.

the Saudi Embassy. There, he met with Prince Abdullah Faisal (who may have been Prince Sultan bin Faisal bin Turki bin Abdullah al-Saud, mysteriously dead four months after being named an al-Qaeda accomplice).[163] The prince handed over $150,000 to train and support the mujahideen and their families.[164] Hampton-El then went to Ft. Belvoir, Virginia (roughly twenty miles from DC and headquarters for the US Army's Intelligence and Security Command), where he was given a list of soldiers who were ending their tours of duty and who would be suitable for recruitment as fighters in the Balkans.[165] A radical cleric called Abu Ameenah Bilal Phillips (born in Jamaica as Dennis Bradley Phillips) got Hampton-El these names. Phillips, a Saudi government employee, was head of the kingdom's "Project Bosnia" in America and, while in Saudi Arabia, preached conversion to Islam to US soldiers stationed there.[166]

How Helpers Helped

Saudi Arabia did more for the destruction of Bosnia than its close "ally" the United States of America has let on. According to Schindler, the CIA believed that one-third of Islamic charities engaged in Bosnia, especially the IIRO, had "facilitated the activities of Islamic groups that engage in terrorism." Moreover, the Saudi High Commission for Relief for Bosnia, set up in 1993, had distributed

---

[163] Anthony Summers and Robbyn Swan, "The Kingdom and the Towers," *Vanity Fair,* August 2011. CIA official John Kiriakou said bin Laden associate Abu Zubaydah fingered the prince as one of three princes who were Al Qaeda members. Sultan died inexplicably in a car crash within a week of the other two passing away under strange circumstances.

[164] J. M. Berger, *Intelwire.com.*

[165] *Road to 9/11,* 149, citing Clement Rodney Hampton-El testimony, United States v. Omar Ahmad Ali Abdel Rahman et al., US District Court, Southern District of New York, 1995; 15629–30, 15634–35, 15654,15667, 15671, 15673.

[166] *Unholy Terror,* 122.

about $500 million in aid. Where it went is unknown, but after the September 11, 2001, attacks, raids on its Sarajevo office turned up before and after pictures of the World Trade Center and information on how to counterfeit US State Department identification badges. Seized records also disclosed minutes of meetings with Osama bin Laden.[167] (N.B. When I was in Jeddah, 1987–1989, Saudi charities and aid to Muslims abroad were part of the US mission's reporting plan; that is, the American government wanted to learn as much as possible about them. Now we know why.)

As Schindler notes, Mustafa Kamel Suleiman, a veteran of both Afghanistan and Bosnia, received orders from an unspecified source and went from Afghanistan, where he had been living, to Bosnia with a group of recruits. First, he traveled to Saudi Arabia, progressing from there to Croatia and then to Bosnia with his mujahideen. A Bosnian military group met them at the Zagreb airport, getting them accredited as "Islamic relief workers" by the Croatian foreign ministry. Other of the "muj" masqueraded as UN staff and journalists.[168] Furthermore, it's Schindler's claim that Osama bin Laden, in Bosnia, transformed the original al-Qaeda from Afghanistan into the "flexible, well-funded multinational jihadi organization it became."[169]

Did he do so with or without American and Saudi and other help? The Third World Relief Agency, which was set up "to spread radical Islam,"[170] funded the war in the Balkans. Between 1992 and 1995, it passed on $2.5 billion in Islamic aid to the Party of Democratic Action, a Muslim political party in Bosnia.[171] Schindler does not specify the sources of the aid other than to note it came from "gov-

---

[167] Ibid., 129, citing *US News and World Report*, December 15, 2003, and *Dani* (Sarajevo news magazine), September 12, 2003.

[168] Ibid., 130, citing *Vecernji List* [*Evening Gazette*] Zagreb, October 16, 2001.

[169] Ibid., 131.

[170] Ibid., 148.

[171] Ibid., 149.

ernments who wished to mask their support for radicalism."[172] Nor does he say exactly where it went. However, Pakistan's ISI, long a supporter and pass-through for the covert cold war against the Soviets, provided antitank missiles to the Bosnian Muslims. Additionally, help came from UN forces in Bosnia, such as Turkey, Malaysia, and Bangladesh. They sold large quantities of ammunition to Bosnian Muslim fighters.[173] The "muj" ran a training camp outside Milan, Italy, which provided refresher instruction when necessary. Some of those trained were traveling with Italian passports.[174] On November 20, 2005, the waynemadsenreport.com noted that additional monies for the Albanian and Bosnian guerrillas in the Balkan war came from an entity titled "The Bosnian Defense Fund," a body created with a special account in the "Bush-influenced Riggs Bank and directed by Richard Perle and Douglas Feith." Richard Perle had been Assistant Secretary for Defense, 1981–1987; Feith had been Undersecretary of Defense for Policy, 2001–2005. The Fund collected monies, according to a later Wayne Madsen report, from various Arab and Muslim countries (such as the United Arab Emirates, Saudi Arabia, and Qatar). Amounting to hundreds of millions of dollars, the cash was managed by Feith's law firm, Feith and Zell, the Riggs Bank, and the Central Bank of Bosnia-Herzegovina in Sarajevo.[175]

Riggs, like BCCI, was a remarkably dirty bank, with questionable clients ranging from African and Latin American despots such as Chilean dictator Augusto Pinochet to Saudi Arabian diplomats (Prince Bandar bin Sultan). One major customer was the CIA, with an unknown number of bank accounts. Fined $25 million for banking violations and investigated by the US Justice Department,

---

[172] Ibid., 148.

[173] Ibid., 154.

[174] Ibid., 164.

[175] "Former 'Al Qaeda member' poised to spill beans on Balkans operations," *waynemadsenreport.com*, Jan. 26, 2009.

Riggs went out of business, with PNC Bank buying the remnants in 2005. Prosecution appeared to evaporate when the bank's ties to American government officials, hush-hush agencies, and US covert operations began to surface. For example, Bandar and his wife denied money laundering or financing 9/11 hijackers but he "fund[ed] the Contras at the behest of the White House, support[ed] the Afghan rebels against the Soviet Union, and serv[ed] as a go-between in the mending of the Libya-US relationship."[176]

Madsen further reported that there was a pipeline carrying money between Osama bin Laden and Bosnia at a time when French intelligence reported that bin Laden and his cohort were in Darunta, Afghanistan, and still under the control of the CIA and British intelligence around 1993. Madsen noted the importance of this link: bin Laden had apparently visited Bosnia and carried "at least one Bosnian diplomatic passport" and had dealt with Bosnian diplomats in Vienna. This money link between Bosnia and bin Laden included the Third World Relief Agency, a Saudi businessman, a Bosnian, the Sarajevo Deposit Bank, and the First Austrian Bank.[177]

"America's financial support for 'Al Qaeda'" also tied the Clinton Administration to backing al-Qaeda training in Bosnia and Kosovo. Rahm Emanuel, at the time assistant to the president for political affairs, was deeply involved in Clinton's foreign policy machinations in Bosnia and Kosovo. Emanuel asserted that Clinton went to both regions to handle al-Qaeda instruction. (Certainly, Clinton supported al-Qaeda training in both areas.) Madsen added that there were believable Serbian reports that fugitive financier Marc Rich (later pardoned by Clinton) had been engaged in arms smuggling to Bosnian Muslims.[178]

---

[176] Jack Shafer, "The CIA and Riggs Bank," *Slate*, January 7, 2005. Timothy L. O'Brien, "At Riggs Bank, A Tangled Path Led to Scandal," *New York Times*, July 19, 2004.

[177] "America's financial support for 'Al Qaeda,'" *waynemadsenreport*, July 5, 2007.

[178] Ibid.

While the United States and the Kingdom of Saudi Arabia poured money into financing the destruction of the Balkans, it fell to Prof. Michel Chossudovsky to illuminate another dark corner of the war's bankrolling: drugs. In a *Global Research* article,[179] Chossudovsky recalls past CIA covert operations such as those in Central America, Haiti, and Afghanistan. Illicit dope funded the so-called "Freedom Fighters" Langley sponsored in those areas. As an example, Chossudovsky noted that Iran-Contra rebels and the Afghan "muj" got their funds through "dirty money" being transformed into "covert money" by way of shell companies and the lending structure. Weapons and drugs and money flowed across the borders of Albania with Kosovo and Macedonia. For hefty commissions, "respectable" European banks, far removed from the fighting, dry-cleaned the dirty dollars. The drugs went one way, and the greenbacks another, helping pay the fighters and their trainers. Writing in *Global Research*,[180] Prof. Chossudovsky added to our knowledge of the sources of support for the Bosnian Muslim Army and the KLA—opium-based drug money direct from the Golden Crescent (Afghanistan, Pakistan, and Iran).

> Mercenaries financed by Saudi Arabia and Kuwait had been fighting in Bosnia.[181] And the Bosnian pattern was replicated in Kosovo: Mujahadeen [sic] mercenaries from various Islamic countries are reported to be fighting alongside the KLA [Kosovo Liberation Army] in Kosovo. German, Turkish and Afghan instructors

---

[179] "Remembering the 1999 NATO led War on Yugoslavia: 'Kosovo Freedom Fighters' Financed by Organized Crime," (March 19, 2009, but written and published April 1999).

[180] "Who Is Osama Bin Laden?" September 12, 2001.

[181] Michel Collon, "Poker Menteur," Editions EPO, Brussels, 1997, 288.

were reported to be training the KLA in guerilla and diversion tactics.[182]

Worse,

The trade in narcotics and weapons was allowed to prosper despite the presence since 1993 of a large contingent of American troops at the Albanian-Macedonian border with a mandate to enforce the embargo. The West had turned a blind eye. The revenues from oil and narcotics were used to finance the purchase of arms (often in terms of direct barter): "Deliveries of oil to Macedonia (skirting the Greek embargo [in 1993–94] can be used to cover heroin, as do deliveries of kalachnikov [sic] rifles to Albanian 'brothers' in Kosovo."[183]

Then there were the shadowy American aircraft that flew into Bosnia.

A Norwegian helicopter pilot, Captain Ivan Moldestad, reported the landing of a mysterious C-130 (Lockheed's large cargo plane) with a fighter escort at Tuzla airbase in Bosnia. When he reported this to NATO's Combined Air Operations Center in Vicenza, Italy, the organization told him no planes had landed, he was entirely mistaken in what he had seen, and then it hung up. However, other Norwegians witnessed similar occurrences and made written reports. Still the talk on the flightline and among intelligence and special operations personnel was that these were American aircraft and that Washington was secretly arming the Bosnians. On

---

[182] "Kosovo in Crisis," Truth in Media, Phoenix, April 2, 1999.

[183] "Who Is Osama Bin Laden?" citing Roger Boyes and Eske Wright, "Drugs Money Linked to the Kosovo Rebels," *The Times*, London, March 24, 1999.

a subsequent visit to Zagreb, Moldestad ran into three American officers who knew of his reports. Displeased, they took him to a fifth floor hotel balcony and suggested "things could get messy" if he stuck with his story.[184]

The Americans had more help from their client state, the Federal Republic of Germany. Its external intelligence service, the Bundesnachrichtendienst (BND), had helped arm the Muslims during the war. Additionally, BND officers had penetrated UN and European programs and sent firearms and other deadly devices to the Muslims through "peacekeeping channels." Moreover, "[T]he head of Germany's team of EU peace monitors was actually a BND officer, and the Germans shipped munitions in food packages, with shells hiding in boxes of powdered milk."[185]

Schindler's *Unholy Terror* goes on to link the Americans and their Bosnian operation to the September 11, 2001, attacks on New York's World Trade Center and the Pentagon. It seems that Khalid Sheikh Muhammad, alleged mastermind behind those events, had fought in Afghanistan (after studying in the United States) and then went on to the Bosnian war in 1992. In addition, two more of the September 11, 2001, hijackers, Khalid al-Mihdhar and Nawaf al-Hazmi, both Saudis, had gained combat experience in Bosnia. Still more connections came from Mohammed Haydar Zammar, who supposedly helped Mohammed Atta with planning the World Trade Center attacks. He had served with Bosnian army mujahideen units. Ramzi Binalshibh, friends with Atta and Zammar, had also fought in Bosnia.[186] This is yet another clear-cut example of officially unofficial US government support for terrorism. Also, it was one more example of the treachery of the American government, both against its own citizenry and its employees. Give the terrorists

---

[184] *Unholy Terror,* 177, 178, citing Cees Wiebes, *Intelligence,* 192.

[185] Ibid., 178, citing *The Daily Telegraph,* April 20, 1997.

[186] Ibid., 281–282.

the tools and means to do the job, even if it means killing people en masse and then prosecuting the crooks afterward for taking care of business. This was also true of Emmanuel "Toto" Constant, death squad leader, human rights abuser, and CIA asset in Haiti. They're like Kleenex—use them for their intended purpose and then throw them away.[187]

Unofficially but officially sending Americans to fight in someone else's war is celebrated in real-life fiction. In 1941, US Army Air Corps pilots resigned their commissions to fly first-line US fighter planes (the P-40 Warhawk) for the Chinese government. They fought against Japan while it was still at peace with America. Yet, the words "covert operation" never seem to be used in connection with this activity, and no one ever seems to question the ends resulting from such means.

Indeed, according to Nafeez Mosaddeq Ahmed, there is reason to believe that the CIA struck a deal with Ayman al-Zawahiri, al-Qaeda jihad group leader. If he and his band of men did not attack US interests in the Balkans, al-Qaeda would be free to engage in anti-American operations elsewhere in the world, including in the United States. Ahmed notes that al-Qaeda (the Arab-Afghans) appeared to accept the arrangement.[188]

In sum, "If Western intervention in Afghanistan created the Mujahideen, Western intervention in Bosnia appears to have globalized it."[189]

---

[187] Cf. the author's interview with him, December 29, 1995. Published in *Unclassified*, Spring 1996 issue.

[188] *War On Truth*, 52.

[189] Ibid., 32, citing Brendan O'Neill, "How We Trained al-Qaeda," *Spectator*, September 13, 2003.

Summary

Throughout this section, we've seen how the US government, which increasingly resembles a terrorist organization, worked with extremists, including its then-asset Osama bin Laden, to destabilize and then destroy Serbia. According to John Schindler, professor of strategy at the US Naval War College, the American Department of State and President Clinton sought to bomb the Serbs to help the Muslims, "following the lead of progressive opinion on Bosnia." Thousands of Arab-Afghans (Saudis, Yemenis, Algerians, Egyptians, Tunisians, Iraqis, Libyans, Jordanians, and others), with extensive combat experience gained fighting the Soviets in Afghanistan on behalf of the Americans, opened a new front in the Balkans. They had weapons procured with help from the US government, as well as money from the Saudis and Americans, including that passed through the al-Farooq mosque in Brooklyn. They had the assistance of the Maktab al-Khidamat (Services Office), set up to recruit, train, and aid fighters for the Afghan war. Richard Holbrooke, Assistant Secretary of State for European Affairs, wanted a repeat of the Afghanistan model in the Balkans, using Saudi Arabia, Turkey, and Pakistan to send arms to the combatants. Front companies, secret arms drops, and Clinton's National Security Council all played a role.

The result was the creation of a larger and more capable cadre of murderers, war criminals, and human rights violators. They enabled the United States to topple a socialist opponent of its policies in Yugoslavia, tap the natural resources of the region, and control the routes from and access to oil and natural gas in Central Asia.

American propaganda that flooded the media about murderers, war criminals, and human rights violators was particularly effective in gaining support in the United States and abroad.

Like actions against the USSR, the United States trained fighters, supplied arms, and provided financial aid to rebels seeking to overthrow their government. Washington and NATO applied economic sanctions to Yugoslavia, hastening the country's collapse. The KLA, directly supported and politically empowered by NATO in 1998, had been listed by the US State Department as a terrorist organization supported in part by loans from Islamic individuals, among them allegedly Osama bin Laden.

According to Yossef Bodansky, an Israeli American, "Bin Laden's 'Arab-Afghans' also assumed a dominant role in training the Kosovo Liberation Army." The former Canadian Ambassador to Yugoslavia James Bissett once stated: "Many members of the Kosovo Liberation Army were sent for training in terrorist camps in Afghanistan. There is no question of their [Al Qaeda's] participation in conflicts in the Balkans..." John R. Schindler, professor of strategy at the US Naval War College, asserted that the United States backed Osama bin Laden and al-Qaeda members in the Bosnia conflict, 1992–1995.

Richard Holbrooke, Assistant Secretary of State for European Affairs (1994–1996), believed that secret American support for the Afghans was an ideal pattern for sending arms to Bosnia through Saudi Arabia, Turkey, and Pakistan. The American Ambassador to Croatia, Peter W. Galbraith, contacted leaders in Croatia and Bosnia about supplying them with arms, with the help of Iranian Boeing 747s as transport. President Clinton's National Security Council oversaw this operation, without informing Congress, not unlike what Ronald Reagan had done during the Iran-Contra operation.

Yet, years later, no one in official Washington acknowledged that it had been US policy to allow al-Qaeda into the Balkans and to provide unofficial American diplomatic and military support. How Osama bin Laden's boys got to the region "were questions no one in Washington seemed eager to ask or have answered."

The US Army helped provide fighters to destroy Washington's "enemies" in the Balkans. Ft. Belvoir, Virginia, (roughly 20 miles from D.C. and headquarters for the United States Army's Intelligence and Security Command), supplied a list of soldiers who were ending their tours of duty and who would be suitable for recruitment as fighters in the Balkans.

The Americans and their Bosnian operation were linked to the September 11, 2001, attacks on New York's World Trade Center and the Pentagon in that some of the same players appeared in both places. Khalid Sheikh Muhammad, alleged mastermind behind those events, had fought in Afghanistan (after studying in the United States) and then went on to the Bosnian war in 1992. In addition, two more of the September 11, 2001, hijackers, Khalid al-Mihdhar and Nawaf al-Hazmi, both Saudis, had gained combat experience in Bosnia. Still more connections came from Mohammed Haydar Zammar, who supposedly helped Mohammed Atta with planning the attacks. He had served with Bosnian army mujahideen units. Ramzi Binalshibh, friends with Atta and Zammar, had also fought in Bosnia.

IRAQ

This section has been remarkably difficult to write due to well-connected, "progressive" Iraqis not responding to requests for interviews or suggestions for sources. These include: Anes Shallal, the owner/operator of Busboys and Poets, Washington, DC restaurants, which he makes available to people and organizations who criticize the US government. Among such are Sibel Edmonds (former FBI translator and alleged whistleblower) and Code Pink. Shallal's sister, May Kheder, also would not talk, even though an attorney, who had defended Arab Muslims that the US government had charged with criminal activity. Also in the group are Aseel Albanna, an activist and member of Iraqi Voices for Peace, Iraqis in Jordan, Iraqi Youth Foundation, and Fuel on the Fire, and, formerly, an official at the Iraqi Cultural Center in Washington, DC. Another US critic is Dr. Sami Albanna, with ties to US government agencies, yet an alleged activist and member of Iraqi Voices for Peace and The International Council for Middle East Studies. None of them would meet with the author, however informally. Additionally, Raed Jarrar, once Communications Director, American-Arab Anti-Discrimination Committee, initially wouldn't even talk to me, then despite help from an intermediary, never followed through on my requests. Asked directly about the Arab-Afghans at the Palestine Center in DC, September 3, 2014, neither Sami Albanna nor Jarrar responded to my inquiry. Rend al-Rahim Francke, Executive Director of the Iraq Foundation, despite phone calls and e-mails, refuses to speak with me. SourceWatch has tied her and her foundation to rightists, such as L. Paul Bremer III, and banksters. Anna Eshoo (D-CA), a supporter of Nancy Pelosi (D-CA) and one of the few Iraqis in government, also did not respond to inquiries.

Whether unknown people or organizations have instructed these individuals to be uncooperative, or whether they fear the consequences of providing firsthand information on a delicate subject, or whether, as some Arabs have told me, persons from the region simply do not cooperate with anyone unless they see an advantage in doing so are questions I can't answer.

Who's the Terrorist Now?

The people of Iraq not only had to contend with the Arab-Afghan Legion, they had to deal with the New Mongols, who employed them. Not since Hulugu, grandson of Genghis Khan, destroyed Baghdad in AD 1258, killing nearly a million people and annihilating the Abbasid Caliphate and Islam's Golden Age, has the Land Between the Dijla and Furat had to contend with such barbarity—until the Americans invaded and occupied the country in 2003.

At the Palestine Center's September 3, 2014, briefing on Iraq in crisis, Sami Albanna, Raed Jarrar, and Adil Shamoo (the last a professor at the University of Maryland and Associate Fellow at the Institute for Policy Studies) squarely blamed the United States for Iraq's troubles. According to Shamoo, America created the internal dissensions and sectorial divisions, now rampant in the country, with its 2003 invasion. Continuing, he indicted Europe, Israel, Kuwait, Saudi Arabia, and the United States for making matters worse. Shamoo asserted that the Islamic State of Iraq and Syria (ISIS) is made up of former Ba'athists, al-Qaeda members, and Sunnis who lost their positions of influence. ISIS funding, he declared, comes from the Saudis and the Gulf states, along with the Islamic State's sales of oil at $25 a barrel, one-quarter of the 2014 world price.

Jarrar, suddenly critical of the United States in public (perhaps reflecting a new job with the American Friends Service Committee), blamed America's invasion and occupation of Iraq for Mesopotamia's problems.

Sami Albanna also jumped on the "Bash America" bandwagon, contending that the CIA had been behind previous coups d'état in Iraq. He emphasized that Langley brought on the 1958 revolt that abolished the British-installed monarchy and later put the Ba'ath (Resurrection) Party into power in 1963. Albanna also stressed that the Kurdish Peshmerga is a US creation.

But What Drove This Train Wreck?

In January 2005, *Newsweek* wrote that the American government was weighing a "Salvador Option" to counter resistance fighters in Iraq. (During the Reagan Administration, US armed forces trained and supported the Salvadoran military, which engaged in outrageous murders, war crimes, and human rights violations, as they fought a popular uprising against a repressive government.[190] Retired four-star US Army general Wayne Downing, former head of all US Special Operations Forces, corroborated this in a January 10, 2005, interview with Katie Couric on the NBC "Today Show." She had asked him about the "Salvador Option" story. He said, "What they're considering is to use a special—or more special Iraqi units trained and equipped and perhaps even led by US Special Forces to conduct strike operations against this—this insurgency, against

---

[190] Cf. citation to Noam Chomsky, "The Crucifixion of El Salvador," zmag.org.

the leaders of it, which of course is a very valid strategy, a very valid tactic. And it's actually something we've been doing since we started the war back in March of 2003."[191]

Max Fuller, the *Newsweek* article's author, went on to note that, in September 2004, Counselor to the Ambassador for Iraqi Security Forces, US Colonel James Steele began work with the Special Police Commandos, formed under Iraq's Interior Ministry. Before working with this "elite" unit, Steele had helped organize and develop similar groups in El Salvador between 1984 and 1986.[192] Steven Casteel, a former assistant administrator for intelligence at the Drug Enforcement Administration, and senior vice president, international business development, Vance International Inc.,[193] aided Steele in this effort. Then working as senior advisor to the Iraqi Interior Ministry, Casteel helped create the Police Commandos, who deliberately cultivated a terrifying appearance. "During raids," said Fuller, "they wear balaclavas and black leather gloves and openly intimidate and brutalize suspects, even in the presence of foreign journalists."[194]

Fuller noted the upsurge in mass executions and mass burials had occurred soon after organization of the Commandos and correlated with locations where they had operated. Iraqi and US government sources, providing sketchy evidence, claimed that the dead were victims of "insurgents." Fuller, however, added that "many, if not all, of the extrajudicial killings in Mosul have been carried out by the Police Commandos."

A cursory read of any newspaper shows that these killings are continuing in 2014, with little or no definitive attribution to individuals

---

[191] Stephen Shalom, "Phoenix Rising in Iraq?" zcommunications.org., February 11, 2005, and cited in Fuller's article.

[192] "For Iraq," citing Peter Maass, "The Way of the Commando," May 1, 2005, in the *New York Times* and in *psychoanalystsopposewar.com.*

[193] "New at the Top," *Washington Post,* February 27, 2006.

[194] "For Iraq," citing Peter Maass.

or groups, other than "Al Qaeda" or "terrorists" or ISIL/ISIS.[195] But, in the past, things were different. According to Fuller,[196] accusations were leveled against the Commandos in three Baghdad massacres. On May 5, 2005, fourteen young men, with their hands tied, were found lying in a shallow grave with gunshots to the head—after torture and beatings. In reality, they had been farmers going to market. On May 15, 2005, fifteen more corpses came to light, again with bound hands and bullets in the head.[197] This wasn't al-Qaeda or ISIS/ISIL in action but governmental forces which the US trained and organized.

"The Association of Muslim Scholars quickly responded to the wave of killings, accusing soldiers and Interior Ministry commandos of having 'arrested imams and the guardians of some mosques, tortured and killed them, then got rid of their bodies in a garbage dump in the Shaab district'"[198]

Now, the Iraqi government is wading deeper into the morass, tying itself to terrorists. According to a *Washington Post* report[199], Nouri al-Maliki's government has been seeking to employ the "insurgents" from al-Qaeda that the United States had previously recruited. Al-Maliki is reviving America's old policy of arming and paying Sunni tribesmen who had initially fought the US invasion and occupation. Called al-Sahwa (the Awakening), Baghdad's puppet government is giving the new recruits millions of dollars along with weapons, such as three thousand Russian machine guns and two thousand AK-47 rifles delivered to Ramadi. Not all Iraqis see

---

[195] Islamic State of Iraq and the Levant/Islamic State of Iraq and Syria.

[196] Citing http://www.guardian.co.uk/ international/story/0,,1488096,00.html, http://abcnews.go.com/International/ wireStory?id'760368.

[197] "For Iraq," citing www.chicagotribune.com/news/ nationworld/ chi-05051700 30may17,0,3795261.story?coll'chi-newsopinionperspective-utl.

[198] "For Iraq," citing www.mg.co.za/ articlePage.aspx?articleid'238784&area' / breaking_news/ breaking_news__international_news/.

[199] Loveday Morris, "In Iraq, seeking a second awakening," January 31, 2014.

this as progress. One unnamed official said, "We reject our sons being rentals. They are used like a disposal tissue, to wipe up the problems and then thrown away." Another, Sheikh Rafai Mishhin al-Jumaili, accused the government "of sectarianism, saying it has branded all rebel tribesmen as al-Qaeda to justify attacks on them." (This has been, as demonstrated here, the practice of the CIA and the rest of the American government through the course of the US "intervention.")

Now, in June 2014, the Awakened Ones appear to be sleepwalking. *The Statesman* ran an AP report on the situation on June 25, 2014.[200] The piece discussed waking up the Awakening, to which the Americans had given more than $370 million between 2006 and 2009.[201] The article continued, touching on new American fears. Worried that the Awakening might become a form of somnambulism, the United States is reputedly concerned that funds and weapons passed to the new recruits might well go to "terrorists" not officially sanctioned by Uncle Sam but supported instead by Jordan and Saudi Arabia. Many of those who awakened but went back to sleep are now joining forces with the Islamic State of Iraq and the Levant (ISIL), along with other Sunnis and about one thousand Ba'athists, holdovers from Saddam Hussein's secular, socialist party.

George W. Bush's personal representative to Iraq, John Negroponte, created death squads there, patterned on the ones he supported in El Salvador, while he was also American ambassador there.[202] Negroponte, as Dr. Elias Akleh noted in "American Terror Strategy in Iraq,"[203] had learned his trade while supervising

---

[200] Lara Jakes, "In Iraq, former militia program eyed for new fight."

[201] Col. Peter Mansoor, USA (ret.) helped create them. He spoke June 23, 2014 at a National Press Club panel organized by the American Task Force for Palestine to promote more intervention in Iraq.

[202] Michel Chossudovsky, "Terrorism with a 'Human Face': The History of America's Death Squads," *Global Research*, January 4, 2013.

[203] Undated article appearing originally at www.inmediares.dk.

the CIA's Phoenix Program in Vietnam. Akleh defined Phoenix as involving "the training and the arming of death squads specialized in torture, forced interrogation, assassination."

Aiding Negroponte in this matter were Political Counselor Robert Stephen Ford (later US Ambassador to Syria) and Henry Ensher (my old "friend" from the CIA base/American consulate general at Jeddah, Saudi Arabia). Ford helped recruit the death squads, using his contacts with Shiite and Kurdish militia groups. Ensher, now American Ambassador to Algeria, played an important role on the "team," reaching out to a wide range of Iraqi extremists.[204]

In corroborating Max Fuller's views and General Downing's remarks, Akleh flatly stated that the American aim in Iraq was *divide et impera* (Imperial Rome's principle of divide and rule). With a goal of "spreading a sectarian hatred between the three major Iraqi sects, Kurds, Shiite, and Sunnis," American agents, ably assisted by Israeli ones, executed Sunni and Shiite leaders while blowing up their mosques and setting off explosives in their communities. This turned the groups from fighting the American invaders to battling each other.

Additionally, Dr. Akleh wrote that US forces targeted civilians and tried to link the attacks to the resistance, attempting to cut them off from the Iraqi population that sheltered them. The assailants weren't the Anglo-Saxon Christians from the American Midwest but were "Al-Qaeda," "Al-Zarqawi," or "foreign terrorists." Following the lead of the Nazi SS in wartime Czechoslovakia, and as they had done with Operation Phoenix in Vietnam, the Americans destroyed entire villages for protecting opponents of the invasion.

US officials, such as James Steele and Steve Casteel, as Dr. Akleh perspicaciously wrote, created sectarian, vigilante militias, placing them under the control of Iraqi politicians, such as Iyad Allawi, "for their protection." Akleh further asserted that directing Kurdish

---

[204] "Terrorism with a 'Human Face.'"

Peshmerga and Shiite militias against the Sunni "increase[d] the likelihood of sectarian hatred and civil war." To its everlasting discredit, the US Marine Corps created its own Iraqi militias. Dr. Akleh stated that, in January 2005, the 7th Marines established a group called "The Iraqi Freedom Guard," paying each member $400 a month (at the 2005 exchange rate, that was nearly 600,000 Iraqi dinars). The 23rd Marines also set up a militia, mostly from Basra, called "Freedom Fighters." Both groups, Dr. Akleh said, were used in attacks in Anbar Province in western Iraq. Continuing, Elias Akleh said that the American forces had worked out an agreement with Moqtada Al-Sadr's Mahdi army, always described in the US press as "anti-American," to pursue and seize members of the resistance.

Robert Dreyfuss wrote in "Phoenix Rising,"[205] that Congress had given $3 billion to the CIA to create militia-run paramilitary units. The object was to kill "nationalists, other opponents of the US occupation and thousands of civilian Baathists up to 120,000 of the estimated 2.5 million former Baath Party members in Iraq." Furthermore, Dreyfuss asserted that the lion's share of this money would help "create a lethal, and revenge-minded Iraqi security force." As Dreyfuss said, citing John Pike in globalsecurity.org, "The big money would be for standing up [sic] an Iraqi secret police to liquidate the resistance." Continuing, Dreyfuss noted that the Iraqi secret police would be "staffed mainly by gunmen associated with members of the puppet Iraqi Governing Council…linked to Ahmad Chalabi's Iraqi National Congress…the Kurdish *pershmerga*…and Shiite paramilitary units…"

Yet, no mention was made of the real saddle tramps, the Arab-Afghans, who undoubtedly formed a goodly number of the people engaged in "extrajudicial" killings in Iraq.

---

[205] *The Prospect*, December 10, 2003.

Distressing Details about the Legion

Methods of implementing *divide et impera* varied. The US-sponsored *Al Iraqiya* TV channel ran a program six nights a week called "Terror in the Grip of Justice." It denigrated opposition fighters as criminals, alcoholics, and homosexuals, people whom good Arabs, Muslims (and others) believe to be sinners. Dr. Akleh also noted that American soldiers would routinely stop a car, confiscate the driver's license, and send the driver off to be interrogated. While he was absent, explosives would be placed in the vehicle. Upon his return, he would be directed to a police station to get his license back. A US helicopter would follow, detonating the bomb by radio just as the car reached the cop shop, thus giving the appearance of another "terrorist" attack.[206]

"Outsiders" helped the Americans wreck Iraq by convoying terrorists into the country and supplying them with weapons. Just as the Americans used the Arab-Afghans in the former Yugoslavia to turn the country into a collection of small, weak statelets, they, the British, and the Israelis used them, in vain to date, to split Iraq into three pieces, the Kurdish north, the Sunni center, and the Shii south.[207]

However, with the recent successes of The Islamic State of Syria and the Levant (ISIL)/Islamic State of Iraq and Syria (ISIS), *RT.com* reported June 27–30, 2014, that the Kurds would likely use the turmoil occasioned by the group's attacks on the Iraqi army to declare the north of the country an independent state, thus beginning the permanent division of Iraq. As one Iraqi American commented, Barack Obama can now say, along with George W. Bush, "Mission Accomplished." The *Washington Post* ever the propaganda organ,

---

[206] "American Terror Strategy."

[207] Elias Akleh, "British Terrorism in Iraq," *Global Research*, September 30, 2005.

added that Massoud Barzani, head of the "largely autonomous Kurdistan Regional Government," seeks a plebiscite on seceding from Iraq.[208] The article asserted that Iraq is separating into three pieces "since "[the] Islamic State [of Iraq and Syria] routed the government's forces and took over a vast stretch of territory...[in June]." As Wayne Madsen wrote June 26–27, 2014: "There are credible reports that US Special Forces in Jordan helped train many of the ISIL fighters [obviously more of the Arab-Afghans] now in control of a large swath of western Iraq, including former US military bases and the Baji oil refinery, Iraq's largest."[209]

Michel Chossudovsky concurs. Writing in *Global Research* he said, "The Islamic State is not an independent political entity. It is a construct of US Intelligence." Continuing, he decried the fact that the CIA, with help from Saudi Arabia, Qatar, and Turkey, is clandestinely backing the Caliphate. Israel is also participating, sending aid to al-Qaeda in Syria through the Golan Heights and to the Kurdish secessionists in Syria and Iraq as well.[210],

Chossudovsky went on to emphasize that there was no al-Qaeda in Iraq prior to the American invasion of 2003[211] and it did not emerge in Syria until the "US-NATO-Israeli supported insurgency in March 2011." Indeed, Chossudovsky remarked that the ISIS attacks are intended to "destroy and destabilize Iraq as a Nation State." Projected to topple Iraq's al-Maliki government, the Islamic State is aiming at breaking up the country into three pieces. It has no

---

[208] Abigail Hauslohner and Loveday Morris, "President of Iraqi Kurdistan calls for independence vote," July 4, 2014.

[209] "R2P architects helped form a new Middle East coalition," *waynemad senreport.com.*

[210] "The Engineered Destruction and Political Fragmentation of Iraq—Towards the Creation of a US Sponsored Caliphate," July 1, 2014.

[211] A point raised many times by Prof. Edmund A. Ghareeb, an internationally recognized expert on the Kurds, Iraq, and media issues.

interest in traditional "regime change." As is the case of Yugoslavia's partition, Washington would find this in its "national interest."

Naturally, as Chossudovsky observes, Iraq's fragmentation will impact Syria. The latter country is roughly an arc-shaped slice of pizza, with Christians, Druze, Shiite Allawi, Sunni, and Yezidi (an obscure, much-persecuted religion[212]) distributed through it.

The article also speculated that asking Iran to help mediate the Caliphate conflict is one way of causing that country's intervention, to its detriment.

Ultimately, Chossudovsky ventured that the map of the Middle East could be redrawn along the lines proposed by Lt. Col. Ralph Peters, USA (ret.): Iraq in three pieces; "Kurdistan" made up of parts of Turkey, Iraq, Armenia; an enlarged Jordan, absorbing part of northwest Saudi Arabia; a truncated Saudi Arabia, with chunks gong to an Arab Shia state (mostly the Eastern Province), an Islamic Sacred State (principally the Hejaz) and Yemen.

The Americans couldn't divide Iraq with their army, navy, and air force in eleven years. But now, with the aid of terrorists from the Arab-Afghan Legion, the United States appears to be succeeding, after years of preparation. From the enthusiastic declarations carried in the "fawning corporate media" about the wild men from ISIL/ISIS, it appears that US policy in Mesopotamia is following that enunciated by Cheryl Benard in describing the destruction of Afghanistan: recruit the most unstable, ruthless fanatics to get the job done.[213]

---

[212] The Yezidi religion blends elements of monotheism from Christianity and Islam, adding a bit of its own. They acknowledge an inactive, static, and transcendental God who created, or "became," Seven Great Angels, the leader of which is Tawsi Melek, the Peacock "King" or Peacock "Angel." Cf. yeziditruth. org. They also seem to add elements of Zoroastrianism and Mithraism. They have a caste system as well. Cf. Sean Thomas, "Death of a religion: Isis and the Yazidi," *The Telegraph*, August 6, 2014.

[213] Cf. Cheryl Benard's comments in Stone and Kuznick, 461, citing Dreyfuss, *Devil's Game*, 290.

The investigative journalist Wayne Madsen blames Dick Cheney and L. Paul Bremer for the collapse of Iraq.[214] They toppled Iraq's secular President Saddam Hussein and engaged in "'de-Ba'athfication' that would erase Iraq's legacy of pan-Arab socialist secular rule." Add to that Bremer's policy of demobilizing the Iraqi army, and you end up with "fertile ground" sown with ISIL's dragon teeth "to germinate and flourish." Madsen also condemns Paul Wolfowitz, Bush Deputy Secretary of Defense, for "eliminat[ing from leadership]…Saddam Hussein's chief officials…[which he says] led to the current rise of ISIL and their Salafist supporters in Iraq and Syria."

Furthermore, as Madsen continued, it was Barack Obama's twin picks for National Security Advisor and Ambassador to the UN, Susan Rice and Samantha Power, respectively, who helped "bring about a Sunni-led…revolt against Syria Baathist leader Bashar al-Assad." With Assad losing power in east Syria, ISIL forces, "backed by Saudi Arabia and Qatar, [were able] to gain a foothold in Iraq and expand the conflict against Assad to threaten the outskirts of Baghdad and the Prime Minister Nouri al-Maliki [sic] government."

> Madsen commented: What the neocons want more than anything else is Arab killing Arab and Muslim killing Muslim. Mossad's fingerprints are found in supporting a number of radical Arab and Islamic factions…for the sole purpose of driving wedges between Arab and Muslim states and peoples. Only through a policy of population cleansing in Syria, Iraq, Palestine, and other Arab states will there be lebensraum (living space) for a greater Jewish state.[215]

---

[214] "They're back! The neocons," *waynemadsenreport.com*, June 27–29, 2014.
[215] Ibid.

Moreover, according to Reuters, the Israeli government told the United States on Thursday, June 26, 2014:[216]

> ...Kurdish independence in northern Iraq was a "foregone conclusion" and Israeli experts predicted the Jewish state would be quick to recognise a Kurdish state, should it emerge...Israel has maintained discreet military, intelligence and business ties with the Kurds since the 1960s, seeing in the minority ethnic group a buffer against shared Arab adversaries.

But the "fawning corporate media" tends to underreport this, a point noted by Marsha Cohen in *LobeLog*:

> A decade ago, Seymour Hersh called attention to Israel's close ties with the Kurds. Hersh's "Annals of National Security: Plan B," published in the *New Yorker*, is noteworthy, particularly in light of mounting criticism against the Obama administration's handling of the current crisis. US officials interviewed by Hersh told him that by the end of 2003, "Israel had concluded that the Bush Administration would not be able to bring stability or democracy to Iraq, and that Israel needed other options." One of those options was expanding Israel's long-standing relationship with Iraqi Kurds and "establishing a significant presence on the ground in the semiautonomous region of Kurdistan."

---

[216] Dan Williams, "Israel tells U.S. Kurdish independence is 'foregone conclusion.'"

Although the reliability of Hersh's sources was challenged at the time, they have been affirmed by more recent articles and reports. Neriah [Jacques Neriah, retired Israeli colonel and foreign policy advisor to PM Yitzhak Rabin], writing in August 2012, cites numerous reports in the Israeli media about the activities of Israeli security and military personnel working for Israeli firms in Kurdistan: According to Israeli newspapers, dozens of Israelis with a background in elite combat training have been working for private Israeli companies in northern Iraq, helping Kurds there establish elite antiterror units. Reports say that the Kurdish government contracted Israeli security and communications companies to train Kurdish security forces and provide them with advanced equipment.[217]

The *Washington Post* reported in June 2014[218] that the "rebels" have erased most of the border between Syria and Iraq, and it seems clear that Washington intended this result. Free to move the extremists it armed and trained between the two countries, the United States now appears able to completely destroy the political integrity of Iraq, having previously obliterated that country's infrastructure, army, and culture. Iran, as Liz Sly reported, denounced continued American interference in Iraq, claiming Washington sought "to dominate Iraq and have its agents rule over the country." Additionally, Teheran argued that "the United States is dissatisfied with the result of elections in Iraq, and they want to deprive the Iraqi people of their achievement of a democratic system..." The *Post's* Loveday Morris and Karen DeYoung quoted Rick Berenson,

---

[217] "Israel: The Silent Stakeholder in Northern Iraq," June 19, 2014.
[218] Liz Sly, "ISIS widens control in Iraq," June 23, 2014.

RAND Corp. analyst, as saying "…I think what we're looking at is the beginning of the disintegration of the state of Iraq."[219]

It's not hard to speculate that the latest attack on Iraq with a "new" set of bogeymen, ISIL, is merely a continuation of the old policy, coupled with the ongoing destruction of Syria. It's significant that the Obama administration was reportedly "undecided" over attacking ISIL. After all, why bomb the people you sent to smash what's left of Iraq?[220] That *Post* article continued the falsehood the US government is not arming and training terrorists in both Syria and Iraq. It also claimed that there were no more American soldiers in Mesopotamia, asserting that US officials can't deal with both countries separately and they must "…build effective partnerships."

Retired DC Superior Court Judge Thomas Andrew O'Keefe had a different view.

> Iraq is still filled with thousands of US military personnel and contractors housed at the US Embassy compound in Baghdad and at US consulates in Basra, Kirkuk, and Mosul who serve as military trainers or security guards. In addition, the US military still helps patrol Iraqi air space and also trains the country's nascent air force. This does not include the thousands of American military contractors [mercenaries] on the Iraqi government payroll who previously were paid by the US Department of Defense.[221]

PRESSTV[222] attributes the disaster that American policy in the region has become to National Security Advisor Susan Rice;

---

[219] "US advisers likely to find broken army," June 23, 3014.

[220] cf. Scott Wilson, "White House grapples with borderless conflict," *Washington Post*, June 20, 2014.

[221] Letters, *Washington* [DC] *Lawyer*, April 2014.

[222] "US policy on Middle East 'monumental failure,'" June 23, 2014.

the US Ambassador to the United Nations, Samantha Power; and former Secretary of State Hillary Clinton. Citing an interview with investigative journalist Wayne Madsen, it asserted that "US policy is constantly shifting like the Middle East sands." Madsen observed that "the recent crisis in Iraq is a result of US activities in the region." According to the interview, ISIL/ISIS in Iraq is directly attributable to America providing weapons and other aid to the Syrian rebels, "many of whom are al-Qaeda affiliates...Some of this weaponry has been used across the border in Iraq." It's clear to the author that any change of heart about ISIL/ISIS by the US government can only come from their possible or projected attacks on the Kurds.

On June 22, 2014, AFP (*Agence France Presse*) reported Iran's President Hassan Rouhani as warning Muslim states supporting Sunni combatants now devastating Iraq that they could become the insurgents' next target. While Rouhani did not name names, "officials and media in...Iran have hinted that...ISIL are being financially and militarily supported by Saudi Arabia and Qatar." Both these American allies against "terrorism" were deeply embroiled in destroying Libya and Syria. AFP quoted Iran's supreme leader, Ayatollah Ali Khamenei, as saying "This is not a Shiite versus Sunni war, unlike what American officials say"...while blaming the United States for "disrupting (Iraq's) stability and threatening its territorial integrity."

According to Al Jazeera,[223] Iraq had been beefing up army units on its western border, hoping to block terrorists from neighboring countries, including Syria, from entering. Citing Iraqi Prime Minister Nouri al-Maliki, the news channel noted that 90 percent of foreign fighters infiltrated the country through Syria, where they had been training. Once there, they engaged in terror bombings, such as those in Baghdad. Additionally, Al Jazeera reported August 21, 2005, that Iraq accused Jordan of hosting people involved in "terrorist acts" in

---

[223] "Inside Story: Iraq-Syria Rift Over Bombings," Sept. 7, 2009.

Mesopotamia. Iraqi government spokesman Laith Kubba announced that 281 foreign fighters had been jailed, including eighty Egyptians, sixty-four Syrians, forty-one Sudanese, twenty-two Saudis, and one Briton. Kubba also noted that hostiles have used Jordan to mount attacks on his country, some perpetrated by exiled Iraqis, such as Saddam Hussein's family and exiled Ba'athists. Continuing, Kubba said that "Jordan, Syria, and the United Arab Emirates are being used as 'safe havens' for elements that 'support and practice terrorist acts in Iraq.'" (He didn't mention the fact that Jordan and the U.A.E. were and are "allies" of the United States or that Jordan is making its land available for terrorist training by Americans and others.)

Syria, on the other hand, declared that it had been doing all in its power to control its six hundred kilometer border (nearly 373 miles) with Iraq. Al Jazeera reported on July 21, 2005,[224] that the Syrian government had told diplomatic missions in Damascus that its soldiers had been attacked "not only by infiltrators and smugglers but by the Iraqi and American forces." Despite one hundred clashes, some involving American soldiers, the US government claimed that Syria had not been doing enough to stop the passage of fighters across the Iraqi border. Also, it was not interdicting the transfer of funds to fuel the opposition to the American occupation of Iraq. In reply, Syria noted that it had caught 1,240 combatants, deporting them to their respective countries. Additionally, the government had investigated, it said, roughly four thousand more individuals who left or attempted to leave for Iraq to join the fighters there. From all indications, just as Moammar Gaddafi was ousted and Libya paid the price for dealing adversely with the Arab-Afghans, so apparently will Bashar al-Assad, if Washington and Israel have their way.

In September 2005, the Iraqis and Americans seized about two hundred men in a "rebellious" section of Tal Afar, a town near the Syrian frontier. According to Iraqi army captain Mohammed Ahmed,

---

[224] "Syria says U.S. forces fired on troops."

one hundred and fifty of those captured were Arabs from Jordan, the Sudan, Syria, and Yemen.[225] Unnamed US government officials insisted that "many foreign nationals" were fighting American forces between the Dijla and Furat. A Syrian had been sentenced to life imprisonment by an Iraqi court after being captured in Falluja and, allegedly, intending to fight the Iraqi forces. Another, a Saudi, also got life after entering Mesopotamia illegally to battle the government. Another Syrian obtained six years "for entering Iraq illegally to join the armed fighters." A Libyan was sentenced to fifteen years for entering Iraq illegally from Syria and conducting "terrorist actions" against Iraqi security forces. An Egyptian received only two years for having "an expired entry visa" after being found with three other combatants in a house with arms and ammunition.[226]

Even the one-time Afghan American Ambassador to Baghdad, Zalmay Khalilzad, asserted that "terrorists" were traveling from Syria to Iraq. Al Jazeera reported that Khalilzad, in remarks to journalists at the US State Department, had threatened Syria for allowing "foreign terrorists" to stream across its border with Iraq. He claimed that would-be terrorists were flying to Syria from other countries in the region (such as Saudi Arabia, Yemen, and North Africa), getting training, and then moving into Iraq. [227] Al Jazeera reported one of the kingdom's dissidents, Dr. Muhammad al-Massari, as saying the Saudis have supplied thousands of fighters to Iraq. Resident in London, al-Massari observed that there were five thousand mujahideen sent to battle the American invader in Baghdad alone, with others joining them from the rest of the Arab and Muslim worlds.[228] The reportage added that L. Paul Bremer III, Administrator of the Coalition Provisional Authority, had expounded the view that

---

[225] "Scores of 'fighters' held in Iraq," *Al Jazeera*, September 6, 2005.

[226] "Foreign fighters convicted in Iraq," *Al Jazeera*, April 4, 2005.

[227] "US Renews Warning to Syria on Iraq," September 12, 2005.

[228] Shaista Aziz, "Saudi fighters join resistance in Iraq," *Al Jazeera*, October 29, 2003.

"most of the 'terrorists' in Iraq were not Iraqis but came from countries such as Syria, Saudi Arabia, Yemen, and the Sudan." Bremer observed that sealing Iraq's frontiers was a demanding, if not impossible, task. Al Jazeera's report contained some of the George W. Bush administration's continued fulminations against Iranian and Syrian guerillas in Iraq. In accordance with its claims, the US government had asserted that "foreign fighters" had instigated four suicide bombings, killing 34 and wounding 230 in Baghdad.

In an earlier statement, Bremer had stressed that, while American government forces had captured nineteen "Al Qaeda" members, he had no idea of their nationalities. Bremer did know, he said, that of the two hundred forty-eight men the US military seized, there were one hundred twenty-three Syrians and many Iranians and Yemenis. His basis for this information was questioning "the usual suspects," plus documents the men were carrying. According to Al Jazeera's Baghdad correspondent Jawad al-Umari, Bremer's remarks were designed to pressure the countries named, such as Syria and Iran, presumably to do more about restricting the flow of combatants.[229]

Hard analysis of the captives' origins wasn't always possible. Al Jazeera reported on October 24, 2010, that identities of thousands of foreign fighters seized by US soldiers were often obscure.[230] When arrested, many had foreign passports or no identification whatsoever. American armed forces guessed at the nationalities of those captured through "accent, dress and mannerisms." The combatants from outside Iraq, according to US authorities were Syrians, Saudis, Egyptians, Yemenis, Libyans, Afghans, Pakistanis, Lebanese, Jordanians, and Algerians, just like in Afghanistan, Bosnia, and Libya. Additionally, some came from "Western countries," that is, the United Kingdom, Canada, and the United States. The Arab-Afghan Legion was and is a remarkably wide-ranging organization.

---

[229] "US holding 250 foreign fighters in Iraq," *Al Jazeera*, September 27, 2003.
[230] Gregg Carlstrom, "The Secret Iraq Files: The War."

The origins of the "terrorists'" weapons weren't quite so obscure. According to *Global Research*, the Israeli paper *Ma'ariv Daily News* announced March 7, 2007, that Shmoel Avivi, a retired Israeli officer, had established a firm in Iraq to covertly sell weaponry to "terrorist groups in Iraq." *Ma'ariv* wrote that Amnesty International had claimed that Avivi was one of the largest arms dealers in the region. The Israeli journal noted that "Iraqi sources" asserted that attacks in the country had been sponsored by Mossad, the CIA, and former agents of Saddam Hussein. Additionally, Hadi Ameri, Iraqi parliament security commission chairman, had charged the occupying coalition of secretly masterminding "terrorist" attacks and organizing "terror" squads in his country.[231]

According to another Al Jazeera story, the Kingdom of Saudi Arabia is at the bottom of many terrorist attacks. [232] In a meeting at Iraqi Prime Minister Nouri al-Maliki's residence, comprising al-Maliki, US Army General David Petraeus, and US Ambassador Ryan Crocker, the prime minister blasted the kingdom and its leadership, saying, "Most terrorists here are Saudis; the Saudi people have a culture that supports terrorism." Furthermore, al-Maliki held the head of Saudi Arabia's General Intelligence service, Prince Muqrin bin Abdulaziz, responsible for provoking sectarian violence in Iraq. Al Jazeera quoted al-Maliki as saying, "I told Vice President Cheney that (Saudi) Prince Muqrin is funding a Sunni army to oppose the Shia army." (Muqrin is now the kingdom's deputy crown prince.)

Global Research News, along with the *FARS News Agency* reported on January 4, 2014, that Saudi Arabia was continuing to support the culture of terror. It asserted that the kingdom is still backing the al-Qaeda "terrorist groups in Iraq, Syria, and Lebanon." Moreover, the House of Saud (which essentially owns the country) has been

---

[231] *Global Research*, March 26, 2007.

[232] Robert Kennedy, "Iraqi PM: Saudi has a 'culture' of terrorism," September 9, 2011.

clandestinely shipping small arms, explosives, anti-armor, and antiaircraft weapons into and through Iraq from the Saudi city of Nakheib and the Ar Ar border crossing.

On March 8, 2014, BBC News reported more of Nouri al-Maliki's extremely negative remarks on Saudi support for terrorism in Iraq. Citing an undated interview with French television channel *France 24*, the BBC recounted al-Maliki as saying that Saudi Arabia and Qatar had "effectively declared war on Iraq" and that Saudi Arabia supported "global 'terrorism'." The Iraqi prime minister charged that the Saudis were attacking his country through Syria. In addition, he alleged, "accusations that he was marginalizing the Sunnis [the minority branch of Islam in Iraq] came from sectarian groups with links to Saudi Arabia and Qatar, which are majority Sunni states." The report noted that UN figures show that violence in 2013 had killed 8,868 people [an astonishingly accurate figure, given the vagueness of the number on Iraqis the Americans have killed since 2003].

The United Kingdom also applied its own highly developed form of terrorism to Iraq, using the Special Air Service (SAS). In September 2005, several SAS members, disguised in wigs as al-Qaeda terrorists, shot two Iraqi police officers who had been watching them. The Britons were soon captured and their vehicle was found to be filled with explosives that they intended to detonate in the middle of Basra, Iraq's chief port. Although the Iraqis jailed the SAS terrorists, the British army, using tanks and helicopters, attacked the prison and freed them for future crimes. Attacks on UN headquarters in Iraq, a plethora of car bombings, as well as strikes on embassies and mosques were seen by the Iraqi man in the street as foreign forces' efforts to destabilize the country and incite communal violence. The intent, by American, British, and Israeli groups, in part using Kurdish Peshmerga guerrilla forces, was to provide reasons to continue the occupation and partition of Iraq into Kurdish, Sunni, and Shii sections, on the model of what had been done to Yugoslavia.[233]

As noted in the *waynenadsenreport.com*,[234] the *Washington Post* had stated on August 14, 2007, that the US military in Iraq was working with Sunni "ex-members" of al-Qaeda in Baghdad, Anbar, and Diyala provinces. Madsen further noted that Langley was also working with pro-al-Qaeda and Taliban elements in Pakistan. In an Al Jazeera "In Depth" report called "Iraq's Summer of Terror,"[235] Brigadier General Saad Mann, the Iraqi Interior Ministry Spokesman, was quoted as saying that most of the attacks in the country can be blamed on al-Qaeda. He also observed that "what is happening in Syria is definitely affecting Iraq." Unnamed Iraqi security officials said that more "foreign suicide bombers" and fighters from North Africa and other Arab countries are coming across the Syrian frontier. Yet, the author, Jane Arraf, wrote that many political organizations, seeing that they were losing at the ballot box, had turned to intercommunal violence to regain their diminished power.

According to the *New York Times*, "Smuggling routes and alliances that moved terrorists and supplies into Iraq during the height of the war, in 2006–2007, have been reversed, allowing fighters and supplies to flow into neighboring countries, particularly Syria."[236]

On August 12, 2013, *PRESSTV*, the Iranian news service, quoted Belfast-based author and Middle East expert Saeb Shaath as saying that Saudi Arabia, together with the United States, Israel, Turkey, and the United Arab Emirates, have been sponsoring sectarian violence in Iraq. Additionally, Shaath noted that the support for Iraqi terrorism included financing and training. Shaath tied Hillary Clinton to this, referring to Clinton's CNN and YouTube clips

---

[233] Elias Akleh, "British Terrorism in Iraq," *Global Research*, September 30, 2005.

[234] August 15, 2007.

[235] July 20, 2013.

[236] Jessica Stern, "Iraq: Where Terrorists Go to School," March 19, 2013.

wherein, he said, she conceded that the United States had created al-Qaeda, which the Saudis financed and the Wahhabi extremists ran. Expanding on his theme, Shaath claimed that the US armed forces and the CIA were partners in a Saudi terror campaign in Iraq.

According to a June 2009 report by United Press International, "insurgents" in Iraq were using recent-model Beretta 92 pistols produced without serial numbers, obviously meant for intelligence operations or terrorist groups having government support. Analysts suggested that the weapons were probably from the CIA or Mossad and were intended for *agents provocateurs* participating in US government-sponsored "insurgent" attacks against civilians. The aim was to delegitimize the resistance.

This apparently led to the import of Afghan [Arab-Afghan?] mercenaries recruited from Taliban ranks into Iraq to fight civilians there. Their role also included attacking Iraqi and occupation military forces. According to Iraqi police reports, the constabulary found thirty to forty Afghan Taliban hidden in a trailer entering Baghdad. When questioned, the fighters said that the US government had brought them there with the goal of creating as much trouble as they could. Senior US military officers then ordered the Iraqi police to release them, which they did.[237]

Earlier, US intelligence had noted senior al-Qaeda financial figures were in Iraq, moving large amounts of untraceable gold in and out of the country, principally through the cities of Baghdad, Falluja, and Samarra (with its two-thousand-year-old gold exchange). The Coalition Provisional Authority of Jerry Bremer allowed free movement for the al-Qaeda personnel, permitting them to exchange the precious metal for cash at money exchanges in Mecca, Amman, Dubai, and London. Saudi Arabia helped with this exchange, funding al-Qaeda in Iraq by transferring gold bars through eight to ten

---

[237] *waynemadsenreport.com*, June 24–25, 2009.

locations.[238] Underwriting al-Qaeda there in fact is sponsoring the Iraqi Branch of the Arab-Afghan Legion.

According to *Global Research*,[239] the American journalist, Seymour Hersh disclosed that "an unknown number" of mujahideen, Taliban, and al-Qaeda, were "flown to safety" in a US-sponsored airlift out of Afghanistan, giving rise to the suspicion that they had moved on to other countries, such as Iraq, with the "tacit" approval of the US Defense Department (apparently in late 2001). *Global Research* suggested that Northern Iraq (where many of the Kurds live) is "virtually a US protectorate." The publication noted that American intelligence and military officials knew of and ignored the influx of these Afghanis as well as terrorist acts taking place in Kurdish areas. Furthermore, the piece suggested that Ansar al-Islam (Supporters of Islam), a Kurdish fundamentalist group, of which many Arab-Afghans were members, received the same support from American intelligence organizations as other al-Qaeda groups in Central Asia. The intent, *Global Research* continued, was to further destabilize Iraq through contrived weakening of the established Kurdish political parties and the creation of a Muslim theocracy. Colin Powell, as Secretary of State and another military man (retired U.S. Army General) claimed in an address to the UN on February 5, 2003, that the head of the Kurdish terrorists was Abu Musab al-Zarqawi, who had "fought in the Afghan war more than a decade ago." What Powell omitted was appropriate background for his remarks. What he did not say was that al-Zarqawi had fought in an American-sponsored war led by the Central Intelligence Agency. Moreover, he was most likely "trained and indoctrinated" in a CIA camp in the region.[240]

---

[238] *waynemadsenreport.com*, November 14, 2005.

[239] "Who is behind the 'Terrorist Network' in Northern Iraq, Baghdad or Washington?" February 15, 2003.

[240] Ibid.

As reported by Thomas Hegghammer, there were four thousand to five thousand "private global foreign fighters" operating in Iraq after the US 2003 invasion. [241] These came from many Arab countries, the United States and Europe, as well as Turkey. One of Hegghammer's tables notes that only one thousand to fifteen hundred of these fighters had been campaigning against America and its NATO puppets in Afghanistan after 2001. Again, the imported combatants came from numerous Arab countries, the United States, and Europe. Hegghammer mentioned that many activists, especially from Saudi Arabia's Hejaz (Western Province), emphasized outside threats to the Islamic *umma* (community). They also established "a global network of charities for the provision of inter-Muslim aid." This enabled them to round up soldiers for Afghanistan, the Arab-Afghans, who then went on to constitute a foreign fighter cadre.[242] The Hejaz supplied most of the Saudi warriors who went to Afghanistan before 1987 (the year I arrived in Jeddah and when the orders to issue visas to questionable applicants began). [243]

Referring to links among the outside combatants, Hegghammer continues his analysis, asserting that "recruitment literature" from previous wars was recycled to promote subsequent conflicts. Personnel also "overlapped" he said, with the Arab-Afghans being originators of at least eight later engagements. While there was no central command, many of the cadre fought in more than one war, with some engaged in five or six different ones.[244]

Brian Fishman, once with West Point's Combating Terrorism Center and now with the New America Foundation, asserted that the

---

[241] "The Risk of Muslim Foreign Fighters—Islam and the Globalization of Jihad," *International Security* 35, no. 3 (2010/11): 53–94. Table 1.

[242] Ibid., 56–57.

[243] "The Risk of Muslim Foreign Fighters—Islam and the Globalization of Jihad," 85, citing Thomas Hegghammer, *Jihad in Saudi Arabia* (Cambridge: Cambridge University Press, 2010), 59–60.

[244] Ibid., 72, citing *Jihad in Saudi Arabia*.

biggest inflow of foreign fighters to Iraq took place in 2006–2007, with six hundred joining the cause.[245]

On July 8, 2013, Ayub Nuri, a Kurdish journalist told the author that, when the United States invaded Iraq in 2003, it bombed Ansar al-Islam in the North, sending foot soldiers there. He was at the front, reporting on the fighting, and saw many of the dead, with their identification papers, including passports. Among the fallen were Algerians, Saudis, Chechens, and Afghans, as well as Syrians, Turks, Iranians, and Iraqis. In fact, he had interviewed one captured soldier, who acted as an interpreter between the Arab-Afghans and the Kurds in Ansar al-Islam. Remarking it was dangerous to arm these kinds of people, my contact added they don't believe in borders, and they would go on to other conflicts because there were no limits against whom they would fight to advance their cause. He contended that al-Qaeda was not different from the Arab-Afghans and that both derived from the US war against the Soviets. In Nuri's view, the groups in Syria opposing Bashar al-Assad's government are the same type, if not more so, as those in Iraq, who fought to destabilize the government there. It is significant that John Schindler's *Unholy Terror* tied Ansar al-Islam to Bosnia. "Ansar's hardcore operatives were experienced fighters who had battled in Bosnia," he states[246]

An *NBC News* analysis, published June 20, 2005, helped substantiate this claim. A report by Lisa Myers and the network's investigative unit noted the national origins of more than 400 "foreign" fighters who had fallen in Iraq since 2003: Saudi Arabia, 55 percent; Syria, 13 percent; North Africa, 9 percent; and Europe, 3 percent. The reasons the Legionnaires, from twenty-one countries, gave for fighting don't really hold up: they were poor, they were rich, they saw

---

[245] Liz Sly, "Foreign extremists' footprint in Syria growing," *Washington Post*, October 2, 2013.

[246] *Unholy Terror*, 306, citing *Saff*, an Islamic youth journal, Sarajevo. May 27, 2004.

the Americans killing Iraqis on TV. Chris Kyle, former Navy SEAL, wrote that he had shot some Chechens in Iraq.[247]

Plausible (?) Deniability

More to the point, the foreign fighters got to Iraq because they had been recruited as terrorists. In a July 24, 2013, telephone call with Bob Baer, former CIA case officer in the Middle East and South Asia, he told me the Arab-Afghans had not been directly recruited by the Agency, but that their gathering had been "outsourced" for "plausible deniability." Milt Bearden, former Pakistan station chief and field officer in Afghanistan; Vince Cannistraro, former case officer and chief of operations and analysis at the CIA's Counterterrorist Center; and Larry Johnson, former CIA analyst and State Department official had all told the author that the CIA only recruited Afghans. All omitted any discussion of their instruction. Baer told me that US policy was to have the Saudis handle the recruitment program. They were the ones who located the Palestinians, Pakistanis, etc. [248] The Saudi official in charge was Ahmed Badeeb, chief of staff to Prince Turki al-Faisal, head of the Saudi Intelligence Presidency. Badeeb had also been a teacher to Osama bin Laden.[249]

Badeeb was also a well-connected bagman. To support operations in Pakistan, he once arrived in Karachi aboard a *Saudia Airlines* flight with "a little extra." Besides his personal baggage, he was carrying

---

[247] Chris Kyle, *American Gun: A History of the U.S. in Ten Firearms* (New York: William Morrow, 2013), 250.

[248] In Prof. Chossudovsky's article, "Who Is Osama Bin Laden," he quotes Abdel Monam Saidali, at Cairo's Al Aram Center for Strategic Studies, as saying Bin Laden and his Afghan Arabs had gotten extremely sophisticated training from the CIA. Citing Eric Weiner and Ted Clark, "Weekend Edition Sunday," NPR, August 16, 1998.

[249] Steve Coll, *Ghost Wars*, (New York: Penguin Books, 2004), 72.

$1.8 million in freshly printed currency, imported directly from the United States. Badeeb conveyed this money in person to Pakistan's president, Zia Ul Haq, and a group of his generals in Rawalpindi. It was part of a payment for Chinese-made, rocket-propelled grenade launchers.[250] The Saudis also channeled funds delivered by Badeeb and others through religious charities to support their intelligence functions. Ultimately, the money went to Afghan commanders outside of ISI or CIA control. Badeeb also set up safe houses for himself and other Saudi intelligence officials with the aid of these charities.

Saudi involvement also kept the beneficiaries of this aid from learning how closely the Americans were involved, the reasoning being that the fighters objected to direct contact with Westerners.[251] The watchword was plausible deniability. Baer added that outsourcing in all this plausible deniability was so effective that everyone concerned was unaware of US involvement, including American intelligence involvement. They believed that this was a do-it-yourself jihad. Besides the Saudis, recruitment was also handled by the ISI, who worked with the Haqqanis (a US-designated terrorist group) and Gulbuddin Hekmatyar.

Training was outsourced as well. ISI could do this because its "military and intelligence officers, bureaucrats, undercover agents and informers" were thought to total about one hundred and fifty thousand men.[252]

According to a January 7, 2008, *Christian Science Monitor* article, "the bulk of foreign fighters [operating in Iraq] originate from countries with whom the United States is allied..."[253] Citing a report produced by the Combating Terrorism Center at the US Military Academy at West Point, the article noted, however, that

---

[250] Ibid., 70, 72.

[251] Ibid., 86, citing Coll's interview with Badeeb, Feb. 1, 2002.

[252] "Who Is Osama Bin Laden," citing Dipankar Bannerjee, "Possible Connection of ISI With Drug Industry," *India Abroad*, December 2, 1994.

[253] Gordon Lubold, "New look at foreign fighters in Iraq."

the individuals fighting in Iraq come also from Libya, Algeria, Morocco, Syria, Tunisia, and Yemen. They entered Iraq through Egypt, Syria, Germany, and Turkey (with the exception of Syria, all countries involved in helping to destabilize the Middle East). The authors of the report, Lt. Col. Joseph Felter and Brian Fishman (neither of whom would speak with me) said that those fighting in Iraq got there through "very established routes," a clear tipoff that the United States is involved.

John Schindler amplified this information, noting that Bosnians had gone on to fight in Iraq. He said that the German BND Director, August Hanning, had confirmed this. According to Schindler, a mosque in Sarajevo operated as the local recruiting station for "muj" bound for Iraq and Chechnya. Not quite twelve hundred volunteers had followed this connection with Iraq in the years between 2007 and 2011. Abu Anas al-Shami, a Jordanian and second only to Abu Musab al-Zarqawi in managing fighters in Iraq, had come from Bosnia after his mid-1990s service there.[254]

SOME Iraqis Do Talk

On August 25, 2013, I spoke with a female Iraqi asylee about her former country. The gist of the conversation was that the United States was deeply involved with terrorism in Iraq.

While my interlocutor was in Jordan, she told me that she interpreted at a 2006 conference facilitated by the Jordanian Ministry of the Interior. At the meeting, a high-ranking US official (whose name she no longer recalls) met with former leaders from Saddam Hussein's government, mostly from the city of Falluja, in al-Anbar province. Discussed in that conference were ways in which the US government could help restore former Iraqi government officials to

---

[254] *Unholy Terror*, 305.

power. (By way of clarification, she noted that Jordan had worked very closely with such people since many from Saddam's regime had gotten sanctuary there. They were given preferences, she said, that others who fled to Jordan from Iraq did not get. In fact, the two countries were so closely connected that Saddam's middle daughter, Raghad, is living there with her family.)

Turning to years of terrorist attacks on the people of Iraq, notably the appalling upsurge now murdering scores of individuals all across the country, she said most people believe that the United States is behind those actions. They frankly don't believe US assertions that terrorists are responsible for the attacks. Not only do Iraqis in Iraq support this view, Iraqis in the diaspora, especially in the United States, hold to this belief as well, she said.

Additionally, my contact said al-Qaeda, America's all-purpose villain, simply consisted of people and their weapons who had been smuggled into Iraq in 2003. After the destruction of the Iraqi government and the dissolution of the army and police force, there were no internal controls nor was there any authority acting to seal the country's borders. Never airtight, they were now wide open to anyone who wanted to enter, or leave.

My informant also told me many Iraqi Sunnis believe that the groups harming buildings, installations, and people there are all supported by Iran, another American bogeyman. Some of this could well be the result of the Sunni lamenting their loss of power. In the past, although they formed only about a third of the population, they dominated the nearly two-thirds that was Shii (Source: *CIA World Factbook*). My contact added that this was likely true. The Sunni in the West are behind the killings, kidnappings, and bomb attacks so that they might regain power. Certainly, Barack Obama believes this. After an October 2013 Washington meeting with Nuri al-Maliki, the American president asserted that Iraq needed an election law "so Iraqis can express their differences politically instead of using violence."[255]

The new Iraqi government, my contact believed, was an American puppet and was doing all it possibly could to destabilize the country. Prime Minister Nouri al-Maliki's administration has so poisoned the well that many Sunni abroad believed that the Shii are at the bottom of Iraq's troubles.

Another Iraqi, a Christian, told me on October 5, 2013, that she had contacted several relatives still in Iraq on my behalf. They told her that they believed the source of all the current violence in the country can be laid at the feet of domestic terrorists rather than foreign fighters, in particular a group known (in translation) as "The Band of People of the Right." It was the old story, she said, of the Sunni versus the Shii. They also asserted the Iraqi government, installed with American help, is astonishingly corrupt, with the current prime minister, Nouri al-Maliki, seeking an unprecedented third term to which he is not entitled by the constitution. In the meantime, she noted, al-Maliki is sending fighters and weapons to President Bashar al-Assad in Syria. Finally, in addition to expressing amazement at other Iraqis' refusal to cooperate with my research, she suggested that, based on her knowledge and her relatives' comments, Iran is the big winner in the "Iraqi Stakes."

Complicating affairs, my August 25 interlocutor, a Shia, asserted that the Kingdom of Saudi Arabia, hand in glove with Israel, supports the Sunni and their actions. The Saudis, as noted elsewhere in this work, did yeoman service in recruiting, training, and financing the Afghans and the Arab-Afghans.

The Saudis, being fundamentalist Sunni (Wahhabis), appear, I was told, to be doing all in their power to incite religious conflict in the region, conceivably as a way to weaken Arab states and

---

[255] Philip Rucker, "Obama, Maliki talk Iraqi security needs," *Washington Post,* November 2, 2013.

their efforts to form more democratic governments. Certainly, the Wahhabis despise the Shii, and are behind, I was told, outrageous threats to exhume from his grave in Najaf, Iraq, Ali ibn Abi Tallib, one of the four "rightly guided caliphs" who succeeded the Prophet Mohammed. He was the first Imam of Shiism and was assassinated in AD 66. Syrian rebels, strongly supported by the Saudis, have also suggested they would imperil the Damascus shrine of Zainab Bint Ali, granddaughter of the Prophet Mohammed and a revered figure for Shia Muslims.

Summary

Following the US attack on and occupation of Iraq, the American Embassy in Baghdad, along with the Department of Defense, and the Central Intelligence Agency created sectarian, vigilante militias, placing them under the control of Iraqi politicians. The US Ambassador, John Negroponte; the Political Counselor, Robert S. Ford; Ford's deputy, Henry Ensher; and the US Army's Special Forces recruited and used death squads to strike at Iraqi resistance leaders.

The American aim in Iraq was *divide et impera*. With a goal of spreading a sectarian hatred between the three major Iraqi groups, Kurds, Shiite, and Sunnis, American agents, ably assisted by Israeli ones, executed Sunni and Shiite leaders while blowing up their mosques and setting off explosives in their communities. Congress gave the Agency $3 billion to create paramilitary units run by militias. The object was to kill "nationalists, other opponents of the US occupation, and thousands of civilian Baathists."

Additionally, and as part of this process, just as it had done in the Balkans, the American government convoyed terrorists into the country and supplied them with weapons. According to Al Jazeera, combatants infiltrated Iraq from Syria to engage in terror bombings. As in similar events in Afghanistan and Bosnia, these included Egyptians, Syrians, Sudanese, and Saudis. Also among the Arab-Afghans, according to Iraqi government spokesman Laith Kubba, were those from safe havens in Jordan, Syria, and the United Arab Emirates. An Iraqi army officer noted that Yemenis, Jordanians, Sudanese, and Syrians had been captured. US soldiers also seized Afghans, Pakistanis, Lebanese, Algerians, Saudis, Syrians, Egyptians, Yemenis, and Libyans. The Israeli press linked a retired Israeli officer to covert sales of weaponry to terrorist groups in Mesopotamia. An Iraqi parliamentarian charged the occupying coalition with secretly masterminding terrorist attacks and organizing terror squads. The Coalition Provisional Authority (the ad hoc occupation government) allowed al-Qaeda financial figures to move large, untraceable amounts of gold in and out of Iraq. An American-sponsored airlift flew many mujahideen out of Afghanistan, presumably into Iraq and other countries. Many Legionnaires had moved to northern Iraq, and former Secretary of State Colin Powell, another retired general, stated that the head of al-Qaeda in Iraq had fought in Afghanistan with the CIA.

Saudi Arabia continued with its successful efforts, perfected in Afghanistan, to create a culture of terror. The kingdom is still supporting the al-Qaeda terrorist groups in Iraq, Syria, and Lebanon. Moreover, the House of Saud has been clandestinely shipping small arms, explosives, anti-armor, and antiaircraft weapons into and through Iraq from the Saudi city of Nakheib and the Ar Ar border crossing. According to Iraqi Prime Minister Nouri al-Maliki, the Saudis have been attacking his country through Syria.

LIBYA

However, please note that Central Asia, the Balkans, and Iraq were not the only places the Arab-Afghan Legion was employed.

As Andrew Kreig wrote, "The North African street protests provided an opportunity to overthrow Libya's longtime director, Moammar Gaddafi. Players included his opponents, such as radical militants as well as Gulf monarchies and NATO allies."[256]

According to Peter Dale Scott:

> It also seems quite clear that Western intelligence (at least British) found al-Qaeda itself to be a useful ally against a common enemy—the secular dictator, Muammar Gadhafi of Libya. As the French authors Jean-Charles Brisard and Guillaume Dasquié have pointed out, Gadhafi's Libya in 1998 asked INTERPOL (International Criminal Police Organization) to issue an arrest warrant for Osama bin Laden. They argue that bin Laden and al-Qaeda elements were collaborating with the British MI5 [sic; MI5 is the

---

[256] *Presidential Puppetry*, 190.

154

Security Service, dealing with counterintelligence and focusing on internal threats] in an anti-Gadhafi assassination plot.[257]

"A leader in the plot was Anas al-Liby, who was later given political asylum in Great Britain despite suspicions that he was a high-level al-Qaeda operative. He was trained in terrorism by the triple agent Ali Mohamed, while Mohamed was still on the payroll of the US Army."[258] Nafeez Mosaddeq Ahmed says al-Liby was more than a suspected high-level al-Qaeda operative. He had been on the FBI's list of Most Wanted Terrorists for allegedly helping blow up US embassies in Tanzania and Kenya. The American government offered $25 million for his arrest and conviction.[259]

How did Syed al-Liby escape such a dragnet? Ahmed makes it clear: "...Anglo-American intelligence agencies have compromised and, indeed, entirely blocked investigations to apprehend Osama bin Laden and al-Qaeda...[so as] to pursue terrorist operations perceived to be within Anglo-American strategic interests....They clearly believe that the end justifies the means..."[260] Continuing, he questions the public statements that al-Qaeda is a group to be apprehended and removed from circulation. Rather, he suggests that for British intelligence employing terrorists is fairly routine.[261]

Al-Liby wasn't a unique case. Another Libyan, Khalifa Hiftar, was a former general who sought refuge in the United States and,

---

[257] *Road to 9/11*, 130–131, citing Brisard and Dasquié, *Forbidden Truth: U.S.-Taliban Secret Diplomacy and the Failed Hunt for Bin Laden* (New York: Thunder's Mouth Press/Nation Books, 2002), 97–102.

[258] *Triple Cross*, 104. Ali Mohamed's background is summarized on pp. xxiii–xxiv in *Triple Cross*.

[259] *War On Truth*, 113, citing FBI "Most Wanted Terrorists," www.fbi.gov/mostwant/terrorists/teralliby.htm.

[260] Ibid., 116.

[261] Ibid., 117.

according to the *Washington Post*, "apparently" became a citizen, voting in 2008 and 2009. Hiftar, residing in CIA-friendly Fairfax County, Virginia, sold his $612,000 house and moved to Libya in 2011, just as the American effort at "regime change" began. Once there, he led rebel forces against the legitimate government, earning accolades for his heroism. Now, Hiftar, after months of plotting, is again working on a new government for Libya, using militia units to attack "Islamist" rivals defending the current administration. In the multicolumn article, the *Post* somehow omitted the origin of resources enabling a "refugee" and his family to exist and buy an expensive house. He was most likely on Langley's payroll, hardly a rarity in such cases. [262]

Although President Barack H. Obama had declared in a speech in Accra, Ghana, in 2009, that "Africa's future is up to Africans," it was really American policy toward Africa, as elsewhere in the world, to remove political leaders that the United States considered "inconvenient". Those who opposed or who were at odds with US plans, such as socialists, communists, and "Islamists" became legitimate targets of Yankee weapons.

On March 19, 2011, Obama began combat against Libya without securing a Congressional declaration of war, as the federal Constitution requires. He also refused to notify Congress that American forces were engaged in combat operations, in violation of the War Powers Act, adopted in response to the reckless, unconstitutional actions by the president in going to war in Vietnam.[263]

The US and NATO air and sea attacks on Libyan soldiers and civilians also included actions by intelligence and special forces designed to disrupt the country's stability. The American president

---

[262] Abigail Hauslohner and Sharif Abdel Kouddous, "Leader of Libya revolt spent years in N. Va.," *Washington Post*, May 20, 2014.
[263] 50 USC, Section 1541 *et seq.*

provided weapons and funds to alleged "rebels" to further desta-bilize Libya.

The British, the French, and the Americans finally succeeded on October 20, 2011, when Libyan President Gaddafi was murdered. This followed eight months of a NATO bombing campaign coupled with internal warfare using outside fighters affiliated with al-Qaeda. Concurrently, the neocolonialists fomented a rebellion supported by foreign weapons and intelligence agencies.

Recently, George F. Will, a conservative columnist writing in the *Washington Post,* put this situation in perspective.[264] He said: "Today, Libya is an anarchy of hundreds of rival militias...This humanitar-ian imperialism ["to protect Libyans...from the supposed threat of genocide..."] quickly became an exercise in regime change. But the prolonged attempt to assassinate Gaddafi from the air made no provision for a replacement regime." Citing Alan J. Kuperman at the University of Texas, Will noted:

> Gaddafi did not initiate violence against peaceful pro-testers. Rather protesters initiated the violence that engulfed four cities. Media reports "exaggerated the death toll by a factor of 10, citing 'more than 2,000 deaths' in Benghazi during the initial days of the uprising, whereas Human Rights Watch (HRW) later documented only 233 deaths across all of Libya in that period." Furthermore, when the United States and a few other NATO nations intervened in March 2011, "Gaddafi already had regained control of most of Libya, while the rebels were retreating rapidly toward Egypt. Thus the conflict was about to end, barely six weeks after it started, at a toll of about 1,000 dead."

---

[264] "A challenge for the GOP," June 19, 2014.

This Didn't Always Work So Well

According to CNN, "Officially, the US presence [in Benghazi] was a diplomatic compound under the State Department's purview."[265] But, "the larger US grouping was in a secret outpost operated by the CIA." Further, like the Agency's consulate at Jeddah, most there didn't work for State. When thirty people were evacuated from this "diplomatic compound" in Benghazi on September 11, 2012, twenty of them were CIA employees. The CNN piece simply provided more cover for Langley, without answering any real questions as to why the spooks were on the loose. For example, it stated that the "Agency had two objectives in Libya: countering the terrorist threat that emerged as extremists poured into the unstable country, and helping to secure the flood of weapons after the fall of Moammar Gaddafi that could have easily been funneled to terrorists." Yet, there was no real hard news provided for just why there was a "terrorist threat" or where this "flood of weapons" came from in the first place. The article did mention comments by Congressman Frank Wolf (R-VA): "There are questions that must be asked of the CIA and this must be done in a public way." Wolf noted that he'd been getting calls from CIA officials who wanted to talk, but "If you're fifty years old and have two kids in college, you're not going to give up your career by coming in [and telling the true story]…give them the protection so they can't be fired [for talking out of school]."

Lacking in CNN's Report Was Any Sort of Background to the Situation.

The United States of America had been providing more than two thousand al-Qaeda fighters with arms and other support in parts of eastern Libya. The guerillas were "Salafists," a militant,

---

[265] "Analysis: CIA role in Benghazi underreported," May 15, 2013.

Sunni extremist group, similar to the puritanical, reactionary form of Islam practiced in Saudi Arabia and Qatar, and to an extent, in the UAE. Those states backed NATO's efforts to unseat Moammar Gaddafi's secular government. The anti-Gaddafi combatants came from Afghanistan, Yemen, Saudi Arabia, Egypt, Algeria, Morocco, and Tunisia, as reliable Libyan journalists stated. [These were the same origins and fit the same pattern as the warriors who had fought in Afghanistan and Bosnia and Iraq.] The same reporters were present when French philosopher Bernard-Henri Levy met with representatives of the revolutionary National Transitional Council. Levy reportedly told the Council that, if they wanted more aid from NATO, "they should establish relations with Israel." Later, the Council announced that, if it won the war against the government, Libya would establish diplomatic ties to Israel. Additionally, Levy reputedly convinced French President Nicolas Sarkozy to be the first to recognize the revolutionaries and send French forces to help them.[266]

Here They Come Again (With More Help)

Patrick Martin, writing in *Global Research*, observed that the difference in manpower between the "diplomatic" and CIA compounds was caused by the main thrust of the US government's plans for Libya.[267] In 2011, it was overthrow Gaddafi. In 2012 and later, it was recruit soldiers and supply weapons to Muslim fanatics trying to overthrow the government of Syria. Martin, quoting the *World Socialist Web Site*, stated that Libyan extremists comprised the largest part of the combatants active in Syria, making up twelve hundred

---

[266] "U.S., NATO supporting 2000 'Al Qaeda' irregulars in Benghazi," *waynemadsenreport.com*, June 5–6, 2011.
[267] "New York Times Report: CIA-Backed Militias Linked to Benghazi, Libya Attack," December 30, 2013.

to fifteen hundred of about thirty-five hundred men sent to Syria from great distances, such as Chechnya and Pakistan. Essentially, they were more Arab-Afghans, in many instances "veterans of guerrilla fighting in Afghanistan, either as part of the US-backed war against the Soviet army in the 1980s, or in the ongoing war against the US-NATO occupation regime established in 2001...The CIA had mobilized Islamic fundamentalists, including veterans of the al-Qaeda and Taliban war in Afghanistan, to fight Gaddafi, and was recruiting them for a new war against Assad."

What CNN likewise omitted was what was carried in the *waynemadsenreport.com*: [268]

> The flow into Libya of "terrorists" and weapons came as the direct result of US government actions. The "El Salvador" option has also been used in Libya, where al-Qaeda irregulars, drawn from Iraq, Afghanistan, and Yemen, have been carrying out murders of Libyan civilians, especially black Libyans and African guest workers, on behalf of the Libyan rebel government. Some of the murders of civilians have been blamed on pro-Muammar Qaddafi forces but they have, in fact, been carried out by al-Qaeda units fighting with the rebels and are being directed by CIA and MI6 advisers. Ford [then US Ambassador to Syria] has been providing advice to the Libyan rebels on how to carry out their death squad attacks.

CNN also didn't report that the US government had sent a Blackwater (later Xe, later Academi, later Constellis) veteran to help the insurgents fight against the lawful governments of Libya

---

[268] "U.S. ambassador to Syria in charge of recruiting Arab/Muslim death squads," September 9–11, 2011.

and Syria. As *Business Insider* reported March 20, 2012, Blackwater's former director, Jamie F. Smith, had provided security for anti-government Libyan National Transitional Council members. Additionally, he had helped train rebel soldiers after imposition of the "no-fly zone" in March 2011. Smith, later chief executive of SCG International, another private security company, stated that his former firm consisted of Defense Department and CIA personnel. The article, by Michael Kelley (based on an *Al Akhbar English* report), noted that Smith "allegedly" participated in the murder of Moammar Gaddafi. Blackwater's one-time director had worked in Libya with Fred Burton, an official at STRATFOR, a private intelligence gathering organization. In the 1990s, Burton had been Deputy Chief of the US State Department's counterterrorism section in the Bureau of Diplomatic Security. Burton claimed that Smith had been in Syria collecting information on the opposition to President Bashar al-Assad. Smith had also been meeting with Syrian insurgents in Turkey. The two had been receiving "air" support from then-Representative Sue Myrick (R-NC), outspokenly anti-Arab and anti-Muslim, who had been a member of the House Permanent Select Committee on Intelligence.

The story told by what former CIA official Ray McGovern calls the "fawning corporate Media" was that Libya, like Iraq, like Iran, like Syria is/was a "bad" country. Maximilian Forte summarized the stories used to justify American, British, and French attacks on that North African state.[269] Under the guise of NATO's "responsibility to protect" the people there, the people with the highest Human Development Index (a UN measurement of well-being) in all Africa, Western military forces destroyed the country. Now, the Index only records the steep collapse of all indicators of well-being.

---

[269] "Destroying Libya: A War for 'Human Rights'?" *Global Research*, December 9, 2012.

One author, Phil Greaves, writing for *Global Research*, cited "Capitol Hill speculation" that US agencies working in Benghazi were aiding the movement of surface-to-air missiles out of Libya, through Turkey, and into the possession of Syrian extremists. Greaves added that the CIA had been "consulting" with Qatar's structure of arms smugglers, run out of the Emir's palace. The intent was to ensure that the Salafist fanatics in Syria had enough guns from Libya's stores. Alluding to a November 2011 London *Telegraph* story, Greaves noted that one of the leaders fighting Gaddafi, Abdel Hakim Belhadj, seen as the local al-Qaeda/LIFG (Libyan Islamic Fighting Group) commander, had visited Turkey, meeting with members of the Free Syrian Army. Principal topics at the conference were sending "money and weapons" to the insurgents and Libyan training of Syrian combatants. Additionally, the piece cited a Fox News report from December 2012 that the arms shipments began in October 2011, following the murder of Gaddafi. Originating at a number of ports and continuing weekly, the goods sometimes moved in six-hundred-ton batches. Fox News' source affirmed that the arms, along with combatants to use them, were definitely going to Syria and that the US government knew everything. This was not unsurprising since there was a citation to a March 30, 2011, *New York Times* report that the CIA had been operating in Libya "for weeks." The British paper, *Independent,* published an account of Obama's seeking Saudi arms for the Libyan "insurgents." The American president also persuaded Qatar and the United Arab Emirates to send weapons to Benghazi, asking them to send non-US weapons to allow "for plausible deniability." This violated Obama's own "No-Fly" Zone and arms embargo policy, not to mention the US Constitution and International Law. Greaves also speculated that the arms traveling to Syria began about the time protests against Bashar al-Assad started, back in the spring of 2011. He suggested that this was when Qatar, with the knowledge and assistance of the CIA, began organizing weapons shipments from Libya to Syria.[270]

As Forte notes:

> We were told that Muammar Gaddafi threatened mass atrocities, even "genocide" against Benghazi. We were told that he fueled his troops with Viagra, so they could go on a systematic spree of mass rape. We were told that he used the air force against unarmed, peaceful protesters. We were told that he imported African mercenaries to butcher his opposition. And we were told that our military intervention would save lives and was designed to protect civilians.

The problem was that none of that was true.

This was instead a series of "incubator babies" stories (Recalling the false Iraqi "atrocities" conjured up by a member of the Kuwaiti ruling family, coached by PR firm Hill and Knowlton, to justify George H. W. Bush attacking Iraq): exaggerate and repeat such fabrications often enough and some of it might seep into public "consciousness" as if it were fact.[271]

Why not? After all, Americans really are pig-stupid and badly educated.[272]

---

[270] Philip Greaves, "CIA Gun-Running, Qatar-Libya-Syria," *Global Research*, August 9, 2013.

[271] "Destroying Libya: A War for 'Human Rights'?" *Global Research*, December 9, 2012.

[272] Cf. Susan Jacoby, *The Age of American Unreason* (New York: Pantheon Books, 2008). In this work, the author recounts, inter alia, that 50 percent of US adults have not read a book in the past year, that 25 percent of Americans believe the sun revolves around the earth, and that 25 percent of US high school biology teachers think that dinosaurs and cavemen coexisted.

It surely worked. Maximilian C. Forte had their measure in *Slouching Towards Sirte, NATO's War on Libya and Africa*[273]. It wasn't a war over oil, although that *was* a factor, nor about saving lives (more were killed with intervention than without). It was about control, about militarizing Africa.[274]

Forte argues in his Preface that

> [I]t is part of an ongoing contest between US power (in decline) against the interests of China, Russia, and other ascendant regional hegmons [sic], to secure access to both material and political resources in an effort to stall the impending demise of the United States while making the world safe for transnational capital. Finally, the intervention was an attempt to control the directions of uprisings in a region of critical geopolitical and economic significance to the United States and Europe. Libya, once prosperous, independent and defiant, is now faced with ruin, dependency and prolonged civil strife, precisely at a time of extreme political and economic volatility and uncertainty in the world system. This is the kind of Libya that has finally met with Western approval.[275]

Cui Bono?

The media, such as Al Jazeera and CNN, parroted US government lies about Libya and Moammar Gaddafi. Yet, they concealed the fact that among the terrorists fighting the legitimate government

---

[273] Maximilian C. Forte, *Slouching Toward Sirte* (Montreal: Baraka Books, 2012).
[274] Ibid., 9, 10.
[275] Ibid., 10.

were foreign combatants, including military aircraft and soldiers from the repressive emirate of Qatar.[276] In arguing for an immediate attack on Libya, newly appointed US Secretary of State John Kerry portrayed himself as "protector of Muslims," just as Italian dictator Benito Mussolini had done while riding his horse into Tripoli on March 20, 1937. A quick, successful war, supposedly waged for humanitarian purposes, would help the world to forget the distasteful image of American aggression in Iraq and Afghanistan. There would be no time for Congressional debate, awkward questions, or criticism.[277]

A major US goal was to capitalize on the possible gains resulting from intervention on the pretext of supporting Libyan street protests similar to those in Tunisia, Egypt, and other countries. The American government could obtain increased access for US corporations to Libyan reconstruction funds, block any Russian or Chinese attempts to secure Libyan oil contracts, install a "friendly" administration, and increase the presence of the newly established AFRICOM (US Africa Command),[278] This tactic would diminish the power of the African Union and remove the possibility of a Libyan-led substitute. Other aims were to "politically stabiliz[e] the North African region in a way that locked out opponents of the US; and drafting other nations to undertake the work of defending and advancing US political and economic interests, under the guise of humanitarianism and protecting civilians."[279] Like Saddam Hussein, Slobodan Milosevic, and Bashar al-Assad, Moammar Gaddafi had run afoul of the United States and Europe: the assassinated Libyan leader had espoused a concept more deadly than supplying weapons

---

[276] Ibid., 12–13.

[277] Ibid., 24, citing John Kerry, "We Must Not Wait for a Massacre," *Al Jazeera English*, March 14, 2011.

[278] Headquartered in Stuttgart, Germany.

[279] Ibid., 25–26.

to help the Irish Republican Army fight British imperialism. His goal was "a central Libyan leadership role in an integrated Africa."[280]

One result? Sirte, Gaddafi's hometown, "used to be a beautiful city, one of the most beautiful in Libya. Today it looks like (postwar) Leningrad, Gaza or Beirut."[281] In just seventeen days, NATO air raids had murdered more than two thousand Libyans in Sirte.[282] Further, it wasn't just Sirte that was destroyed—it was the whole of Libya. Thomas Gaist, in *Global Research,* noted that the US and European forces had flown more than twenty-six thousand sorties against Libyan targets, "carpet-bombing" Tripoli and Sirte. On the ground, Western lawbreakers relied on "Islamist and al-Qaeda elements as proxies to help conquer Libya, devastating the country in the process."[283] That devastation was calculated and long planned.

At a Group of Eight (France, United States, United Kingdom, Russia, Germany, Japan, Italy, Canada) meeting in L'Aquila, Italy in mid-2009, newly elected President Barack Obama would not meet with Gaddafi, a man George H.W. Bush had brought into the US sphere. As Forte noted, this "was a major shift in stated US policy." Obama's "administration [proved] more severe toward Libya than Bush's, with little awareness by the US public and with all of the 'strategic ambiguity' that Obama swore he would eliminate."[284]

Under Obama's policy, Libya was turned into an arsenal of fascism. With weapons shipped into the country by Europe, the United States, and the repressive Gulf monarchies, added to Libya's own

---

[280] *Slouching Toward Sirte,* 27.

[281] Ibid., 31, citing Zarouk Abdullah, quoted in Associated Press, "Gaddafi Hometown Pays Heavy Price in Libyan Battle," Oct. 28, 2011.

[282] "Over 2,000 killed in NATO airstrikes on Gaddafi's hometown," *Global Research,* September 17, 2011.

[283] "Mass Anger Builds in Libya After US Special Forces Raid," October 9, 2013.

[284] *Slouching Toward Sirte,* 52.

supply, there were more arms in the Libyan Jamahiriya[285] than in the entire arsenal of the British army. Disturbingly, as many as three thousand surface-to-air missiles disappeared following the assassination of Gaddafi. Altogether, more than one million tons of Libyan weapons were looted by insurgents after Gaddafi's murder. Worse, according to *Akhbar Alaan TV,* Libyan extremists had been shipping these weapons to Syrian terrorists for more than a year. Turkey was the middle man in this deal. Qatari C-17 cargo planes (sold by the United States) used their seventy-ton payloads to fly armaments from eastern Libya and deliver them to the Turkish-Syrian frontier and the savages waiting for them. Some of the arms were also flown to Jordan, whose former king, Hussein I, had long been in the pay of the CIA. From there, they were then, presumably, trucked across the line to Syria.[286]

The British-Libyan merchant of death, Abdul Basit Haroun, asserted that not all the arms to Syria went by air. He claimed, in a statement to the Reuters news service, that a great deal of weaponry was off-loaded from ships that had sailed from Libya. True to their clandestine nature, "guns for the death of Syria" were hidden in the midst of humanitarian aid. Except, there wasn't much stealth to the nature of these deliveries. Haroun, a brigade commander during the insurgency, declared that the authorities knew and that "everybody knows" about the shipments.[287]

---

[285] *Jamahiriya* can be translated as a state ruled by the people. Libya's official name was Great Socialist People's Libyan Arab Jamahiriya.

[286] *Global Research,* "Afghanistan, Iraq, Libya, and now Syria: Cheer-leading Another Blood Bath in the Name of Peace," citing www.dailymail.co.uk/news/article-2342917/Don't-turn-Syria-Tesco-terrorists-like-Libya-generals-tell-Cameron; http:English.al-akbar.com/node/16164; Felicity Arbuthnot, June 23, 2013, and also http://in.reuters.com/article/2013/06/18/libya-syria-idINDEE95H0CP20130618.

[287] Ibid.

It's All about Control

The real US goal was controlling and directing the "Arab Spring" in such a way as to derail and destroy the people's legitimate aspirations for justice and democracy. As Forte puts it:

> US strategy became one of steering events towards the preservation of hierarchies in allied states which were critical to the US either for their oil resources (Saudi Arabia), their provision of military bases (Bahrain), or their subservience to US "counterterrorism" strategy (Yemen). At the same time it encouraged rebellion in "adversary" states, especially those with friendly or close ties to Iran (Libya, Syria), while controlling rebellion and maintaining military dominance in others (Egypt).[288]

In *Slouching Toward Sirte*, Maximilian C. Forte states that the British government had previously tried to murder Moammar Gaddafi. In March 1996, when Gaddafi was traveling in a motorcade through Sirte, MI6, used and paid an al-Qaeda cell, the Libyan Islamic Fighting Group (LIFG) to place a bomb under what they believed was his car. Abd al-Muhaymen, in charge of the attack, had trained and fought in Afghanistan with the mujahideen against the Soviets, making full use of his access to CIA and British intelligence officials, who had helped create the "muj."[289] Shayler told the court at his trial for violating the Official Secrets Act that MI6 had also backed the assassination plot and had worked with the LIFG. MI6

---

[288] *Slouching Toward Sirte*, 258–259.

[289] Ibid., 79–80, citing David Shayler, one-time MI5 officer, in Martin Bright's "MI6 'Halted Bid to Arrest Bin Laden;' Startling Revelations by French Intelligence Experts Back David Shayler's Alleged 'Fantasy' About Gadaffi Plot," *The Observer*, Nov. 10, 2002.

officers Richard Bartlett and David Watson had overall responsibility for the action.[290] Continuing, Forte refers to "credible reports" from "French intelligence" (which I presume was DGSE, Directorate General for External Security) that not only al-Qaeda and LIFG were connected at that time but also that MI6 turned over large sums of money to an al-Qaeda cell.[291] The United Kingdom also granted asylum to "Libyan Afghans" who then issued propaganda statements from their refuge in Blighty,[292] declaring Gaddafi's government "an apostate regime that has blasphemed against God" and asserting that it must be overthrown.[293] One leader of the LIFG named al-Hasidi admitted that he had fought in Afghanistan. Additionally, he noted that his guerrillas had ties to al-Qaeda.[294]

Egypt also helped arm the Libyan "insurgents." The *Wall Street Journal* of March 17, 2011, (after Mubarak's overthrow) reported that the Egyptian military, according to US and Libyan sources, was sending weapons to arm Gaddafi's enemies, who at that time were losing ground to government forces. According to Hani Souflakis, a Libyan businessman, the Egyptian military council wanted to keep a low profile on its weapons shipments. "Americans have given the green light to the Egyptians to help. The Americans don't want to be involved in a direct level, but the Egyptians wouldn't do it if

---

[290] Ibid., 80, citing Bright, Nov. 10, 2002. Adel Darwish, "Did Britain Plot to Kill This Man?" *The Middle East*, Sept. 4–6, 1998. Immigration and Refugee Board of Canada [RBC], "Libya: Information on an Attempted Attack on President Gaddafi by a Religious Group in 1996, Possibly Affiliated With A Group Called Al-Sahwa of Islam," 1998, *Refworld* [UNHCR], July 1.

[291] Ibid., 80.

[292] From the Hindi and the days of the Indian Empire, *bulayati*, "my country," by way of the Arabic, *wulayati*.

[293] Peter Dale Scott, "Who are the Libyan Freedom Fighters and Their Patrons?" *Global Research*, March 25, 2011, citing Dan Lieberman, "Muammar Al Gaddafi Meets His Own Rebels," CounterCurrents.org, March 9, 2011.

[294] Ibid., quoting *Daily Telegraph* [London], March 25, 2011, "Libyan rebel commander admits his fighters have al-Qaeda links."

they didn't get the green light," he said. Unnamed "Western" and Libyan officials apparently asserted that the United States wanted to stay out of the limelight because its past disasters in Iraq and Afghanistan had created such anger and suspicion.

Further, unlike the United States, Moammar Gaddafi obtained a March 1998 International Criminal Police (INTERPOL) warrant for CIA asset Osama bin Laden's arrest.[295] Forte quite rightly questioned US plans for the overthrow of Gaddafi, noting that, if the fake uprising, against a "dictator" whom "all Libyans hated," was really "popular" and "national," how was it that there was such unflagging resistance in Sirte and elsewhere?[296]

LIFG's origins are not surprising. Mujahideen veterans who had fought the Soviets in Afghanistan founded it in 1995. Although the group had first organized in Afghanistan, its members, upon their return to the Jamahiriya "reasoned" that Libya had become corrupt and impious. They believed "regime change" was needed. They began with a series of assassinations of policemen and soldiers, a tactic now much used in Iraq, with many suicide bombers there coming from the Libyan city of Derna.[297]

Go back an additional ten years and you will find more of Gaddafi's antagonists. In Peter Dale Scott's previously cited article, the same old snakes then crawled out of the ground.[298] As noted in the Paris-based *African Confidential* newsletter (January 5, 1989, edition), Israel and the United States had established bases

---

[295] *Slouching Toward Sirte*, 80, citing Bright, Nov. 10, 2002.

[296] Ibid., 80–81.

[297] Pewter Dale Scott, "Who are the Libyan Freedom Fighters and Their Patrons?," *Global Research*, March 25, 2011, citing Center for Defense Information, "In the Spotlight: The Libyan Islamic Fighting Group [LIFG]," January 18, 2005.

[298] Ibid.

in neighboring Chad and other "nearby" but unnamed countries to train two thousand Libyan rebels.[299]

There were others gunning for Gaddafi. US records demonstrate that Saudi, Egyptian, Moroccan, and Israeli money fueled the Chad-based clandestine attack on Libya. The Saudis kicked in $7 million to one opposition group, "the National Front for the Salvation of Libya" (also backed by French intelligence and the CIA). The United States tried and failed to involve the Egyptians. However, after the military overthrew President Hosni Mubarak, Egypt became more helpful.[300]

Impenetrable Transparency

Demonstrating that Gaddafi was no longer in favor, the US government refused all requests from the Libyan government to send a high-level delegation there in 2009 to help celebrate the 1969 revolution's fortieth anniversary. Although Gaddafi had personally extended an invitation to the new American president, Obama "for some reason could not come." Obama also did not meet with Gaddafi at the 2009 UN General Assembly meeting.[301]

"Regime change," the tired mantra of the Bush administration, "was one of the actual, immediate goals to which Obama himself admitted" of his administration's policy toward Libya. "Later, according to the *New York Times*, Hillary Clinton publicly revealed that the former CDA [Chargé d'Affaires] in Tripoli, Christopher Stevens, was sent back to Libya in the early days of the 2011 'revolution' to

---

[299] "Who are the Libyan Freedom Fighters and Their Patrons?," citing Joel Bainerman, *Inside the Cover Operations of the CIA and Israel's Mossad* (New York: S.P.I. Books, 1994), 14.
[300] Ibid., citing Richard Keeble, *The Secret War Against Libya* (MediaLens, 2002).
[301] *Slouching Toward Sirte*, 81.

covertly work with the insurgents in order to overthrow Gaddafi."[302] Moreover, at the time, the CIA had been "interrogating, recruiting, and/or imprisoning suspected radicals."[303] Kreig further noted that Stevens, an Arabist (but, as I understand the term, not in the sense of one who favors Arab interests and positions), "was engaged in dangerous, ultrasecret efforts to facilitate radical Muslim armed support for the rebel insurrection in Syria, a violation of public US policy."[304]

Moreover, Kreig observed that "The CIA [and] Brennan's counterterrorism office in the White House were engaged in especially dangerous outreach to jihadists." He cited World Net Daily (WND), for additional details:

> WND has filed numerous reports, quoting Middle East security officials who describe the [US] mission in Benghazi as a meeting place to coordinate aid for the rebel-led insurgencies in the Middle East. Middle Eastern security sources further described both the US mission and nearby CIA annex in Benghazi as the main intelligence and planning center for US aid to the rebels that was being coordinated with Turkey, Saudi Arabia and Qatar.
>
> Many rebel fighters are openly members of terrorist organizations, including al-Qaida. [sic]

---

[302] Ibid., 83, citing Hillary Clinton, "Remarks on the Deaths of American Personnel in Benghazi, Libya"; *US Department of State*, September 12, 2012.

[303] *Presidential Puppetry*, 159, citing Eric Schmitt, Helene Cooper, and Michael S. Schmidt, "Deadly Attack in Libya Was Major Blow to CIA Efforts," *New York Times*, September 23, 2012.

[304] Ibid., 159.

> Among the tasks performed inside the building was collaborating with countries, most notably Turkey, on the recruitment of fighters 'including jihadists' to target Assad's regime, the security officials said.[305]

Additionally, Forte, in *Slouching Towards Sirte*, commented that Gaddafi often admonished the United States and Saudi Arabia for supporting extremists. Forte added that the United States and the United Kingdom had previously collaborated with Islamic radicals, first in Afghanistan, then Bosnia and Kosovo. Many of them subsequently targeted Gaddafi for assassination.[306] Quoting the late US Ambassador Christopher Stevens, killed at the CIA's Benghazi consulate in 2012, Forte said that Syria, demonstrating its opposition to terrorism, had transferred over one hundred foreign fighters to Libyan government custody in a two-year period, thus diminishing the ranks of jihadists. The stream of these men from Libya to Iraq and the blooded, trained veterans back to Libya diminished due to Gaddafi's cooperation with other states. "Worried that the fighters returning from Afghanistan and Iraq could destabilize the regime, the GOL [Government of Libya] has aggressively pursued operations to disrupt foreign fighter flows, including more stringent monitoring of air/land ports of entry, and blunt the ideological appeal of radical Islam."[307]

Obviously, Gaddafi had to die and Libya be destroyed because he was creating problems for the Arab-Afghan Legion. He was pulling them back from other countries, "disrupting their flow," and urging the United States to rein in Saudi Wahhabi fanaticism. He

---

[305] Ibid., 263, citing Aaron Klein, "Media ignore Hillary's bombshell Benghazi claim; Secretary insists she did not know about gun-running at U.S. mission," January 24, 2013.

[306] *Slouching Toward Sirte*, 293.

[307] Ibid., 294, citing secret cable from Embassy Tripoli, August 28, 2008, "Scenesetter for Secretary Rice's Visit to Libya."

warned Tom Lantos (D-CA), one of Israel's strongest supporters in Congress, about the threat to US interests posed by Saudi Wahhabi/Salafi extremism.[308]

NATO's bombing of Libya ended the day Gaddhafi was murdered. Moreover, the speedy transfer of military and other personnel to Libya since February 2011 underscored the intent of Western states to use local protests as a smokescreen for overthrowing Gaddafi and the al-Fateh revolution (the 1969 coup against the King). As Forte wrote, the *New York Times* had reported that, by the end of March 2011, CIA officials had been operating inside Libya for "several weeks," that is, it's apparent that Agency men landed in the Socialist Arab People's Republic around February 2011, the time the so-called protests began. Dozens of British special forces and MI6 officers joined them. Simultaneously, Barack Obama secretly authorized the CIA to give weapons and "other support," that is, covert actions, to the Libyan insurgents. USAID (US Agency for International Development, often viewed as a front for CIA activities) had sent a team to Libya in early March.[309]

Martin Iqbal, writing in *Global Research* reported that NATO admitted to bombing the Gaddafi's convoy as it was moving near Sirte the morning of October 20. American government sources

---

[308] Ibid., 294, citing Embassy Tripoli cable, August 15, 2005, "Libyans Pleased with Saudi Decision," and Embassy Tripoli cable August 31a[sic], 2006, "Congressman Lantos Stresses Bilateral Achievements and Regional Challenges With Libyan Leaders."

[309] Ibid., 119–120, citing M. Mazetti and E. Schmitt, "C.I.A. Agents in Libya Aid Airstrikes and Meet Rebels," *New York Times*, March 30, 2011. G. Thomas, "US May Use Covert Action Against Gadhafi," *Voice of America*, March 30, 2011. J. Lee, "The President on Libya: 'The Violence Must Stop; Muammar Gaddafi Has Lost the Legitimacy to Lead and He Must Leave,'" *The White House Blog*, March 3, 2011. "Obama Signed Secret Libya Order Authorizing Support for Rebels," *Reuters*, March 30, 2011. *DipNote* (State Department Blog), "U.S. Announces Additional Humanitarian Assistance in Response to Violence in Libya," March 10, 2010.

claimed that a US Predator drone had fired on the column as did French warplanes. Iqbal also cited the Israeli intelligence news organization, DEBKA, as recounting that its military contacts said NATO Special Forces had located, captured, and shot Gaddafi. [310]

Summary

Central Asia, the Balkans, and Iraq were not the only places the Arab-Afghan Legion was employed. The North African street protests provided an opportunity to overthrow Libya's longtime director, Moammar Gaddafi. Players included his opponents, such as radical militants, as well as Gulf monarchies and NATO allies. A leader in the plot was Anas al-Liby, who was later given political asylum in Great Britain despite suspicions that he was a high-level al-Qaeda operative. He was trained in terrorism by the triple agent Ali Mohamed while Mohamed was still on the payroll of the US Army. The United States of America had been providing more than two thousand al-Qaeda fighters with arms and other support in parts of eastern Libya. These guerillas were "Salafists." The anti-Gaddafi combatants came from Afghanistan, Yemen, Saudi Arabia, Egypt, Algeria, Morocco, and Tunisia, as reliable Libyan journalists stated. These were the same origins and fit the same pattern as the warriors who had fought in Afghanistan and Bosnia and Iraq.

"Justification" for American and European misadventures in Libya came down to cock and bull stories concocted for the "fawning corporate media," such as

We were told that Muammar Gaddafi threatened mass atrocities, even "genocide" against Benghazi.

---

[310] "The 'Rebel' Assassination of Muammar Gaddafi: a NATO Operation from A to Z," October 22, 2011.

We were told that he fueled his troops with Viagra, so they could go on a systematic spree of mass rape. We were told that he used the air force against unarmed, peaceful protesters. We were told that he imported African mercenaries to butcher his opposition. And we were told that our military intervention would save lives and was designed to protect civilians.

The problem was that none of that was true.[311]

A quick, successful war would help to heavily overpaint the distasteful image of American aggression in Iraq and Afghanistan. There would be no time for Congressional debate, awkward questions, or criticism.

The aim was to move against Libya as an apparent way station on the road to Damascus. In 2011, it was overthrow Gaddafi. In 2012 and later, it was recruit soldiers and supply weapons to Muslim fanatics trying to overthrow the government of Syria. The *World Socialist Web Site* stated that Libyan extremists comprised the largest part of the combatants active in Syria, making up twelve hundred to fifteen hundred of about thirty-five hundred men sent to Syria from great distances, such as Chechnya and Pakistan. Essentially, they were more Arab-Afghans, in many instances "veterans of guerrilla fighting in Afghanistan, either as part of the US-backed war against the Soviet army in the 1980s, or in the ongoing war against the US-NATO occupation regime established in 2001." The CIA had mobilized Islamic fundamentalists, including veterans of the al-Qaeda and Taliban war in Afghanistan, to overthrow Gaddafi, and then was recruiting them for a new war against Assad.

The flow into Libya of "terrorists" and weapons came as the direct result of US government actions. The "El Salvador" option

---

[311] "Destroying Libya: A War for 'Human Rights'?" *Global Research*, December 9, 2012.

has also been used in Libya. Al-Qaeda irregulars, drawn from Iraq, Afghanistan, and Yemen, had been carrying out murders of Libyan civilians, especially black Libyans and African guest workers, on behalf of the Libyan rebel government. Some of the murders of civilians have been blamed on pro-Gaddafi forces but they have, in fact, been carried out by al-Qaeda units fighting with the rebels and are being directed by Agency and MI6 advisers. Robert S. Ford (then US Ambassador to Syria) had been providing advice to the Libyan rebels on how to carry out their death squad attacks.

There was Capitol Hill speculation that US agencies working in Benghazi were aiding the movement of surface-to-air missiles out of Libya, through Turkey, and into the possession of Syrian extremists. According to *Akhbar Alaan TV*, Libyan extremists had been shipping these weapons to Syrian terrorists for more than a year. Turkey was the middle man in this deal.

SYRIA

- In May 2012, Syria's UN envoy Bashar Ja'afari declared that dozens of foreign fighters from Libya, Tunisia, Egypt, Britain, France [and] elsewhere had been captured or killed, and urged Saudi Arabia, Qatar and Turkey to stop their sponsorship of the armed rebellion.[Yacoub, Khaled (May 9, 2012)].
- Syria rebels kill 7, bomb explodes near UN monitors. (Reuters).
- Syria's UN ambassador says two Britons killed in Idlib. (BBC News, May 17, 2012.)
- Jihadist leaders and intelligence sources said foreign fighters had begun to enter Syria only in February 2012. (Macleod, Hugh; Flamand, Annasofie, May 13, 2012).
- Iraq-style chaos looms as foreign jihadists pour into Syria. (The Sunday *New York Times*.)
- In June, it was reported that hundreds of foreign fighters, many linked to al-Qaeda, had gone to Syria to fight against Assad. (Jaber, Hala. June 17, 2012).
- Jihadists pour into Syrian slaughter. (The Sunday *New York Times*.)
- In July, Iraq's foreign minister again warned that members of al-Qaeda in Iraq were seeking refuge in Syria and moving there to fight. (Peel, Michael; Fielding-Smith, Abigail, July 5, 2012).
- Iraq warns over al-Qaeda flux to Syria. (FT.com)

- According to the Associated Press, Foreign weapons sent to rebels in Syria worry Iraq, September 26, 2013; Lara James. Iraq's Foreign Minister, Hoshyar Zebari, asserted that "foreign intelligence" had confirmed that 10,000 foreigners were fighting against the Syrian government.

Yet, this was not the beginning. First in Egypt, then in Syria, American and British intelligence services worked to overthrow men and governments they didn't like. First, there was that "socialist" Nasser, president of Egypt, whom they tried to get rid of in 1956 and 1958. When that failed, they took aim in the late 1950s at Syria for not being anti-communist enough. Their means? They did what they do so well—buying potential revolutionaries (as is being done today in Thailand, the Ukraine, and Venezuela). Unfortunately for the plotters, the Syrian intelligence officers didn't stay bought and the coup failed. (See the end of this book: "Let's Wrap This Up, If We Can").

Still, practice makes perfect. If, at first you don't succeed, try, try again.

Building on extensive experience, successful practice, and perfected propaganda, used and refined in Afghanistan, the Balkans, Iraq, and Libya, the United States, aided by repressive governments in the region, again moved against the Syrian Arab Republic, using its favorite cat's paw, the Arab-Afghan Legion. The attack began, if not in concert with the alleged "spontaneous" uprising in March 2011, then not long afterward.

Indeed, in George Will's *Washington Post* column of June 19, 2014, he flatly said, "The [NATO] intervention [in Libya] encouraged peaceful protesters in Syria to use violence in the hope of attracting an intervention. This increased the rate of killing there tenfold. And since Gaddafi fell, sophisticated weapons from Gadhafi's arsenal—including up to fifteen thousand man-portable, surface-to-air missiles unaccounted for as of 2012—leaked to radical Islamists throughout the region."

Train Those Terrorists!

According to a *News Pakistan Online* article, the CIA had been secretly training Syrian "rebels" since November 2012. Citing an undated *Los Angeles Times* report, the account noted that the Agency, along with US Special Operations forces, began instructing Assad's enemies in late 2012, just days after President Barack Obama declared he would arm those opposing the Syrian government. Preparing these terrorists for action included education in the use of antitank and antiaircraft weapons at locations in Turkey and at a US base in southwest Jordan. US Special Forces soldiers chose the fighters to be trained while Saudi Arabia, Qatar, and other unnamed Arab states supplied the heavy weapons.[312] The *Washington Post* claimed that the Agency "has organized the training effort." Every month, the *Post* said, two hundred and fifty fighters graduate from training programs supervised by the CIA's auxiliary army.[313] As Reuters reported December 13, 2013, American forces in Jordan now total at least fifteen hundred men. Quoting the Obama White House, the news service said they "will remain there until the security situation improves [and] they are no longer needed." The US military presence includes soldiers to operate Patriot missile batteries and fly combat aircraft.

Conceivably, the Obama Administration had begun arms shipments to the Syrian terrorist groups earlier than acknowledged. CNN reported on August 1, 2013, that "Speculation on Capitol Hill has included the possibility that US agencies operating in Benghazi

---

[312] Reprinted in *Global Research News* on June 22, 2013.
[313] David Ignatius, "The spymasters tackle Syria," February 20, 2014.

were secretly helping to move surface-to-air missiles out of Libya, through Turkey, and into the hands of Syrian rebels [sic]."[314] The program further mentioned that the CIA was going to amazing lengths to conceal its activities in Benghazi. *Global Research*, in a piece by Brad Michelson, commented that the Benghazi "consulate" was a secret CIA safehouse.[315]

Whatever the start date, the Legionnaires were marching.

And They Might Come Home!

Citing a recent study, *Global Research News* reported May 22, 2013, that "between 2,000 and 5,500 foreign nationals are active in Syria." European Union (EU) counterterrorism officials asserted that at least five hundred of these come from European countries, including twenty from Germany. According to an interview with the German newsmagazine *Der Spiegel*, German Interior Minister Hans-Peter Friedrich claimed that some of these had even brought their families to the Syrian war zone. Gilles de Kerchove, EU antiterror head, further noted that Britain, France, and Ireland had the greatest number of "militants" fighting the government of President Bashar al-Assad. European government officials, *Global Research* went on to say, are now worrying about the consequences of these foreign legionnaires returning home.[316] To misquote the post-World War I song: *How Ya Gonna Keep'em Down on the Farm, Once They've Learned How to Bomb Paree?*

---

[314] Jake Tapper, "Dozens of CIA operatives on the ground during Benghazi attack," *The Lead*.

[315] "CIA Was Smuggling Weapons to Syrian Rebels During Benghazi Embassy [sic] Attack," August 5, 2013.

[316] "Western Mercenaries Have Integrated the Ranks of Al Qaeda Rebels in Syria," *Global Research News*.

On April 12, 2013, *Global Research* quoted a much higher figure for "soldiers of fortune." It reported the Russian Federal Drug Control Service Director Viktor Ivanov as saying that 20,000 foreign mercenaries were active in Syria and they were financed by organized crime groups. Ivanov stated that they, and not the Taliban, pose the greatest threat. Russian Foreign Ministry spokesman Alexander Lukashevich asserted earlier in April 2013 "that Syria was turning into a 'center of attraction' for international terrorists."[317]

According to the *Washington Post*, the US government also shares this view. Unnamed "senior US intelligence officials said" that thousands of combatants from outside Syria are streaming into the country and that they will eventually go home, spreading their belief systems and targeting Western institutions.[318] The unidentified sources also noted that the majority of the fighters came from the Middle East and North Africa, with about seven hundred arriving from Europe with "Western" passports. These same contacts went on to relate that the volunteers (recruited, they claimed, through Twitter and YouTube) would gain combat experience and "indoctrination" and would then form "future terrorist cells and threats much the way Afghanistan did in the 1980s." More surprisingly, in the light of fifty-two recruiting offices in the United States set up during the Afghan war in the 1980s (see footnote 18, above), the anonymous officials believed that there are no Syrian recruiting efforts taking place in America because "of the distance between the two countries."

Later, the *Washington Post* reported more on the story of foreign fighters in Syria.

Griff Witte, in a dispatch from London, asserted that "returnees from the Syrian war, hardened and trained by their experiences in

---

[317] "America's Undeclared War: Nearly 20,000 Foreign Mercenaries Fight in Syria," *RTT News*, April 11, 2013.

[318] Greg Miller, "U.S. officials warn of fighters entering Syria," November 21, 2013.

battle, will seek to carry out terrorist attacks." Citing the head of Scotland Yard's counterterrorism command, he wrote such strikes are "almost inevitable."[319]

Witte went on to quote unnamed sources (a *Post* specialty) as claiming that there were more Britons fighting in Syria than had fought in either Afghanistan or Iraq. These were "two other conflicts that attracted [sic] radicalized young fighters from the West..." According to the *Post* story, security officials in Washington and Europe are "distressed." James R. Clapper (Lt. General, USAF, ret.), Director of National Intelligence, is reported as saying that the [American] war in Syria had "attracted" approximately seven thousand combatants from fifty countries and that one of the main groups there [which the United States has been supporting] "aspires to carry out an attack in the United States."

Witte's piece, apparently intended to keep the fear alive, noted that the British were still anxious following the July 2005 London transit bombings and were afraid that the radicals would return and seek regime change at home. French Minister of the Interior Manuel Valls was cited as saying that foreign fighters coming home represented "the biggest threat that the country faces in the coming years." However, in an odd twist in the article, Margaret Gilmore, a terrorism analyst with the Royal United Services Institute, was quoted as saying the British government knows little about what is actually happening in Syria.

Put in context and shorn of the propaganda needed to keep people accepting increased limits on their freedom, Americans and Europeans appear to be having second or third or fourth thoughts about the wisdom of recruiting and training terrorists assigned to the Arab-Afghan Legion. The Arab states apparently had the same fears after the people they helped enlist for Afghanistan started to return home. Governments, such as Saudi Arabia, had blocked them

---

[319] "European combatants in Syria war alarm West," January 30, 2014.

from coming back, thus helping provide more "saddle tramps" for the Legion. If the Americans and Europeans fear history repeating itself, what will they do? Keep them out? Intern them? Or add them to another division of the Legion?

Garbage about Garbage Trucks, Nonlethal Bombs, and "Intelligence" Services

On the page opposite from Witte's story was an article headlined, "US resumes sending nonlethal aid to rebel-held areas in Syria." Anne Gearan wrote that, following radical "rebel" attacks on a US warehouse, "ambulances, garbage trucks, generators, school supplies and office equipment…are being delivered to civilian local governments and charity groups…" According to State Department spokesman Jen Psaki, "These deliveries are helping those local groups provide essential services for the Syrian people and counter violent extremists." No explanation was given (or can be conceived of) for needing garbage trucks and office materials in rebel-held areas. Curiously, while talking about "nonlethal" provisions, Psaki would not respond to questions about "ammunition, body armor, and other direct battlefield supplies."

Like those already seen in Afghanistan, the Muslim republics of the USSR, the Balkans, Iraq, and Libya, the "insurgency" in Syria is maintained by the "financial, logistical, and military support of external players…[with] most of the…deaths…caused by foreign terrorists from outside Syria…rebellion 'leaders' have been supplied by recruiting programs run by the CIA, Britain's MI6 [the Secret Intelligence Service], Israel's Mossad [external intelligence service], and the French DGSE [external] intelligence service." As is clear, "The CIA has dusted off its old playbook from the Afghan mujaheddin [sic] war against the Soviet Union and is, once again, relying on the Saudi 'Al Qaeda' database run jointly by Langley and the Saudi Mukhbarat General Intelligence Directorate to drum up personnel, money laundering facilities, and other logistics support for Jihadists, including veterans of insurrections in Iraq, Libya, Afghanistan, Somalia, Yemen, Chechnya, and Algeria, to enter and fight in Syria."[320]

The Ottoman Empire Strikes Back

Echoing Wayne Madsen's remarks, the FARS News Agency reported on March 26, 2013, that thousands of tons of arms and ammunition have already been provided to Syrian "rebels."[321] Beginning in early 2012, the news agency related that Qatar, Saudi Arabia, and Jordan flew weapons acquired in Croatia to Turkey, which then delivered them by the truckload to insurgents attempting to overthrow the legitimate Syrian government. The news service quoted Hugh Griffiths of the Stockholm International Peace Research Institute as saying that the enterprise is a "well-planned and coordinated clandestine military logistics operation." This is not unsurprising since FARS stated that former CIA Director and retired army general David H. Petraeus played a central role in setting up this program, with additional input from other CIA officials as alleged "consultants." Commenting on the hundreds of weapons flights into Turkey, Attila Kart, a member of the Turkish CHP (Republican People's Party), forming the main opposition to Prime Minister Erdogan's government, said "The use of Turkish airspace at such a critical time, with the conflict in Syria across our borders, and by foreign planes from foreign countries that are known to be central to the conflict, defines Turkey as a party in the conflict." Kart, according

---

[320] "Sequestration does not impair U.S. support for Syrian rebels," March 15–17, 2013, *waynemadsenreport.com*.

[321] "CIA Aids Huge Arms Smuggling to Syria."

to an Abu Dhabi English-language paper, the *National*, asserted that sixteen Saudi Air Force planes delivered military goods or fighting men to Ankara during the first four months of this year. The Saudis had also sent an unknown number of aircraft making additional deliveries in mid-August.[322]

On June 15, 2013, SANA (Syrian Arab News Agency) reported Bulent Esinoglu, Deputy Chairman of Turkey's Labor Party, as saying that the CIA had recruited six thousand Arabs, Afghans, and Turks to commit terrorist acts in Syria. Esinoglu added, it was said, that Black Water [sic] had been paying extremely well for its operatives to engage in murder and destruction in the Syrian Arab Republic. [Erik Prince's Blackwater, a US corporation notorious for employing former American Special Forces and providing them as mercenaries to foreign governments, changed its name to Xe Services, then to Academi, and now Constellis. The name changes came after repeated charges of murder, war crimes, and human rights violation were laid at its door. It's also an infamous private security contractor providing mercenaries for use as security forces by the US Department of State.] The Deputy Chairman continued, saying that Turkey's war against Syria is controlled by the United States and Israel, thus transforming the Turkish armed forces into mercenaries.

Hundreds more combatants came from the Agency's war in the Balkans. Eldar Kundakovic was one. A Bosnian Muslim from Sandzak, he died fighting to break out Syrian insurgents from prison. According to Radio Free Europe/Radio Liberty, both covertly-organized and funded CIA radio stations, he was one of many individuals recruited from Serbia, Montenegro, Bosnia-Herzegovina, Macedonia, Kosovo, and Albania. Pawns being used in a campaign to overthrow the legitimate government of Syria, many had no idea of the country's location or how

---

[322] Thomas Seibert, "Turkey being dragged into Syria's war: opposition," September 4, 2013.

to get there. Often engaged by Salafists, including some through intermediaries in Vienna, many joined the al-Nusra Front, listed as a "terrorist" group by Washington. The Salafists were seen as Saudi-funded "leftovers" who had established themselves in Bosnia-Herzegovina during the 1992–1995 US war against Serb and Bosnian-Serb forces.[323]

The status of some of these combatants may now have been altered by changes in American foreign policy. On April 12, 2007, BBC News announced that Bosnia was stripping about four hundred former combatants of their citizenship. The piece's author, Nicholas Walton, wrote that Bosnian news media viewed the crackdown as compliance with a US request to fight terrorism. Bosnia asserted it was investigating their origins and how they came to settle in the country. Their origins were clear enough. The Turks, Egyptians, Syrians, Algerians, Tunisians, Sudanese, and Russians had all come to Bosnia-Herzegovina after fighting in Afghanistan. The Arab-Afghans joined the war in Bosnia, seeing it as a defense against a Serbian attack on Islam. Their leaders stated that their actions had "the tacit support of the international community." Their settling in the area was no mystery: after the war, many of them married local women and took up residence throughout the country.

Balkan Links

On March 8, 2013, Richard Spencer, Middle East Correspondent for the British paper *Telegraph*, filed a story sourced by *Jutarnji List* [*Morning Gazette*], a Croat journal. In it, he said that the British Foreign Secretary, William Hague, had provided more support than previously thought for the terrorists fighting the Syrian government. Despite politicians claiming that Britain was providing only "nonlethal" assistance

---

[323] Teodorovic Milos and Ron Synovitz, "Balkan Militants Join Syria's Rebel Cause," *Radio Free Europe/Radio Liberty*, June 8, 2013.

and training, the article recorded that weapons came from Britain, as well as several other European countries. British military advisors, along with American and French ones, were also operating in lands neighboring Syria, instructing rebel leaders. In addition, Americans were offering aid in securing chemical weapons inside Syria. (Perhaps this aid guaranteed rebel control of the poison gas that America, the United Kingdom, France, and Israel insisted was used by the legitimate government.) First spotted by arms expert Eliot Higgins, the "nonlethal" aid consisted of rocket launchers, recoilless guns, and M79 antitank weapons. The article included unattributed statements from Western officials to the *New York Times* that Saudi Arabia supplied the funds to buy the arms and that Turkish and Jordanian International Air Cargo planes delivered them.[324]

Patrick Henningsen, a 21st Century Wire writer, added more information. On March 10, 2013, in "Open War Crimes: US and British-Backed Weapons Airlift from Croatia to Terrorists in Syria," he noted that "NATO and the Gulf States initial destabilization plans for overturning the government of Syria" were behind schedule.[325] Failing in their attempt to duplicate their previous Libyan success, they apparently became committed to a long, drawn-out ground war. Because arming insurgents directly doesn't look good to the public, Henningsen suspected that the British were transferring chemical weapons stocks from Libya to terrorists in Syria, with Qatar footing the bill. The idea was that the alleged rebels would use them and blame the action on Bashar al-Assad. The next step was war matériel—seventy-five planeloads of military weapons. Three thousand tons of rifles, bullets, and hand grenades, paid for by Saudi money, was a major windfall for the alleged "Free Syrian Army," or the "Syrian Rebels," or the "Syrian Opposition."

---

[324] Richard Spencer, "US and Europe in 'major airlift of arms to Syrian rebels through Zagreb'", *The Telegraph*, March 8, 2013.

[325] Henningsen, "Open War Crimes: US and British-Backed Weapons Airlift from Croatia to Terrorists in Syria", *21st Century Wire*, March 10, 2013.

These were not just war surplus, but UK and other European arms, whose supply the United States organized.

Croatia, one of the participants in the war against Serbia, had worked with the Americans to bring this about, meeting with US officials in 2012 and suggesting that arms be moved into Syria from and through its territory. (Henningsen cited the *New York Times* of Feb. 25, 2013, which based its story on "anonymous" interviews with US officials.) The details were somewhat embarrassing. Ignoring and violating the European Union Arms Embargo, the United Kingdom used its soldiers and support staff in Jordan to distribute these weapons over the Hashemite frontier to Deraa (in southern Syria, near the Jordan border), to Aleppo [Halab], and Idlib. This began in the autumn of 2012.

Foreign Policy, on March 29, 2013, carried an article by John Reed, providing additional information on Jordan's involvement with Croatia in supplying heavy weapons to anti-Assad "insurgents" in Syria. According to the Organized Crime and Corruption Reporting Project (OCCRP), a nonprofit association of investigative centers and investigative media, the Croats sold two hundred and thirty tons of rocket and grenade launchers, field artillery, mortars and ammunition in December 2012 to the Hashemite Kingdom of Jordan. That sale, set forth in UN trade statistics, was the largest in Croatian history. Although Croatia denied participation in what the article asserted was a *New York Times*–reported CIA pipeline to Syrian "rebels" (March 2012), the OCCRP said that a variety of Yugoslav-designed weapons began appearing in pictures of rebel fighters not long after the transaction. *Foreign Policy* noted Croatian denials of its arms sales. Using specious reasoning, the Republic of Croatia claimed that the weapons transactions didn't violate the European Union's embargo on providing arms to combatants. It had simply peddled the weaponry to Jordan, not a belligerent power in Syria. Besides, the Croats argued, the armaments were simply surplus, left over from the 1990s Balkan wars.

Extra Help

Henningsen added that the German newsmagazine *Der Spiegel* was reporting uniformed Americans engaged in training Syrian insurgents and Jordanian intelligence officers at unnamed locations in the Hashemite Kingdom. Additionally, Henningsen cited *Real Syrian News* (no date) as stating large cargo planes were traveling from France to Jordan, supposedly carrying "aid and medical supplies" for refugees. What eighty-five French military staff were doing onboard one of those flights has yet to be clarified. It was also unclear if the "aid and medical supplies" were just that or if they included something a bit more dangerous than sharp needles. Continuing, Henningsen opined that it is still unknown what Jordan has been given or been promised for its help in fomenting a regional war.

Henningsen also quoted Izzat al-Shahbandar, an aide to Iraqi premier Nuri al-Maliki, as saying that the same terrorists still engaged in murder in his country are also fighting the Syrian government. Al-Shahbandar had been speaking to the *New York Times* and had said that these al-Qaeda operatives, whose names they knew through coordination with al-Assad's government, were engaged in crimes in both countries.[326]

Investigative journalist Wayne Madsen reported in September 2011, at the beginning of the effort to overthrow the Syrian government, that the US Ambassador to Syria, Robert S. Ford, "is the key State Department official who has been responsible for recruiting Arab 'death squads' from al-Qaeda-affiliated units in Afghanistan, Iraq, Yemen, and Chechnya to fight against Syrian military and police forces in embattled Syria."[327] Earlier, Ford had learned his trade as Political Counselor at the American embassy in Baghdad

---

[326] Henningsen, "Open War Crimes: US and British-Backed Weapons Airlift from Croatia to Terrorists in Syria".

[327] "U.S. ambassador to Syria in charge of recruiting Arab/Muslim death squads," September 9–11, 2011, *waynemadsenreport.com*.

when John Negroponte was ambassador. Negroponte had been a principal figure in the secret program to arm the Nicaraguan Contras and back brutal paramilitary units in Honduras during the 1980s. Madsen's narrative continued, recounting how Negroponte had ordered Ford to follow Central American death squad practice, this time using Iraqi Shii irregulars and Kurdish Peshmerga paramilitary forces, to assassinate, kidnap, and torture Iraqi freedom fighter leaders in both Iraq and in Syria.

Furthermore, Madsen stated that Ford's terrorists not only "carried out attacks on Syrian security forces but have also massacred civilians in 'false flag' operations later blamed on Syrian government forces. WMR [Wayne Madsen Report] has been informed that Ford's operations in Syria are being carried out with the assistance of Israel's Mossad." According to the US Department of State and other sources,[328] Ford's deputy in Baghdad was my old "colleague" from the Jeddah consulate, Henry S. Ensher, who once demanded I give visas to rather peculiar people. Henry has been well rewarded for his services: in May 2011, he was appointed US ambassador to Algeria by Barack Obama.

Michel Chossudovsky, president and director of the Centre for Research on Globalization (CRG) and editor of GlobalResearch. ca, has declared that Israel is deeply involved in the destruction of Syria.[329] Writing in *Global Research*, he stated that Israel has proposed a "buffer zone" reaching ten miles into Syria along its forty-six-mile border with that country. Characterizing this plan as a "pretext to channel Israeli support to the terrorists in liaison with Washington," Chossudovsky referred to a May 8, 2013, report by DEBKA, the Israeli intelligence news agency, that al-Nusra casual-

---

[328] Mideastwire Blog (Oct. 2, 2011), and Michel Chossudovsky ("Terrorism With a Human Face"), Global Research Jan. 4, 2013.

[329] "Israeli Army Vehicle Enters Syria, Israel Supports Al Nusra," May 21, 2013. [Al Nusra has been described as Syrian mujahideen, back from various jihad fronts.]

ties are being given "medical care in an Israeli hospital facility in the Golan Heights," the Syrian territory seized by Israel in 1967's Six-Day War and annexed by Israel in 1981. To rescue the wounded, Israeli military vehicles travel into Syria proper, with the assistance of Israeli special forces, operating covertly in battle zones. In the piece, Chossudovsky notes that al-Nusra, on the US State Department's terrorist list since December 2012, is sustained by the United States "and its allies, including Saudi Arabia, Qatar, Turkey, and Israel." He stated that "al-Nusra is largely made up of mercenaries recruited in Turkey, Saudi Arabia, and Qatar. Covert (Western) special forces and military advisors have also integrated their ranks...Confirmed by CNN, the al-Nusra terrorists have also been trained in the use of chemical weapons by special forces on contract to the Pentagon." That training, CNN's December 9, 2012, story said, was taking place in Jordan and Turkey and not all of the trainers were US citizens.

"Why would the Israelis aid a 'rebel' army made up almost exclusively of hardened *jihadists*...?" asked Justin Raimondo, editorial director of Antiwar.com.[330]. Most simply, because it helps fulfill Israel's long-term goals: "by weakening, containing, and even rolling back Syria...[and] as a means of foiling Syria's regional ambitions."[331]

In a June 19, 2013, article, Wayne Madsen noted that Israel has been operating a clandestine base for an air fleet in eastern Algeria, near the Libyan frontier. Zimex Aviation, Ltd., a Mossad-owned front company with close ties to Langley, evidently helped destabilize countries such as Libya, Syria, Iraq, and Iran, at one point shuttling Mossad operatives between Iraq and Iran.[332]

---

[330] *Antiwar.com*, May 6, 2013.

[331] Ibid., citing Richard Perle, James Colbert, Charles Fairbanks Jr., Douglas Feith, Robert Loewenberg, David Wurmser, Meyrav Wurmser, "A Clean Break: A New Strategy for Securing the Realm." [All US government officials and/or members of right-wing think-tanks.]

[332] "Mossad's secret base in Algeria," *waynemadsenreport.com*.

According to the *Beijing Review's* August 6, 2012, interview of Imad Moustapha, former Syrian ambassador to the United States (and, at that time, ambassador to China), America is the chief destabilizing agent in Syria. He charged that the United States is doing "anything possible to introduce death and destruction to Syria," in the hope of triggering a civil war or a United Nations–backed war of aggression against his country. Ambassador Moustapha also noted that the belligerence now directed at the Syrian Arab Republic is intended to destroy its cities and "dismantle its social fabric," exactly what had previously been done to Iraq and Libya. Moustapha continued, adding that the terrorism, to date, had been also directed at "infrastructure, like electricity plants, water supply units, dams, bridges, hospitals, and schools."

Plans for the New Syrian Disorder

American actions in Syria, in concert with Britain, France, Saudi Arabia, the Gulf States, and, likely, Israel, were and are intended to *dehouse, deculturalize, destabilize, and destroy* the country. In other words, to break it into pieces, to "Balkanize it." According to the *Jerusalem Post* (May 16, 2012), Kurdish leader Sherkoh Abbas, speaking in Washington, DC, called for Israel to splinter Syria, turning it into ethnic enclaves for Kurds, Druze, Alawite, and Sunni. He made no mention of where to put the 10 percent of the population that is Christian. The Strategic Culture Foundation of September 9, 2013, carried a Wayne Madsen article on the consequences of this policy.[333] Madsen concluded, "The al-Qaeda and al-Nusra Front Salafist Forces being unleashed by Bandar [Prince Bandar bin Sultan bin Abdul-Aziz, former Chief of Saudi General Intelligence]

---

[333] "Obama Administration Stoking Sunni Violence Against Alawites and Shi'as in Syria."

and Brennan [John O. Brennan, CIA Director] are setting the stage for the worst sectarian genocide in the Middle East since the Christian Crusades." On November 6, 2013, the FARS News Agency reported that Kevin Barrett, PhD, a critic of the questionable GWOT, Global War on Terror, termed Saudi Prince Bandar "the operations chief of al-Qaeda, the Arab legion of mujahideen fighters, ever since the Afghan war of the 1980s. It is these CIA-supported, Mossad-supported al-Qaeda fighters that Bandar commands in Syria."

Global Research (January 31, 2013), carried a reprint of a June 2012 piece describing plans for the balkanization of Syria: to foster sectarian divisions, leading to internal war. "Opposition militants" had been sent to Kosovo to participate in terrorist training sessions given by the US-supported Kosovo Liberation Army. The article described closed-door meetings at the State Department involving then-Ambassador to Syria, Robert Ford, the Kurdish National Council, and Assistant Secretary of State for Near Eastern Affairs, Jeffrey Feltman. Given Abbas's preceding statement, it might be possible to conclude that dividing Syria was one of the topics on the agenda.

According to Tony Cartalucci, writing in *Global Research*, the US government confirmed that "al-Qaeda" is running the Syrian alleged rebellion. In the article[334], Cartalucci cites the *Wall Street Journal*[335] as stating that the al-Nusra Front is moving fighters through Turkey and Iraq to overthrow the Syrian government. As Cartalucci affirmed, this "undercuts the West's year and a half-long narrative that Syria's violence was the result of a so-called 'uprising' by the people of Syria." Referring to a *New York Times* article,[336] Cartalucci continued, the CIA and other US government agencies have organized and

---

[334] "U.S. Treasury Confirms that Al Qaeda Runs Syrian Rebellion," July 27, 2012.

[335] Seth G. Jones, "Al Qaeda's War for Syria," July 27, 2012.

[336] Eric Schmitt, "CIA Said to Aid in Steering Arms to Syrian Opposition," June 21, 2012.

directed this pipeline of weapons and militants. Deciding which opposition fighters would get the largesse, the Americans used the Syrian Muslim Brotherhood to distribute rifles, rocket-propelled grenades, and antitank weapons, bought and paid for by Turkey, Saudi Arabia, and Qatar.

Raimondo clarified the reason for this action:

> Bin Laden's legions fought in the Kosovo war on the side of their Kosovar Muslim brothers and NATO: many present-day jihadists are veterans of that conflict, just as they are veterans of Afghanistan, Libya, and Chechnya—all regions where the jihadists and the Americans are de facto allies. In the Balkans, we used them to block Russian influence in Europe, in Syria, we are using them to run interference with the Iranians.[337]

Noting that hundreds of "Libyan militants" had been traveling to Syria (six hundred in 2011 alone), Cartalucci expanded on the topic by saying that they had brought with them weapons and funds provided by NATO during its effort to overthrow Muammar Gaddafi. Indeed, one of the leaders in that was Abdul Hakim Belhadj, one-time commander of the Libyan Islamic Fighting Group (LIFG), an entity listed by the US State Department as a Foreign Terrorist Organization. Belhadj, involved in fighting in Afghanistan and Iraq, brought fighters, funds, and firearms to Syria once he had helped NATO dispose of Gaddafi.

In a similar vein, *Global Research* noted that these six hundred militants were really soldiers in the post-Gaddafi army and that they joined the "Free Syria[n] Army." According to the Egyptian news website, Al Ray Al Arabi, the terrorists entered Syria through

---

[337] *Antiwar.com*, May 6, 2013.

Turkey. Citing British media, the invasion was likely the outcome of a secret Istanbul meeting between the Libyan National Transitional Council envoys and Syrian rebels pledging "arms, money, and fighters to the Syrians."[338]

In one of *Epitoma Rei Militaris'* ("Summary of Military Matters") "Phantom Reports," a Libyan General National Council advisor heading its disarmament program said the country's principal goal is shipping radical Muslims and their weapons out of the country and into Syria.[339] Based on an undated report carried by the Media Line, the gist of the story was that foreign fighters numbering in the tens of thousands, if not more, are leaving Libya for the Syrian Republic, intending to topple Bashar al-Assad's government. Non-Syrians engaged in the three-year "civil" war are Americans, Bosnians, Egyptians, Libyans, Moroccans, and assorted other nationalities. According to one source for the report, Libya has been providing weapons and training for these Arab-Afghans in secret desert camps.

The number of combatants with outside backing ranges from a low of ten thousand (PRESSTV) to one hundred fifty thousand, attributed to a "Syrian military source" not permitted to speak on the record. Noting the increase from October 2012, the Syrian said that there were, then, about seventy thousand foreign fighters, hailing mainly from Afghanistan, Libya, and Tunisia. One of the "insurgents" interviewed noted that he, Basel, a Syrian, had been trained in various antiaircraft weapons, such as SAM-7 missiles, in the early days of the Libyan uprising.

In a *Guardian* article dated September 23, 2012, the "insurgents" were said to need a variety of frontline interpreters speaking

---

[338] "Report: New Libyan Regime Sends 600 Troops To Fight In Syria," November 30, 2011.

[339] "Libya transporting weapons and fighters to Syria: Americans, Moroccans, Libyans, Bosnians fighting alongside rebel forces," February 19, 2013.

"Chechen, Tajik, Turkish, French, Saudi dialect, Urdu."[340] After all, the men were "jihadi veterans of Iraq, Yemen, and Afghanistan." Just as the non-Afghan recruits for the war against the USSR were called "Arab-Afghans," the Syrian terrorists fighting Bashar al-Assad now have the sobriquet "Turkish brothers." Of course, there are some problems with truthfulness among the brothers, according to the *Guardian*. "When the Syrians [from the "Free Syrian Army"] asked them where they were from, a blond French speaker said they were Moroccans, the Chechens said they were Turks, and the Tajiks said they were Afghans." In response to criticism that their behavior endangered NATO supplies reaching the "Free Syrian Army," unidentified jihadis replied that they were there to "stop NATO." Lies and thievery often go together. In Abdul-Ahad's piece, "The jihadis had looted and stolen from the local people and demanded protection money from local businesses in order not to steal their merchandise."

A Lose-Lose Situation

US policy, according to the *Washington Post*, is directed at ensuring victory by neither side in the terrorist war against Bashar al-Assad (American journalist Barbra Nimri Aziz noted this first in her September 3, 2013, blog on Radio Tahrir.).[341] In a Greg Miller–authored front-page article, the CIA has been enlarging a "clandestine" effort to instruct opponents of the Assad government in the ways of war.[342] Citing unnamed US government officials (a forte of the *Post*), the recruits trained are so few they will make no difference in the

---

[340] Ghaith Abdul-Ahad, "Syria: the foreign fighters joining the war against Bashar al-Assad."

[341] WBAI-FM, NYC, "Is the Confusion about Syria Manufactured or Real?"

[342] "CIA steps up effort to train rebels," *Washington Post*, October 3, 2013.

conflict. In fact, Langley's aim, defined by the White House, is to seek a "political settlement" through stalemate. American backing for "its" insurgents will "provide enough support to help ensure that politically moderate militias don't lose but [won't] win." Nevertheless, Miller asserted that the Agency has been sending "additional paramilitary teams" to double the number of insurgents being trained and armed at secret locations in Jordan. Apparently, according to another "unnamed source," Langley has been redoubling its efforts because "its" side is losing, both tactically and strategically.

Jordan, the *Post* said, was chosen because of its intelligence services' long-standing ties to the Agency. The CIA's access to military bases guarded by Jordanian soldiers was also a benefit. Trainers come from Langley's paramilitary branch, the Special Activities Division, an organization reliant on contractors and former US Special Forces members.

In an earlier article, the *Washington Post* noted that American weapons have been flowing to the Syrian insurgents.[343] Quoting more unnamed US officials, the paper did not specify the types, amounts, or value of the arms, other than to note that they were "light weapons and other munitions." The paper did allow that "The CIA shipments are to flow through a network of clandestine bases in Turkey and Jordan that were expanded over the past year as the agency sought to help Middle Eastern allies including Saudi Arabia and Qatar, direct weapons to moderate [sic] Syrian rebel forces."

A Myriad of Myrmidons

Despite the rattling fusillade of media reports about American, European, and Israeli involvement in overthrowing the legitimate

---

[343] Ernesto Londoño and Greg Miller, "U.S. arms reach rebels," *Washington Post*, September 12, 2013.

Syrian government, the *Washington Post* reported in its article "Foreign extremists' footprint in Syria growing:"[344]

> Foreign fighters from across the Arab world and beyond are playing an increasingly dominant role in the battle for control of Syria, which has emerged as an even more powerful magnet for jihadist volunteers than Iraq and Afghanistan were in the past decade.[345]

> The number of Syrians battling to overcome the regime led by President Bashar al-Assad outstrips by a large margin the thousands of Arabs and other non-Syrian Muslims who have streamed into Syria over the past two years to join in the fight.[346]

> But the flow of jihadist volunteers has accelerated, and non-Syrians have begun taking the lead in a variety of roles as the al-Qaeda-affiliated Islamic State of Iraq and Syria (ISIS) attempts to assert control over large areas of the rebel-held north.

> Foreign fighters man checkpoints, serve as commanders on the battlefield and have become the de facto rulers of towns and cities in areas under rebel control, giving them a visible and much-feared presence across large swaths of territory, according to [unnamed] Syrians living in the north as well as [unnamed] analysts.

---

[344] Liz Sly, October 2, 2013.
[345] Magnet? Overlooks recruitment!
[346] No basis for this claim provided, and it seemingly flies in the face of other reporting.

Saudis, Tunisians and Libyans are among the most frequently encountered nationalities, the residents and
analysts say but men from Chechnya, Kuwait, Jordan,
Iraq, and the United Arab Emirates also are present.

In this article, the *Post* relied on Brian Fishman (who had de-
clined to speak with the author) to frame the issue of "foreign
fighters."[347] "There's a lot more foreigners [in Syria] than we ever
saw in Iraq, and there's going to be a lot more," Fishman was quoted
as saying. He continued, articulating "They control territory, they've
established governance, and you see these foreigners playing more
dynamic roles. They're getting trained and leading people and il-
lustrating a level of ability we didn't see in Iraq."

Another expert quoted by the *Post* for Sly's article was Nada
Bakos, "who tracked al-Qaeda for the US government." Omitted was
her background as a CIA "targeting officer" in Iraq, who, according
to CNN, "used to go to work with a Glock [a plastic-framed pistol]
strapped to her thigh."[348] In Bakos's view, the "insurgents" now control more real estate in Syria than they did in Iraq or Afghanistan.

Yet, this *Washington Post* story defies reality. Despite credible reports that Britain and France provide "advisors," weapons, and training to the Arab-Afghan Legion, it claimed that "the United States'
partners in Europe have long expressed reluctance to intervene
in Syria without a mandate from the United Nations or NATO."[349]

---

[347] Fishman is now with the *New America Foundation*, a think-tank with,
SourceWatch.org says, ties to establishment figures such as Francis Fukuyama
and Steve Coll, the latter once refusing to talk with the author. *New America* also
receives funding from George Soros's *Open Society* and the US Department of
State. As the Esteemed Reader should know, the establishment works hard to
control public dialogue and media access.

[348] Suzanne Kelly, "Women in intelligence seek balance in life, value in work,"
CNN, May 11, 2012.

[349] Karen DeYoung and Bob Woodward, "Gulf allies tire of waiting for U.S. to
lead on Syria," November 3, 2013.

In another bit of remarkable obfuscation, the *Post* asserted in the same story that "a parallel operation independent of US efforts is being discussed by the Saudis with other countries in the region, according to officials from several governments that have been involved in the talks."

Months later, the *Post* continued its misinformation. In a front-page article above the fold, the paper "discovered" that President Barack Obama had asked Congress for $500 million "in direct US military training and equipment for Syrian opposition fighters, a move that could significantly escalate US involvement in Syria's civil [sic] war."[350] The funds (see the parallel with my account of the Afghanistan war's beginning under "Asleep At The Switch," *supra*) would enlarge an existing and furtive CIA training agenda. According to DeYoung, the aid would be going to "moderate" groups fighting the government of Syria. No mention was made of Jabhat al-Nusra, a "moderate" group that had previously received funding, even though it was on a State Department terrorist list.

The *Post* added, incredibly, that this tidal wave of money would be "the first direct US military participation in the Syrian conflict."[351]

Additionally, DeYoung noted that these monies resulted from the recent strides that ISIS has been making in the region, which, apparently, helped in concentrating Obama's mind on "terrorism." Iran's PRESSTV had a slightly different slant on that. It quoted investigative journalist Wayne Madsen as saying that John Brennan, the Agency's Director, is playing a significant part "in the creation and rise of the so-called Islamic State of Iraq and the Levant (ISIL)," sometimes known as the Islamic State of Iraq and Syria (ISIS).[352] Observing that the United States had been behind the creation of

---

[350] Karen DeYoung, "Obama seeks funds to train Syrian rebels," June 27, 2014.

[351] Granted the *Post* is not a paper of record, but you'd think their journalists would read previously printed articles on the subject.

[352] "Saudiphile CIA Director behind ISIL," June 30, 2014

al-Qaeda to fight the Soviet Union in Afghanistan, Madsen stated that "we've once again supported and trained and given cash to the same elements and now we've got the rise of ISIL in Iraq and Syria..."

PRESSTV added that Senator Rand Paul (R-KY) had declared that the United States had been providing weapons to ISIL in Syria. On CNN's "State of the Union" program, Rand said, "I think we have to understand first how we got here. We have been arming ISIS in Syria."[353]

Confirming the foregoing, on October 8, 2014, the Australian journalist John Pilger wrote:

> ISIS is the progeny of those in Washington and London who, in destroying Iraq as both a state and a society, conspired to commit an epic crime against humanity. Like Pol Pot and the Khmer Rouge, ISIS are the mutations of a western state terror dispensed by a venal imperial elite undeterred by the consequences of actions taken at great remove in distance and culture. Their culpabilities is unmentionable in "our" societies.[354]

Madsen's conclusion was that there is "a terrorist threat against the United States and that [it] is the CIA director" who is training and financing terrorists.

According to *Washington Post* journalist, David Ignatius (who often writes favorably about U.S. intelligence services), American spooks "are working with their counterparts in the Middle East and Europe to track ISIS and al-Nusra Front operatives and to monitor

---

[353] June 22, 2014.

[354] "From Pol Pot to ISIS: 'Anything that flies on everything that moves," johnpilger.com.

foreign fighters who have traveled to Syria to join the jihad."[355].
Although Ignatius omitted mentioning continued US support for
Jabhat al-Nusra, he wrote that there were about one hundred and ten
thousand "opposition fighters in Syria…[Bilad al-Sham]" ISIS men,
many with experience in guerrilla war in Iraq, numbered between
five thousand and ten thousand, he said, while al-Nusra totaled
five thousand to six thousand combatants. Furthermore, another
Sunni group, Ahrar al-Sham, according to Ignatius, claims to have
ten thousand to fifteen thousand soldiers. He went on to declare
that ten thousand to fifteen thousand foreigners have already made
their way to Bilad al-Sham from "Chechnya, Australia [an American
"ally"], Libya [where they had been recruited to overthrow Gaddafi],
Belgium [a NATO member], and the United States."

The United States and its repressive confederates, if the
Washington Post's numbers are correct, have already turned Syria
into another Iraq.[356] In a December 15, 2013, front-page story written
by Kevin Sullivan and filed from Kilis, Turkey, the *Post* claimed that,
according to UN and regional governments, "between 2.3 million
and 2.8 million Syrians have fled their homeland."[357] That number is
rising, with three thousand people a day leaving the country. Before
the Americans and their associates began their work on Syria, the
paper said that there were already twelve million refugees in the
area, traceable to the Zionists' ethnic cleansing of Palestine in 1948
(and, presumably, to the two million who fled for their lives from
Iraq after 2003). Besides the 6.5 million (40 percent of the population) now internally displaced, most Syrian exiles "live" (if that is a
proper word for their condition) in Lebanon, Turkey, and Jordan.
With one million Syrians sharing space with 4.4 million Lebanese

---

[355] "A growing Syrian threat," May 14, 2014.

[356] Cf. J. Michael Springmann, "Caught Between Iraq and a Hard Place," *The Public Record*, March 21, 2009.

[357] Kevin Sullivan, "Changing Regions Changing Lives," *Washington Post*, Dec. 15, 2013.

and three hundred thousand Palestinians, things are tight there.[358] The Turkish government, one of the states that fomented the war, estimates that seven hundred thousand people have fled the Syrian Arab Republic for the country of its former colonial master. As for Jordan, with a population of 6.5 million, it now hosts 2.6 million refugees of which nearly six hundred thousand are Syrian.

Sullivan's story quotes Helen Clark, head of the UN development program in the region, as saying "These places will never be the same. Many of these people will never go home." As happened with Iraq, "The massive influx of refugees is crippling fragile economies and damaging delicate political and religious balances in the region." By way of comparison, Clark noted that the million Syrian exiles living in Lebanon is "the equivalent of the entire population of Mexico taking refuge in the United States."

A World Bank report, the article claimed, described multiple disasters resulting from neocon policy: Lebanon's gross domestic product will likely be cut by nearly three percentage points annually between 2012 and 2014. Billions of dollars' worth of economic activity will disappear, with wages, due to increased competition for the remaining jobs, being cut. The jobless rate, currently 10 percent, may well double and the number of those below the poverty line (now one million people) may rise nearly 20 percent.

Essential services in the region such as sewage, electricity, and garbage collection are collapsing. Water is becoming scarcer. With its water already directed to Israel in disproportionate amounts, the per capita volume of the life-giving fluid in Jordan is being reduced by the influx of refugees. In Jordan, nearly $2 billion will be

---

[358] Lebanon, once the Switzerland of the Middle East (as local businessman Paul Garmirian once said), has been bled white by fifteen years of civil war (1975–1990), two conflicts with Israel (1982 and 2006), and the strife following Prime Minister Rafik Hariri's assassination in 2005. The American-generated war in Syria has, on occasion, spilled over into Lebanon since 2011.

needed to provide housing and services to the six hundred thousand refugees from Syria.

What hope is there for the future of these refugees? In sixty-six years, the United States, which helped create the Palestinian refugees in their millions, has only added to the number of exiles in the area. It has not resolved the Palestinian problem, and it will not settle those of the Iraqis and Syrians.

Summary

Beginning in the 1950s, first in Egypt, then in Syria, American and British intelligence services have worked to overthrow men and governments they didn't like. With past attempts unsuccessful, the United States, aided by repressive governments in the region, moved against the Syrian Arab Republic in the new century, using its favorite cat's paw, the Arab-Afghan Legion. The attack began, if not in concert with the alleged "spontaneous" uprising in March 2011, then not long afterward. Conceivably, the Obama Administration had begun arms shipments to the Syrian terrorist groups earlier than acknowledged. Reports surfaced in May 2013 that between two thousand and fifty-five hundred foreign nationals were active in Syria, including hundreds from countries such as Britain, France, and Ireland. European government officials are now worrying about the consequences of these foreign legionnaires returning home.

In later stories, the numbers changed. The war in Syria had allegedly attracted approximately seven thousand combatants from fifty countries and that one of the main US-sponsored groups there "aspires to carry out an attack in the United States." US Special Forces are preparing these terrorists for action at locations in Turkey and at an American base in southwest Jordan. Rebellion leaders have been supplied by recruiting programs run by the CIA,

Britain's MI6 [the Secret Intelligence Service], Israel's Mossad [external intelligence service], and the French DGSE [external] intelligence service." Beginning in early 2012, the FARS News Agency related that Qatar, Saudi Arabia, and Jordan flew weapons acquired in Croatia to Turkey, which then delivered them by the truckload to "insurgents" committed to overthrowing the Syrian government. Hundreds of combatants came from Langley's war in the Balkans.

Other things came from the Balkans, too. As part of a deal worked out with the Americans, Croatia sold two hundred and thirty tons of rocket and grenade launchers, field artillery, mortars, and ammunition in December 2012 to Jordan, which were fed into a CIA pipeline to opponents of the legitimate Syrian government.

At the beginning of the anti-Assad rebellion, the US Ambassador to Syria, Robert S. Ford, was the key State Department official recruiting Arab death squads. They were brought in from al-Qaeda-affiliated units in Afghanistan, Iraq, Yemen, and Chechnya to fight military and police units.

American actions in Syria, in concert with Britain, France, Saudi Arabia, the Gulf States, and, probably, Israel, were and are intended to *dehouse, deculturalize, destabilize, and destroy* the country.[359] To further this aim, American policy is now to prevent victory by either side in the terrorist war against Bashar al-Assad. Therefore, the fact that, according to one CIA official, the "insurgents" now control more territory in Syria than they even did in Iraq or Afghanistan is a matter of concern to US policymakers.

The United States and its associates, if the *Washington Post*'s numbers are correct, have already turned Syria into another Iraq. Between 2.3 and 2.5 million Syrians have already fled the country (roughly 10 percent of the 2010 population, according to UN

---

[359] Israel's policy is to ensure that no country in the Middle East can have foreign or domestic policies that Tel Aviv opposes. Statement by David MacMichael to author, 2014.

figures). Forty percent of the inhabitants (6.5 million people) are "internally displaced." The World Bank reported that Syrian refugees, just like Iraqi ones, have stretched the resources of the countries absorbing them to dangerous limits.

LET'S WRAP THIS UP IF WE CAN

The Origins of the Train Wrecks Go Back to the Establishment of the National Security State and its Central Intelligence Agency during the Administration of Harry S. Truman (D-MO).

The man from Missouri created the CIA and the NSA, organizations that believe they have carte blanche to overthrow governments and spy on American citizens and others. They operate without executive, legislative, or judicial control.

The current foreign policy train wrecks are nothing new. American international relations was a disaster in the first half of the twentieth century. Following the so-called professionalization of the State Department's Foreign Service and its merger with the CIA's not-very Clandestine Service in the late 1940s, it then became an unmitigated disaster. Consider just a few operations in the past that I've earlier mentioned and draw the ties to, and the parallels with, the present. Think of the progressives who say, "Why do we need to talk about the past? There is no link to the present." Recall:

• The overthrow of Mohammad Mossadegh, prime minister of Iran—and current US hostility toward that country.

208

• The overthrow of Jacobo Arbenz Guzman, president of Guatemala—and waves of illegal aliens flooding across the US border, attempting to escape the consequences of America's policy of revolution and repression in the region.

The Security State's Reach—Why Limit Things to Just One Continent, Or Region?

Congress passed the National Security Act in July 1947. Included in the Act was the CIA's creation. Truman, who signed the Act, ignored the opposition of his Secretary of State, George C. Marshall, a former career U.S. Army officer. Marshall opposed the law, saying it "abridged the constitutional authority of the president and secretary of state." Yet, in making the Act law, Truman himself "feared that the CIA could turn into a 'Gestapo' or 'military dictatorship.'"[360] Seizing on a vaguely worded portion of the legislation empowering it to engage in "other functions and duties relating to intelligence affecting the national security," the Agency began directing hundreds of clandestine acts abroad, including eighty-one during Truman's second term alone.

In 1947, George F. Kennan, then head of the State Department's Policy Planning Staff, pushed the Secretary of Defense and anti-Soviet, hard-liner James Forrestal to create a "guerrilla warfare corps," something opposed by the general staff. [Now, it's called the Arab-Afghan Legion, or, al Qaeda, or ISIL and the entire government embraces it.] Then, at the end of that year, Truman approved a secret national security council memorandum, NSC 4-A, authorizing Langley to engage in "covert" operations. The next year, 1948, he approved another such, NSC 10/2, providing for "propaganda,

---

[360] Stone, Kuznick, 212–213, citing Arnold A. Offner, *Another Such Victory: President Truman and the Cold War, 1945-1953* (Stanford: Stanford University Press, 2002), 192.

economic warfare; preventive direct action, including sabotage, antisabotage, demolition and evacuation measures; subversion against hostile states, including assistance to underground resistance movements, guerillas, and refugee liberation groups, and support of indigenous anti-Communist elements in threatened countries of the free world."[361]

Money was secretly diverted from the Marshall Plan, designed to revitalize the European economy, devastated by six years of war, to the Agency. As Stone and Kuznick write, the Agency used the funds to set up "phony front organizations that recruited foreign agents as frontline warriors in the propaganda wars that ensued. Sometimes they went beyond propaganda, infiltrating unions and other existing organizations and establishing underground groups. Forrestal and the Pentagon wanted the programs to go further, including 'guerrilla movements...underground armies...sabotage and assassination.'"[362]

It seems that the CIA had problems distinguishing between underground groups and above-ground armies. Langley used Marshall Plan money to support a guerrilla force in the Ukraine, called "Nightingale." Originally established in 1941 by Nazi Germany's occupation forces, and working on their behalf, "Nightingale" and its terrorist arm (made up of ultranationalist Ukrainians as well as Nazi collaborators) murdered thousands of Jews, Soviet Union supporters, and Poles. Allen Dulles brought Mikola Lebed, its leader, to the United States in 1949. The CIA head successfully resisted Justice Department attempts to deport Lebed as a war criminal,

---

[361] Ibid., 213.

[362] Ibid., 214, citing Col. R. Allan Griffin, recorded interview by James R. Fuchs, staff interviewer, February 15, 1947, Harry S. Truman Library Oral History Program. Garry Wills, *Bomb Power*, 78, 88–89. Tim Weiner, *Legacy of Ashes: The History of the CIA* (New York: Cambridge University Press, 2005), 249–253.

asserting that the terrorist chief was of "inestimable value to this Agency 'and was assisting in' operations of the first importance."[363]

These were precedents for US actions taking place in the Balkans, Iran, Iraq, Libya, Syria, and elsewhere, much closer to the present than the 1940s. (Don't forget current events in the Ukraine). Sergei Lavrov, Russian Foreign Minister, certainly sees them as such. On May 30, 2014, Russia's Interfax news service quoted him as believing the Ukrainian coup is very similar to recent events in Iraq and Libya. Lavrov said, "What we see at the forefront today is the crises that were created by similar methods and appeared as a result of policies aimed at changing the regimes in North Africa and the Middle East—Iraq and Libya. And [the crisis] in Ukraine was motivated by the same causes."

Arbenz Was Not a One-Time Intervention

Ronald Reagan picked up where Eisenhower left off, creating a greater nightmare for the people of Central America and the United States.

Ronald Reagan, the fortieth president of the United States, worked with Bill Casey, his presidential campaign manager, whom he named head of the CIA, to fund destabilizing forces in Central America. Aided by Israeli arms dealers and Latin drug merchants, Langley and its politicians sold weapons to Iran and illegal narcotics to American citizens. They used the enormous profits therefrom to finance the attempted overthrow of the legitimate Sandinista government of Nicaragua by reactionary forces (the Contras). Some of them were homegrown, while others were

---

[363] Ibid., 214, citing Norman J. W. Goda, "Nazi Collaborators in the United States, What the FBI Knew," in *U.S. Intelligence and the Nazis*, ed. Richard Breitman, Norman J. W. Goda, Timothy Naftali, and Robert Wolfe, (New York: Cambridge University Press, 2005), 249–253.

mercenaries recruited from Guatemala and El Salvador.[364] Casey also collaborated with another repressive but close ally of the United States, the Kingdom of Saudi Arabia, to attempt the murder of an Arab Muslim, Sheikh Muhammad Hussein Fadlallah. A Lebanese citizen born in Iraq, Fadlallah's writings and sermons inspired Hezbollah (Party of God). On March 8, 1985, in an action eerily similar to the 2005 killing of Rafik Hariri, Lebanese prime minister, CIA operatives—with alleged Saudi help—exploded nearly five hundred pounds of dynamite in a car bomb near the sheikh's home in Beirut. Although failing to slay him, the US attack slaughtered eighty other people, wounding another 256, mostly girls and women, who had been leaving a nearby mosque. The ferocity of the blast "burned babies in their beds," "killed a bride buying her trousseau," and "blew away three children as they walked home from the mosque."[365]

Fallout, Blowback, Whatever—It's A Continuing Train Wreck

The international terrorists the United States recruited for the wars in Afghanistan and Bosnia thirty-odd years ago are still involved in the fighting elsewhere today. Bosnia wasn't the only place those saddle tramps and gunslingers were employed. The visas the State Department issued to them *then* are *now* tied to the current administration's continuing wars in Afghanistan, Iraq, Libya, and Syria. The fanatics I saw get travel papers during my time at Jeddah are either directly involved in or trained those directly involved in fighting US

---

[364] Ibid., 431. NB: Many of the anti-Sandinistas had been veterans of the Nicaraguan National Guard of US-supported dictator Anastasio Somoza.

[365] Ibid., 436; Wikipedia citing Noam Chomsky. Elmandjra. February 26, 2008. NB: *Wikipedia* is not a reliable source, and some journalists believe its information is controlled by intelligence services and Zionists.

forces today.[366] Former Senator Mike Gravel (D-AK), told me last year that those originally recruited for the anti-Soviet operation in Afghanistan are still being used to destabilize governments the United States doesn't like. Now they've got the assistance of mercenary armies enlisted by US firms closely tied to American agencies, such as the infamous, name-changing Blackwater/Xe Services/Academi/Constellis that performs "security" for the State Department.[367]

CIA excesses, propaganda, and other illegal actions have never been restricted to the few events mentioned earlier. While Langley insists that its primary mission is the collection and analysis of foreign intelligence information for use by our nation's leadership and that the Agency has no police, subpoena, law enforcement, or internal security functions, its primary activity is the conduct of covert operations.

While at INR, I attended an Agency briefing at Langley. Of the Agency's four chief divisions (Intelligence, Operations, Science and Technology, Administration), the largest portion of its invisible budget goes to Operations (clandestine activity). The CIA refuses to obey one of the most basic tenets of the Constitution: *No Money shall be drawn from the Treasury, but in Consequence of Appropriations made by Law; and a regular Statement and Account of the Receipts and Expenditures of all public Money shall be published from time to time.* Article I, Section 9. Its budget is never published and its funds are, for the most part, hidden in the accounts of allegedly legitimate agencies. This voodoo bookkeeping helps deceive the American people and their representatives in Congress about the Agency's real activities. No numbers are ever available for its "front" companies' resources.

Langley has traditionally distorted "intelligence," most notably in the "justification" for America's illegal and unconstitutional attacks on Iraq in 1991 and 2003. The Agency is deeply involved with

---

[366] My conversation with Lt. Col. Anthony A. Shaffer USA (ret.), September 26, 2012, National Press Club (Washington, DC).

[367] Response to my May 2, 2013, question posed to former US Senator Mike Gravel (D-Alaska) at the National Press Club (Washington, DC).

domestic law enforcement through participation in "Fusion Centers' that involve cooperation and information sharing with all levels of federal, State, and local police forces, particularly in New York City. There, the CIA had "embedded" at least four of its officers to help the New York Police Department spy on Muslims. New York also had substantial help from Langley in revolutionizing its police department's intelligence division. Naturally enough, anything picked up by Agency officials goes into DC databanks.[368]

Moreover, despite the Congressional ban on domestic spying, Langley has large, essentially ineffective, stations in New York City, Miami, and elsewhere. James Risen, the journalist now an Agency target, wrote this in the *New York Times* (November 4, 2001):

> The Central Intelligence Agency's clandestine New York station was destroyed in the Sept. 11 attack on the World Trade Center...
>
> The agency's New York station was behind the false front of another federal organization, which intelligence officials requested that the *Times* not identify. The station was, among other things, a base of operations to spy on and recruit foreign diplomats stationed at the United Nations, while debriefing selected

---

[368] *NSA Government Surveillance Directorate*: The National Counterterrorism Center (NCTC) operates as a partnership of more than sixteen organizations, including the CIA, FBI, State Department, Defense Department, Homeland Security, and other agencies that provide unique expertise such as the Departments of Energy, Treasury, Agriculture, Transportation, and Health and Human Services.

The NCTC is the primary organization for analyzing and integrating all foreign and domestic terrorism-related intelligence possessed or acquired by the United States. It was also recently given the authority to examine the government files of US citizens for possible criminal behavior, even if there is no reason to suspect them.

American business executives and others willing to talk to the C.I.A. after returning from overseas...

The agency's New York officers have been deeply involved in counterterrorism efforts in the New York area, working jointly with the Federal Bureau of Investigation and other agencies...

The agency is prohibited from conducting domestic espionage operations against Americans, but the agency maintains stations in a number of major US cities, where C.I.A. case officers try to meet and recruit students and other foreigners to return to their countries and spy for the United States.

As activist Rich Ray has suggested, Tax Fraud is another charge that could be laid, but never is, at Langley's door. Here are interesting excerpts from the US Attorney's Manual, Title 9, Section 109 and 18 US Code § 1961 that should be applicable to CIA front company or commercial cover operations that generate a substantial amount of income for the Agency, enabling it to do more with its secret subventions. Think what taxes on gunrunning, drug dealing, and money laundering could do for the Internal Revenue Service and the average American's tax burden.

The Racketeer Influenced Corrupt Organizations Act[369] says:

It is unlawful for anyone employed by or associated with any enterprise engaged in, or the activities of

---

[369] The US Code (18 USC § 1961) defines "racketeering activity" as (A) any act or threat involving murder, kidnapping, gambling, arson, robbery, bribery, extortion, dealing in obscene matter, or dealing in a controlled substance; (B) bribery; counterfeiting; and a myriad of other crimes including but not limited to visa fraud, obstruction of justice, and retaliation against witnesses.

which affect, interstate or foreign commerce, to conduct or participate, directly or indirectly, in the conduct of such enterprise's affairs through a pattern of racketeering activity or collection of unlawful debt.[370]

A violation of Section 1962(c), requires (1) conduct (2) of an enterprise (3) through a pattern (4) of racketeering activity.[371]

Noam Chomsky said, "Propaganda is to a democracy what the bludgeon is to a totalitarian state."

As can be imagined, Langley was and is adept at manipulating the public through the mass media. According to Alexander Cockburn writing in the *Free Press:*[372]

> Later that year [1948], Wisner [Frank G. Wisner Sr.] set [up] an operation codenamed "Mockingbird" to influence the domestic American press. He recruited Philip Graham of the Washington Post to run the project within the industry.
>
> [Joe] Trento writes that "One of the most important journalists under the control of Operation Mockingbird was Joseph Alsop, whose articles appeared in over 300 different newspapers." Other journalists willing to promote the views of the CIA,

---

[370] 18 USCA § 1962(c).

[371] *Sedima, S.P.R.L. v. Imrex Co.*, 473 U.S. 479, 496, 105 S. Ct. 3275, 3285, 87 L. Ed. 2d 346 (1985).

[372] "All The News That's Fit To Buy," December 9, 2005, freepress.org.

included Stewart Alsop (New York Herald Tribune), Ben Bradlee (Newsweek), James Reston (New York Times), Charles Douglas Jackson (Time Magazine), Walter Pincus (Washington Post), William C. Baggs (Miami News), Herb Gold (Miami News) and Charles Bartlett (Chattanooga Times).

"By 1953, Operation Mockingbird had a major influence over 25 newspapers and wire agencies, including the New York Times, Time and CBS. Wisner's operations were funded by siphoning of funds intended for the Marshall Plan. Some of this money was used to bribe journalists and publishers." In his book "Mockingbird: The Subversion of the Free Press by the CIA," Alex Constantine writes that in the 1950s, "some 3,000 salaried and contract CIA employees were eventually engaged in propaganda efforts."

Now, given the tall tales told by the news media, particularly the *Washington Post* about the Arab-Afghan Legion, and the Fourth Estate's vicious attacks on gallant, courageous men such as Edward Snowden, John Kiriakou, and Thomas Drake, we should not be surprised. Operation Mockingbird is obviously still alive and flying high, dropping its guano on Americans and others. Certainly, the cold shoulder by journalists I have approached about my dismissal from the Foreign Service supports that.

The extent of Langley's ability to control the federal government (and organizations outside it) can best be seen in Alyssa Röhricht's article about John Kiriakou in the January 6, 2014, edition of *CounterPunch*.[373] Kiriakou, a former CIA analyst, revealed to

---

[373] "Thou Shalt Not Bear False Witness Against Thy Government: John Kiriakou."

ABC News in 2007 that the Agency used torture as official policy. After investigating and hounding him for years, the US government prosecuted and convicted him, sentencing him to jail for thirty months in federal prison in February 2013. (The torturers themselves, who were "just following orders" have been ignored, if not rewarded, for their actions.)

According to Röhricht, the Agency's aim is to "either dismiss [any] leaks and their importance...[then] discount the heroic efforts of the leakers [like Kiriakou or Snowden, turning] them into crazed homosexuals...a hacker without a cause...or a tool for the enemy." The charge of "aiding the enemy" is most effective since it helps keep fear alive among citizens. This provides a semblance of "peace of mind" to those who dread imaginary terrors and "happily ignore" illegal governmental activities carried out "to protect them." As a result, the sheeple "fall into line and cry traitor" when prompted.

Besides being impoverished by loss of his pension and staggering legal bills, Kiriakou, Röhricht said, has been blocked from seeing his family. The United Services Automobile Association (USAA) also cancelled his car and home insurance, asserting that they insure neither felons nor their families. (USAA, which insures mainly military and diplomatic personnel, has as its motto: *We Know What It Means To Serve.*)

Americans, even educated ones, readily believe the lies, half-truths, and evasions of fact put out to support the existence and the excesses of the Arab-Afghan Legion. Frank Zapatka, a retired professor at American University in Washington, DC told me June 1, 2013, that Syria's hands are not clean because it is being helped by Hezbollah. By implication, there is nothing wrong, then, with the United States, France, Britain, Israel, Saudi Arabia, and the Legion aiding the alleged "Free" Syrian Army in its effort to overthrow Bashar al-Assad's government. Of course, Americans sometimes have help in reaching their beliefs. On September 15, 2013, while attending a program at WHUT (Howard University Television),

I heard American University's Mohamed Abu Nimer, a professor of International Peace and Conflict Resolution, spout the government line on Syria, urging Arabs to join the fight against Bashar al-Assad. Nimer holds two degrees from Hebrew University in occupied al-Quds (Jerusalem).[374] (N.B. The sesquicentennial of the War Between the States is under way. In the 1860s, the Union was vehemently opposed to Britain and France backing the Confederate States' struggle to free themselves from what they saw as an overly centrist and controlling government in Washington.)

The propaganda put forth in support of "regime change" in Syria even comes from supposedly knowledgeable, trustworthy sources, such as *The Washington Report On Middle East Affairs,* a magazine that asserts on its masthead: *Telling the Truth for More Than 30 Years.* In the June/July 2013 issue, one author, Pat McDonnell Twair, wrote about a university panel discussing what she termed the "Crisis." In it, she noted the need for "diplomatic engagement" in Syria, using Yemen as an example. She quoted a university professor from Buenos Aires, Ricardo Arredondo, who seemed to argue for an invasion of Syria. The academic compared Syria to Yugoslavia, saying that, in a state that won't protect its people, such as Kosovo, the UN approved the intervention of other governments. In the same issue, Assistant Editor Dale Sprusansky reported on an event hosted by the Middle East Institute (MEI), "Syria at the Crossroads." Former American Ambassador to Syria, Edward Djerejian, a speaker there, stated that Bashar al-Assad, unlike his father, can't be trusted and that the United States should furnish more military aid to al-Assad's

---

[374] Georgetown University's Center for Contemporary Arab Studies' director, Osama Abi-Mershed, PhD, refused to discuss this book's topic with me. Others connected to the CIA and teaching at the university on subjects relevant to this work also never responded to requests for information. This shouldn't be surprising, since Georgetown has long had a reputation for being a home to many right-wing, anti-communist "intellectuals" such as Jan Karski, Eleanor Lansing Dulles, and Jeanne Kirkpatrick.

opponents. Explaining this, an expert source on the region told me that the *Middle East Report* receives substantial financial contributions from the Kingdom of Saudi Arabia, one of the financiers of the Syrian revolt.

(By way of background, MEI is composed of a number of former State Department and other US government officials. Its president is Wendy J. Chamberlin, past US Ambassador to Pakistan. The chairman is Richard A. Clarke, previous holder of high "national security" positions in the Defense Department, the State Department, and the White House. Michael Ryan, an adjunct scholar at MEI is also a senior fellow at the Jamestown Foundation, a group closely connected to the Central Intelligence Agency. Ned Walker, once Deputy Chief of Mission in Saudi Arabia when the Legion was being recruited there, had been MEI president from 2001 to 2006. Allan Keiswetter, Political Counselor in Riyadh when I was in Jeddah, is another MEI scholar. Both Walker and Keiswetter did not reply to letters asking about the Jeddah visas for the Legion's terrorist recruits from the kingdom. Perhaps, I should have asked Walker in my letter about his appearance on a Fox News TV program in Florida several years ago. He and Jay Freres had been interviewed on terrorism. On the broadcast, both conveniently left out any mention of the United States' role in creating the Legion. (The link to the show no longer exists on Google.)

Afghanistan, Serbia, Iraq, Libya, and Syria

Until the creation of the Arab-Afghan Legion, usually referred to as *Al Qaeda*, the United States worked to overthrow governments it didn't like on an ad hoc basis. Remember what was done to Mohammed Mossadegh in Iran and Jacobo Arbenz Guzman in Guatemala. Additionally, the United States did its best to overthrow Fidel Castro in Cuba (who had dared to nationalize foreign-owned property) and the socialist Sandinistas in Nicaragua. "The City Upon A Hill," that professes American values, (whatever they might be), currently has destabilizing operations underway in Venezuela, the Ukraine, and Russia, but without any group more organized than "Pussy Riot."

But, as noted in *The War On Truth*,

> ...the CIA had always seen vast potential to use the terrorist network, established by bin Laden during the Cold War in an international framework in the post–Cold War era against Russian and Chinese power (i.e., in Eastern Europe, the Balkans, and Central Asia). From the beginning of US policy in Afghanistan, the CIA had hoped that the network of terrorists being spawned by Osama bin Laden, with assistance from Saudi Arabia and Pakistan would continue to be used after the Afghan war against Soviet occupation. Indeed, US intelligence maintained its co-optation of al-Qaeda by proxy as a means of expanding US power in the Balkans wars.[375]

> The degree to which al-Qaeda provides an often convenient—if highly dangerous—instrument of Western statecraft for the orchestration of illegal and corrupt covert operations can be understood in this context...al-Qaeda...[is] not an "enemy" to be fought and eliminated, but rather an unpredictable intelligence asset to be controlled, manipulated, and co-opted as much as possible to secure covert strategic ends.[376]

---

[375] *War on* Truth, 31.
[376] Ibid., 31.

On the other hand, there has been the long-term involvement of the United States with Islam.

Over the years, the United States had been working diligently (but, before Afghanistan, without a blueprint) to use extremist elements from the Muslim world. The goal was expanding the American empire and its control over the lands stretching east from the Pillars of Hercules to the Sutlej, if not as far as Indonesia.

> The US proxy war in Afghanistan, which cost $3 billion and several hundred thousand lives [conservatively], took America's decades-long alliance with ultraconservative political Islam to a new, more aggressive level.

> Until Afghanistan, the dominant idea was Islam-as-bulwark, that is, that political Islam was a barrier against Soviet expansion. But in Afghanistan, the paradigm was Islam-as-sword. The Islamic Right became an offensive weapon, signaling a significant escalation in the policy of cooperating with the Islamic brotherhood in Egypt, the Saudi Arabia–led Islamic bloc, and other elements of political Islam.[377]

The Afghan "jihad," based on the master plan, had "empowered its most violent fringe," created a cadre of combatants skilled in guerrilla war, intelligence "trade craft," assassination, and bomb making. It multiplied the connections and ties among fighters from North Africa, Egypt, the Gulf States, Central Asia, and Pakistan.[378] The "jihad" got the United States control of lands previously outside its area of influence: the Middle East, the Persian Gulf, and Central

---

[377] *Devil's Game*, 245.
[378] Ibid., 245.

Asia. Further, it used its new power to establish bases encircling Russia, Iraq, Afghanistan, and the remainder of the core of Asia, "assembl[ing] a proto-occupation force for the Gulf and surrounding real estate."[379]

However, before the arrangement with the Arab-Afghan Legion, spontaneous, erratic American interference in the region's internal affairs, as noted, was the norm.

Back in the mid-1970s, Henry Kissinger, the infamous National Security Advisor and Secretary of State in the Nixon Administration had an absolutely lunatic idea. He thought of seizing Arabian oil and having Texans and Oklahomans run the extraction facilities. Henry the K wanted to show the Saudis "who's boss" and suggested that the Agency overthrow a sheikhdom or two in the region, presumably as a way of concentrating their minds.[380]

Even before Kissinger's proposal, American and British efforts to effect "regime change" in the Arab world went back farther to the 1950s and 1960s. According to Robert Dreyfuss, in his book *Devil's Game,* the Anglo-American intelligence services sought to overthrow Gamal Abdel Nasser, president of Egypt and the first Arab to challenge European colonialism in the region. Their tool of choice was the Muslim Brotherhood.[381]

However, in Syria, plans to remove the country's left-leaning government, with the assistance of Saudi Arabia, appeared to aim at a "twofer." In 1958, Yusuf Yasin, an adviser to the Saudi King, was implicated in a conspiracy to assassinate Nasser on a visit to Damascus. The project fell apart after the Saudis offered a 1.9 million Syrian pound bribe (about US $575,000) to the Syrian chief of intelligence to help with the murder (and, presumably, the subsequent destabilization of Syria). Earlier, in 1956–1957, Langley tried

---

[379] Ibid., 245–246.
[380] Ibid., 247–248.
[381] Ibid, 94–95.

to overthrow the Syrian government single-handed.[382] Bill Blum elaborated on this attempt, as reported in his book, *Killing Hope, U.S. Military and CIA Interventions Since World War II*.[383] Wilbur Crane Eveland, from the US National Security Council, and old Agency hands Archibald and Kermit Roosevelt, planned a repeat in Syria of Langley's actions in Iran. They planned a coup using senior Syrian army colonels. Blum noted that the operation disintegrated after the money had changed hands because Israel had attacked Egypt in the Suez Canal Crisis of 1956. The would-be revolutionaries said they couldn't attack their own government when another Arab state was embroiled in war with the Zionists.

Kermit Roosevelt tried again in 1957, Blum asserted. Teddy's grandson lost once more because the Syrian army officers assigned key roles in the plot turned in their pay to the country's chief of intelligence, Col. Sarraj, and named the American spooks who had hired them. Col. Robert Molloy, US Army attaché, and Francis Jeton, a career CIA official, whose diplomatic cover was second secretary for political affairs, were declared persona non grata and kicked out of the country.[384]

After this failure, the Americans began to plan and to organize.

Dreyfuss asserted that George W. Bush and his allies used fearsome descriptions of the dangers of the "Islamist Threat" to develop a pretext for expanding US imperialism in the Middle East.[385] Following this statement, Dreyfuss goes on to propose that there

---

[382] Ibid, 124, citing Joel Gordon, *Nasser's Blessed Movement* (New York: Oxford University Press, 1992) 105.

[383] Bill Blum, *Killing Hope, U.S. Military and CIA Interventions Since World War II* (Monroe, Maine: Common Courage Press, 2004), 86–87. Citing Dwight D. Eisenhower, *The White House Years: Waging Peace, 1956–1961;* New York, 1965, 198.

[384] Ibid., 88. Additional details on American efforts to control the region can be found in Blum's book at *13. The Middle East 1957-1958*, 89–99.

[385] *Devil's Game*, 305.

were other American goals in the Middle East, ones that had little to do with combating terrorism. Examples were: two-thirds of the world's oil supply being located in Saudi Arabia and Iraq as well as Bush's close ties to Ariel Sharon and the Israeli right wing. After all, if the real enemy is Islamist terrorism, why fight Iraq, Syria, and the Palestine Liberation Organization (PLO)? Bashar al-Assad, Syrian president; Yasser Arafat, PLO Chairman; and Saddam Hussein, Iraqi president, were all opposed to the Muslim Brotherhood. Saddam was no friend of the "Islamists," Shiite and otherwise, while the Ba'ath Party in both Syria and Iraq was a socialist, secular entity.[386]

But, maybe, it was Saudi money going into Bush pockets?

Citing Craig Unger's book, *House of Bush, House of Saud*, Andrew Kreig noted that the Kingdom of Saudi Arabia crossed the palms of George H.W. and George W. Bush, James Baker, family advisor and Secretary of State, as well as Vice President Dick Cheney with nearly $1.5 billion. (To be sure, some of this money went to companies affiliated with the foregoing individuals.)[387]

The real threat, not the imaginary one the United States was hyping, was "right-wing Islamic groups, institutions, and political parties in the Muslim world." They reflected a constellation that represented a significant menace "to governments, intellectuals, and progressives, and other free thinkers, from Morocco to Indonesia."[388] That is, these were the instruments to change regimes, economic value systems, and ideas successive American administrations opposed. They did not endanger the United States because the United States was allied with them and used them for its own ends.

While the United States ceaselessly proclaimed the need for democracy, self-determination, and noninvolvement by outside forces in the Middle East, the United States did not withdraw from the

---

[386] Ibid., 305–306.
[387] *Presidential Puppetry*, 104–105, and *House of Bush, House of Saud*, 308.
[388] *Devil's Game*, 306.

region. Nor did it end its support for Israel. Instead, the American government embraced the Neocon ideas espoused by the American Enterprise Institute, the Hudson Institute, and the Project for a New American Century, that is, that wars in Afghanistan and Iraq were the beginning of an effort to control Iran, Syria, Saudi Arabia, and the Gulf states.[389] Geopolitics seemed to rule foreign policy and control regional destinies: Syria lies between Israel and American-occupied Iraq while Iran is wedged between occupied Iraq and NATO-controlled Afghanistan. It's always easiest to move against your "enemies" from two directions.[390]

As Ahmed says in *The War On Truth*:

> ...the Western strategic alliance with al-Qaeda [the Arab-Afghans] never ceased. Rather it merely shifted to a new theater of military operations—from Afghanistan to Eastern Europe, Central Asia, and the Balkans. The strategic objective of the policy is the destabilization of the last remaining vestiges of Russian power in this region and the consolidation of Anglo-American hegemony in Eurasia.
>
> Al-Qaeda terrorism through the post–Cold War period is therefore not merely a form of "blowback" from past Western military intelligence operations supporting the mujahideen during the Cold War...[391]

However, people and nations in control never want to relinquish that control. Rather, they seek to maintain, if not expand it. Listen to Walter Pincus.

---

[389] Ibid., 307.
[390] Ibid., 309.
[391] *War On Truth*, 53.

Walter Pincus, one of the Agency's men at the *Washington Post*,[392] reported December 12, 2013, in that paper, the United States was not leaving the Middle East. In fact, he said, Secretary of Defense Hagel had confirmed this view in a December 6, 2013, speech in Bahrain. Hagel reassured his listeners at a news conference that the United States intended to upgrade and increase its already extensive military presence in Southwest Asia. Some of what Hagel did not say, and what Pincus emphasized, was: the siting of X-band radar directed against Iran and located atop Mt. Keren in the Israeli Negev desert as well as at Turkey's Kurecik Air Force Base, 240 miles (about 386 km) from Iran. Pincus cited the *Wall Street Journal*'s report that a similar radar would be placed in a secret location in Qatar. Qatar already houses the Combined Air Operations Center at the Al-Udeid air base, a hub for US, UK and Australian air strikes against Afghanistan. Pincus added more detail, noting, inter alia, that the US Army Corps of Engineers, along with a contractor, Stanley Consultants, "will replace an existing temporary camp at the United Arab Emirates' al-Dhafra air base and provide force protection to [US Air Force] personnel." This means, according to Pincus, "housing, dining, recreation, administrative, medical, fire, communications, security, post office, and morale facilities."

Pincus's story included a chilling quote from Hagel: "The US military is building a new strategic agility in the Middle East." The "journalist's" narrative went on to say that he believed Hagel meant these regional actions were for "enhancing programs and facilities that proved useful for the Iraq and Afghan wars and would provide the security necessity for any future fighting." [Syria? Iran?] Pincus's commentary also included Hagel's statement that there were already thirty-five thousand American soldiers, sailors, and airmen in the region. Expanding on America's imperialist presence, he asserted

---

[392] Cf. Angus MacKenzie, *Secrets, The CIA's War At Home* (Berkeley: University of California Press, 1998).

that the United States has "prepositioned," that is, already shipped, weapons, ammunition, and other combat matériel to Kuwait and Qatar "for immediate contingency challenges." Also, according to Pincus, there is $1.2 billion in US military equipment, including missiles, armored vehicles and artillery ammunition currently stored in Israel, for use by American or Israeli forces.[393]

There are some people willing to speak on the record about the United States and efforts to destabilize governments around the world. One of them is Hamid Karzai, president of the Islamic Republic of Afghanistan.

As stated by Kevin Sieff in the *Washington Post*, the president of Afghanistan, a former fighter against the Soviets and Deputy Foreign Minister in the Mujahideen Government of 1992, "has been building…a case against the Americans…" Karzai, "according to senior Afghanistan officials" is said to have accused the United States of working with "insurgents" to undercut and weaken his government. Compiling a list of "dozens of attacks" organized by or involving the Americans occupying his country, Karzai included the most recent and spectacular: the assault on the Lebanese restaurant in Kabul (*La Taverna du Liban*) that killed twenty-one people. Besides trying to weaken his position (from which he has demanded peace talks with the Taliban and the removal of foreign forces from his country), Karzai claimed that the Americans "planned…to foment instability in Afghanistan…" Presumably, this would either give the United States another reason to keep control of the Islamic Republic or ensure that the country will remain a fragmented, dysfunctional Muslim land, just like Iraq, Libya, and Syria.

The American response?

---

[393] Walter Pincus, "Hagel's verbal assurances for continued U.S. presence in the Middle East come with action," *Washington Post*, December 12, 2013. Al-Dhafra is currently home to KC-10 aerial refueling tankers and U-2 spy planes.

The *Post* quoted the US Ambassador James B. Cunningham as saying "It's a deeply conspiratorial view that's divorced from reality."[394]

Some Talkers Talk

Cunningham's quote is simply one example of a remarkably vast cover-up. Washington's policy is to fire or marginalize anyone in government who questions the official story. Additionally, the policymakers ensure that the official story is heard and heard, time and again. To do that, the United States keeps its propaganda machine going, using CIA official Frank Wisner's "Mighty Wurlitzer" to drown out any counterarguments. Going beyond propaganda are the clandestine efforts to destabilize and overthrow legitimate governments to justify the official story. That's the role of the Arab-Afghan Legion.

The Legion and its operations, as has been seen throughout this work, have been shrouded in secrecy. This includes and is linked to actions by Barack Obama. Whether it's the man's school records, family history, work experience, or foreign and domestic policy, the New Wizard of Oz and his Witches operate from hiding. This is a pattern and practice long associated with the CIA, and goes a great way toward explaining the steady march of the Legionnaires. They have, and have long had, cover from the top:

> The president and his staff have successfully hidden
> or kept unavailable his significant school and uni-
> versity records in a manner that is unprecedented
> in modern times. His and his family's passport and

---

[394] Kevin Sieff, "Karzai said to suspect U.S. in insurgent attacks," *Washington Post*, January 28, 2014.

similar records are unavailable...The vast bulk of Dunham-Obama family records from a variety of institutional archives are reported as lost or sealed... In general, however, declassified CIA records and other authoritative sources illustrate a long-standing pattern of Cold War recruitment of personnel from precisely the schools Obama and his family favored: the East-West Center at the University of Hawaii, Occidental College, Columbia University, and Harvard Law School...Was [Elliott] Haynes... [correct] in describing Barack Obama's future employer [Business International Corp.] as a CIA front? Probably.[395]

The Agency's "Stealth" president Obama has worked hand in glove with Agency man John Brennan. Former assistant to the president for homeland security and counterterrorism, as well as a twenty-five-year career man at Langley, Brennan is now director of his old employer, the CIA. As Andy Kreig put it, Brennan's prior experience as station chief in Riyadh[396] led to his involvement in other Middle East policies that would prove disastrous:

> Brennan, drawing on his extensive Saudi experience, fostered a recruitment strategy for ground troops in Libyan and Syrian battlefields that was popular with the president. This strategy involved recruiting local fighters, in cooperation with monarchies, dictatorships, and other forces friendly to the United States. This seemingly adroit "solution" developed

---

[395] *Presidential Puppetry*, 28–29. Elliot Haynes, with his father, Eldridge, founded BIC. Cf. Wayne Madsen, *The Manufacturing of a President* (LuLu.com, 2014), 209.
[396] *North Bergen Record*, December 5, 2009.

the same problems as a similar US technique used three decades previously against Russian troops in Afghanistan: the most committed rebel freedom fighters were likely to be Muslims so radical as to become difficult for the United States to control in the long run. Visible help to those who might seem like Taliban or al-Qaeda counterparts would not be good public relations for US voters.[397]

Additionally, Kreig noted that

...the liaison role of Brennan between the Saudis, Bush Family, and Obama administration, and the 'Intelligence-Industrial Complex' cannot be overestimated [sic]...Significant evidence exists that the CIA's operation in Benghazi during 2012 included the smuggling of arms and fighters to rebels in Syria, as I told CBS radio affiliate WWL AM/FM in New Orleans during an interview. Any such operations would have been part of Brennan's responsibility at the White House in coordination with CIA Director David Petraeus."[398] [It was also Brennan, as CIA chief during a secret April 2014 visit to Kiev, who apparently directed the putschists to send the army against dissidents in the Eastern Ukraine.[399]]

Presidential Puppetry also offers an explanation for why the United States and its repressive allies opposed some "Muslim firebrands,"

---

[397] *Presidential Puppetry,* 278–279.

[398] Ibid., 299.

[399] Wayne Madsen, "Ukraine's secret recipe: 'Brennan Kiev'," *Strategic Culture Foundation,* April 15, 2014.

murdering them through waves of drones but supported others. Moammar Gaddafi and Bashar al-Assad "had flirted with Russia through the years." The kingdom and other states dependent on oil "had their own reasons to sponsor rebellions. They are highly undemocratic, and thus fear rebellion…" evidently hoping to promote it elsewhere, and far away. One example is among the Alawites in Syria, who profess a variant on Shia Islam, and are thus anathema to the Wahhabi and Salafi radical Sunni.[400]

American experts had long been involved in planning war and making war in the Middle East. (These were two of the charges against the Nazi defendants at the Nürnberg war crimes trials.) Andrew Kreig, citing Tony Blair, former British prime minister and unindicted war criminal, added that Dick Cheney, vice president under George W. Bush, had planned a series of wars against secular states East of Gibraltar. Targets were Iraq, Libya, Syria, Lebanon, the Sudan, Somalia, and Iran.[401] If you count internal instability created by American efforts, notably in Lebanon and Somalia, all of Cheney's conflicts have succeeded. One possible exception is Iran. And there, assassinations, computer viruses, and mysterious explosions point to a covert US war in full operation.

Everything the American Government Does Is Shrouded in Secrecy—to Its Detriment

Throughout the preceding pages, the reader has seen how the American government has operated amid great secrecy. Not only did the left hand not know what the right hand was doing, but each of the fingers thereon did not know what was happening.

---

[400] *Presidential Puppetry*, 279.

[401] Ibid., 114, citing Tony Blair, *A Journey: My Political Life* (New York; Alfred A. Knopf, 2010); citing Robert Parry, "Blair Reveals Cheney's War Agenda," *Consortium News*, Sept. 6, 2010.

The attorney Pat Frascogna, a man with FOIA expertise, once wrote about secrecy and its purpose: "Thus whether it be learning the dirty and unethical business practices of a company or the secrets of our government, the same deployment of denials and feigning ignorance about what is really going on are the all-too-common methods used to keep the truth from the light of day."[402]

Langley recruited the Arab-Afghans so clandestinely that the terrorists didn't know they had been recruited. They thought that they had found a battlefield on their own, or through the Internet or through Twitter or through television. The Agency didn't even bother to tell the non-CIA Americans involved in giving them US visas about they were doing, either out of sheer stupidity, an excess of caution, or the bureaucratic mindset.

The secrecy was so pervasive it even covered religious rituals. Jay Freres used the Holy Church of the Consulate for spiritual services. Not only did he hide that from the Saudis (supposedly), he hid it from the Americans. He also concealed the reasons why some Americans at the consulate could buy liquor but not others. Freres obscured consulate liquor sales to US firms, such as Mobil, operating in the Hejaz. He camouflaged the real reason that the University of Maryland could not teach college-level courses for credit at the consulate. (He insisted that a "State Department" employee, that is, a CIA employee, had to monitor each and every course. This was entirely unacceptable to the school and the prospective teacher, Jackie Black.) Additionally, the consulate had a boat available for rent. However, it really belonged to the CIA Base and the vessel was never free for use by nonspooks due to "mysterious" problems: the engine needed work, the propeller had lost a blade, etc. Even years later, the federal government wouldn't own up to what had happened, because, in one knowledgeable contact's phrase, "it's still going on." Ali Ahmad Jalali, the former Afghan Interior Minister,

---

[402] *Encounter*, 226.

army officer, and resistance planner, simply wouldn't talk. (As a likely CIA asset, that might offend his masters.) The Iraqi puppet government and its embassy in Washington, DC never replied to my questions about terrorist activity in that unhappy country. Anes Shallal (who allowed his Busboys and Poets restaurant to be used for arguing for greater US intervention in Syria) didn't respond to my earlier questions about the Legion in Iraq.[403] Milt Bearden and Marc Sageman, Agency company men, wouldn't talk and kept telling me that the CIA hadn't been involved in recruiting the Arab-Afghans. Houeida Saad, who nursed them, and Phyllis Bennis who knew or should have known of them, claimed they didn't exist. The well-informed Clovis Maksoud and the Albannas, with their ties to the United States and other governments, either professed unbelievable ignorance or said nothing. Yet they were and are willing to speak on almost any subject regarding the Middle East.

Somehow, there was always a "responsibility to protect," either secrecy or people, in Agency jargon, "R2P," yet, somehow, the US government hid what it was doing and concealed the real results. This resulted in almost no "protection."

In Libya, for example, more people died and more infrastructure was destroyed by attacks from American, British, and French warplanes than would have died or been destroyed if the new colonialists had stayed home. Yet, America's tame press never published this information.

"Secrecy" harms everyone. I once had a client on an entirely different matter, persecuted by the FBI and Justice Department for seeking information on the welfare and whereabouts of a close relative. The Justice Department, specifically Assistant US Attorneys Harvey E. Eisenberg and Jason Weinstein, along with their FBI friends, relentlessly harassed the client, her husband, and her mother, eventually driving them out of the country. According to

---

[403] *Washington Report on Middle East Affairs*, March/April 2014, 58.

what journalist Scott Armstrong told me at the time, one branch of the government likely had the client's relative for whom they were searching, but hadn't bothered to tell the rest of the alphabet soup about its prisoner.[404]

"Secrecy" certainly harmed me. The federal government never told me why it fired me. It never told me why I, despite my qualifications, could not find a job for three years. It never told me why my attempts to learn what had happened got classed as a threat to "national security," a concept used, more often than not, to hide corruption, mismanagement, and abuse of authority, if not murder, war crimes, and human rights violations.

"Secrecy" certainly covered how so-called progressives ignored me and my writing. (I was, on occasion, told that some people actually believed I worked for the CIA, despite the harm Langley did to my career at State and my utter contempt for its activities.) Although personally known to people opposing the out-of-control intelligence services, I learn about their activities, meetings, and receptions only from the daily newspaper. Initially able to publish articles with ease on the Internet, I suddenly found that few, if any, organizations had an interest in what I wrote. (Paul Craig Roberts, a far more accomplished individual than I, once noted that he had been almost completely frozen out of the mainstream media.)

In the past, CIA "Secrecy" was not seen as a good thing. Mel Goodman wrote a glowing article for *CounterPunch* about the history of the Pike and Church Committees investigating CIA assassinations of Third World leaders and the Agency's engaging in "regime change."[405] The committees looked deeply into COINTELPRO. (This was an FBI and CIA program to monitor, manipulate, and disrupt domestic social and political activities in the 1960s, much

---

[404] J. Michael Springmann, "Email Spying and Attorney Client Privilege—US Government Reads All About It," *CounterPunch*, March 29, 2004.
[405] "The Congressman Who Exposed Covert Crimes," January 22, 2014.

like what was recently done to the Occupy Movement). At one point, the Committees noted that such actions, even if directed at known criminals, would have been intolerable in a democratic society.

However, despite his experience as CIA division chief and senior analyst in the Office of Soviet Affairs from 1976 to 1986, Goodman professed to me no knowledge of what went on in Afghanistan and the Middle East during and after Carter's Proxy War against the Soviet Union. Given his position, he should have had a wealth of pertinent knowledge and contacts. He certainly used some of that to draft another *CounterPunch* article. In it, he remarked that "CIA's support for the anti-Soviet mujahideen in the 1980s proved particularly damaging because the mujahideen provided weaponry to fuel conflicts in the Balkans and the Sudan and trained the terrorists who would attack us at home, including the bombing of the World Trade Center in 1993."[406]

The US Department of State and the CIA, while greatly prizing such individuals as Kathy Hennessey, Andy Weber, Karen Sasahara, Henry Ensher, and Greta Holtz, had no regard for people such as myself—those of us who thought, who analyzed, who questioned, and who engaged other cultures. Indeed, any employee who showed initiative at State somehow didn't make it. The kind of mentoring, training, and tutelage that well-run organizations normally use to improve their workforce is not found at State or in its consulates and embassies around the world.

The Department of State, the intelligence services and the politicians who allegedly control them, certainly have a remarkably poor track record. Spooks manipulating foreign policy is a guarantee of disaster. Look at Afghanistan, the Balkans, Iraq, Libya, and Syria (if not Pakistan and Yemen). America, a country of supposed "democratic values" seems to have a history of supporting repressive governments and overthrowing those of nontotalitarian states. Yet, the

---

[406] "Blowback and the Cycle of Violence," April 26, 2013.

clearly biased propaganda that supports these policies always depicts the despots as "allies" who are "Western oriented" with "democratic" or, at least, "representative" governments. Somehow, these "allies" oppose variously oriented "Axes of Evil" without permitting any sort of free and open societies at home, viz. Saudi Arabia, Bahrain, Qatar, and Israel. In America's lexicon, persecution, religious fanaticism, and violence are the hallmarks of countries and governments, usually Arab and/or Muslim, that need regime change. The fawning corporate mainstream media happily repeat the lines given them, such as "the Free Syrian Army" or the "Kosovo Liberation Army" who are battling the "insurgents" engaged in mass atrocities and uncountable Viagra-fueled rapes. America and its allies have a "clear responsibility to protect (R2P)" those resisting the "freedom fighters."

As journalist Wayne Madsen mentioned, to achieve this, the United States, the United Kingdom, Canada, Australia, and New Zealand have combined psychological operations with their electronic deception programs, particularly on the World Wide Web.

> These include alias development and masquerading (which includes the employment of "sock puppet" personae already in use by the US military to disrupt and influence the Internet), mass messaging (or spamming) and "call bombing" [jamming a phone with myriad calls], propaganda, and "pushing stories." These tactics have been refined since the CIA and its George Soros-financed nongovernmental organization activist allies brought about the "Arab Spring" overthrow of governments in Egypt, Tunisia, Libya, and Yemen, as well as the bloody civil war in Syria.[407]

---

[407] *Waynemadsenreport.com*, "British GCHQ uses Tavistock mass mind control techniques in cyberspace," February 26–27, 2014.

H. G. Wells wrote *War of the Worlds*. No one, beyond George Soros (Hungarian-born multibillionaire) and Victoria Nuland (former career FSO, now Assistant Secretary of State for European and Eurasian Affairs), seem to know who is writing *War of the Words*.

Political Costs

The *War of the Words* hasn't been too favorable to the United States. It's not hard to see why. In a 2013 Pew Research poll on global attitudes toward America, countries receiving Uncle Sam's money (but not the business end of his weapons) love the United States. Israel, the Philippines, Ghana, Kenya, Senegal, and South Korea rate America highly (above 75 percent). While Iraq, Afghanistan, Serbia, and Syria were not covered, some Arab and Muslim states were. At the bottom of the pile, Pakistan, target of drones, had an 11 percent favorable view of the United States. Egypt, and the Palestinian Prison Camp, along with Jordan, had ratings approving the United States ranging only from 14 percent to 16 percent. In a 2009 Gallup poll of Syria, just 15 percent of the population held a positive opinion of America. In that same questionnaire, Serbia clocked in at 14 percent, but Libyans were not polled. According to an undated BBC online survey:

> **United Arab Emirates:** Views of the United States in the UAE are quite unfavorable, with a solid majority (57 percent) saying they have a mostly negative view of US influence in the world, and just one in four (25 percent) says they have a mainly positive view. Emirates have largely negative views of the United States on its foreign policy issues, though they are somewhat less negative than other publics in the region. Four in five disapprove of US handling of the Israel-Hezbollah conflict (81 percent), the war in Iraq

(80 percent)...Emirates clearly see the US military presence as a destabilizing factor in the Middle East: 66 percent says the United States is provoking more conflict than it prevents, and only 17 percent says it is a stabilizing force.

Lebanon: Lebanese views of the United States remain largely negative. A majority (58 percent) sees the US influence in the world as mainly negative, while about one-third (34 percent) sees it as mainly positive. Attitudes about US foreign policy are unfavourable across most areas and mirror those of neighbouring Arab republics. Overwhelming majorities disapprove of the US handling of the war in Iraq (90 percent), the Israel-Hezbollah war (82 percent)...Respondents in Lebanon decidedly see the US military presence in the Middle East as provoking more conflict than it prevents, with more than three-quarters (77 percent) holding this view.

Syrians and Libyans were not surveyed. Neither were Iraqis or Afghans. Kevin Drum clearly explains negative assessments of America: "We've launched a significant overseas assault every 40 months since 1963."[408] This means:

> **...if you're wondering why people all over the world view the United States as an arrogant bully, reserving for itself the right to rain down death from above on anyone it pleases whenever it pleases, well there you go.** [Emphasis in original.] It doesn't matter whether

---

[408] *Mother Jones Review*, "How the Rest of the World Views the American Military," August 29, 2013.

you think some or even all of those actions were completely justified and morally defensible. From here, we tend to look at each of these engagements in isolation, asking whether there are good reasons to go in and whether we can accomplish important goals for ourselves and others. But when a new American military campaign begins, people in the rest of the world see it in this broader historical context.

This is a perspective that's sorely missing from most mainstream discourse. Too many Americans have a seriously blinkered view of our interventions overseas, viewing them as one-offs to be evaluated on their individual merits. But when these things happen once every three years, against a backdrop of almost continuous smaller-scale military action (drone attacks, the odd cruise missile here and there, sending "advisers" over to help an ally, etc.), the rest of the world just doesn't see it that way. They don't see a peaceful country that struggles mightily with its conscience and only occasionally makes a decision to drop a bunch of bombs. They see a country that views dropping bombs as its primary means of dealing with any country weaker than we are.

Add to Mr. Drum's remarks the effects of the Arab-Afghan Legion, and you will better put justifiable hatred of America in the proper perspective.

American politicians in their arrogance and American voters in their ignorance have destroyed not only major portions of the world and the peoples therein, they have cost the United States its ability to accomplish any goal without the use of force. America does not have any concept of its own interests or those of other countries and cannot figure out any way to reconcile them. This is largely because the Department of State itself does not know what these interests are or how to reconcile them. Diplomacy is not "the art of letting the other fellow have your way" (written on a brass plaque in the Henry Lawson Bar at the Australian High Commission in New Delhi). Nor is it "saying the nastiest things in the most pleasant way possible," as a Frenchwoman, Irène Goyeau-Laurens, remarked. It is, rather, "the conduct of relations between states based on tact and common sense." [409] No democracy can conduct worldwide terrorism campaigns using a war budget greater than any country on earth. (The "peace-loving" United States accounts for almost half, 39 percent of all military expenditures by all countries on the globe).[410] According to the *Washington Post*'s story about data released by Edward Snowden, the alleged total budget for espionage was $52.6 billion for fiscal 2013.[411] (The *Post* said it withheld an unknown amount of information from the story at the US government's request).

One contact, an Arab American attorney, suggested that US citizens reexamine the federal Constitution and the concept of democracy. He advised that, in light of an out-of-control government that goes to war around the world justified solely by lies, false pretenses, and politicized "intelligence," democracy is in peril. If government actions are grounded on information supplied by an alphabet soup of supersecretive spy agencies, a dictatorship is clearly in the offing. Unchecked, unexamined power, ignored by the US corporate-controlled mainstream media as well as by the citizenry itself, permits disasters to flourish, criminals to hide, and fraud, mismanagement, and abuse of authority to go unpunished. The

---

[409] I found this wonderful phrase written under the glass top of my desk in Stuttgart.

[410] Anup Shah, "World Military Spending," June 30, 2013, *globalissues.org.*

[411] Barton Gelman and Greg Miller, "U.S. spy networks' successes, failures, and objectives detailed in 'black budget' summary," August 29, 2013.

woefully abused American concept of secrecy appears designed to hide, "gover-up," and condone illegal and unconstitutional behavior, such as the recruitment, training, and implementation of the Arab-Afghan Legion.

If the federal Constitution had not been abolished by Barack Obama and his predecessors, and if the Congress were not so corrupt, incompetent, and illegitimate, the solution would be simple. Implement Article II, Section 4 of America's Basic Law:

> The President, Vice President and all civil officers of the United States, shall be removed from office on impeachment for, and conviction of, treason, bribery, or other high crimes and misdemeanors.

Material Costs

According to the *News Pakistan*,[412] Sabir Shah wrote a summary of Harvard's Kennedy School of Government analysis of what happens when the US imperial wars are costed out.

> The decade-long American wars in Afghanistan and Iraq would end up costing as much as $6 trillion, the equivalent of $75,000 for every American household...

> The Iraq and Afghanistan conflicts, taken together, will be the most expensive wars in US history—totaling somewhere between $4 trillion and $6 trillion. This includes long-term medical care and disability compensation for service members, veterans and

---

[412] September 20, 2013; reprinted in *Global Research* September 20, 2013.

families, military replenishment and social and economic costs. The largest portion of that bill is yet to
be paid.

Another major share of the long-term costs of the
wars comes from paying off trillions of dollars in debt
incurred as the US government failed to include their
cost in annual budgets and simultaneously implemented sweeping tax cuts for the rich. In addition,
huge expenditures are being made to replace military
equipment used in the two wars.

Shah added: "The authors of this report have warned that the
legacy of decisions taken during the Iraq and Afghanistan wars
would dominate future federal budgets for decades to come." What
was omitted from this report were the costs to the Afghans and Iraqis
of these wars. No words were directed toward the expenses of the
wars in the Balkans, Libya, and Syria, either. However, Libya was
"cheap" according to the *Daily Beast*, at "only" one billion dollars. [413]

What is usually omitted from the puffery of the American mili-
tarists, unchained spooks, neoconservatives, and their supporters in
the "fawning corporate media" is how far "only" one billion would
go toward rebuilding a failed United States.

First, there is health care for the forty-seven million uninsured
or underinsured Americans (2012 numbers. Obamacare deals
only with about seven million people, many already protected.).
According to the Kaiser Family Foundation, covering those forty-
seven million at an annual, individual cost of $5,884 would total
nearly $277 billion. [414] That's a lot of money, but it's still considerably
less than the price tag for the Afghanistan and Iraq wars plus the

---

[413] John Barry, "America's Secret Libya War," August 30, 2011.
[414] Confirmed by Jennifer Dornan, *AFL-CIO*, October 14, 2014.

unknown costs of continued fighting in Libya and Syria, and against the allegedly "new" enemy, ISIS/ISIL/IS, in Iraq.

Next, here are some costs for refurbishing the United States' collapsing infrastructure from an American Society of Civil Engineers 2013 estimate. Compare them with the money wasted on recruiting training, and implementing the Arab-Afghan Legion in Afghanistan, the Balkans, Iraq, Libya, and Syria:

> The Association of State Dam Safety Officials estimates that it will require an investment of $21 billion to repair...aging, yet critical, high-hazard dams.

> There are an estimated 240,000 water main breaks per year in the United States. Assuming every pipe would need to be replaced, the cost over the coming decades could reach more than $1 trillion, according to the American Water Works Association (AWWA).

> The Federal Highway Administration (FHWA) estimates that to eliminate the nation's bridge backlog by 2028, we would need to invest $20.5 billion annually, while only $12.8 billion is being spent currently...

> However, 42 percent of America's major urban highways remain congested, costing the economy an estimated $101 billion in wasted time and fuel annually...Currently, the Federal Highway Administration estimates that $170 billion in capital investment would be needed on an annual basis to significantly improve conditions and performance.

What kind of mental process is needed to ignore the great funds required to repair a crumbling or broken foundation in favor of continual war in the Balkans and Middle East, using the Arab-Afghan Legion as proxy?

It's Curious, Is It Not?

For more than ten years, the United States of America, an allegedly free and democratic country interested only in peace, has been spending billions of dollars annually to destabilize and break up weak, impoverished lands.

First, there was Afghanistan, used as a means of disintegrating the Soviet Union. Jimmy Carter, who, according to his online biography at the Jimmy Carter Presidential Library and Museum website, championed human rights throughout the world, and Zbigniew Brzezinski, the would-be Polish "nobleman," recruited and trained terrorists. Subsequent administrations sent them across the Amu Darya river to split the Muslim Socialist Republics from the USSR—and thereby weakened a multiethnic state with its own internal tensions. These men knew full well that the Soviet Union had never fought the United States; it had only sought to thwart its influence around the world. Russians today well remember American efforts to destroy communism (and a weak, embattled USSR) between 1918 and 1920. Nearly thirteen thousand US soldiers fought the legitimate government of the Soviet Union near Archangel and Murmansk and in Siberia at the behest of President Woodrow Wilson (D-NJ). Moreover, some American history books fail to recount the martyrdom of between twenty million and thirty million of the USSR's people during World War II.

The American government ignores the past, present, and future. History appears to be something that happens somewhere else.

Realizing that the Afghan Legion engaged to fight the Soviets in Central Asia could be profitably employed elsewhere, the United States, supposedly a constitutionally based, federal republic with a strong democratic tradition, deployed them in socialist Yugoslavia, another weak state with internal ethnic and political tensions. Aiming at undermining Soviet influence in Europe and gaining control over oil and gas routes through the Balkans, the Americans, with the aid of their client states Germany and Britain, successfully used the Arab-Afghan Legion's assassins and saboteurs to dismember Yugoslavia, asserting that closer ties to Europe and the United States would be beneficial. To successfully demolish the country, turning it into wrecked statelets, they induced Slovenia and Croatia, the more industrialized and economically advanced sections, to break away and declare their independence. A provoked -war split Bosnia into several pieces and Kosovo was removed through bloody fighting.[415]

Seeing another "enemy" in Iraq, and correctly viewing the possibilities of causing splits between and among the Kurds, the Sunni, and the Shii, the United States, using dubious pretexts, twice invaded the country, in 1991 and 2003. Although the Americans successfully used the Legion to divide the three groups, Iraq still remained more or less unified for another decade. Only after the Legion's second wave of bombings, murders, and destruction beginning in the summer of 2014 has there been talk of the Kurdish north declaring itself independent (with the aid of Turkish oil purchases and Israeli influence). Now, after years of American-stimulated uproar in Iraq, the UN High Commission for Refugees (UNHCR) estimated in January 2014 that there are still one million internally displaced Iraqis, as well as nearly five hundred thousand asylees and refugees from Mesopotamia. Additionally, with conflict in Syria, perhaps US-instigated, there are

---

[415] Michael Parenti, "The Rational Destruction of Yugoslavia," www.michaelparenti.org.
Michel Chossudovsky, "Dismantling Former Yugoslavia, Recolonizing Bosnia-Herzegovina," Feb. 19, 2002, globalresearch.ca.

an additional three hundred and fifty thousand refugees from there in Iraq, along with sixty thousand or so returned Iraqi refugees, presumably from Syria and other neighboring countries where conditions, because of American actions, have gone from bad to worse.

US policy had caused most of the educated and middle-class, the doctors, lawyers, and the Iraqi equivalent of Indian chiefs, to leave Iraq—permanently. These are the individuals whom no country can afford to lose and still progress. The American intent was to ensure the complete destruction of both the material and immaterial aspects of Iraq, to dehouse, deculturalize, destabilize, and destroy the country. After all, which nation is stronger? And which nation, with five thousand years of recorded history, invented the wheel and writing?

As for Libya, while it was not riven by ethnic and/or religious tensions, it was still a weak state. According to a State Department orientation I had attended at FSI, the country's principal export, prior to the discovery and development of its oil resources, had been scrap metal left over from military operations during World War II. The country's 2010 population of 6,351,112 (World Bank) was 97 percent Berber and Arab while its religion is 96.6 percent Sunni Muslim.[416] Far from having a mighty military, Libya, the fourth largest country in Africa, had an army that seemed, at least on paper, to be inadequate for even keeping order over its 1,759,540 square kilometers (679,362 square miles, slightly larger than Alaska or seven times the size of the United Kingdom; with a population density of about 3.5 people per square kilometer):

> By 2002 the Libyan Army numbered some 45,000 men, including 25,000–40,000 draftees. Recent years saw the army undermined by the rise to power of the 40,000-strong Revolutionary Guard. The army

---

[416] *CIA World Factbook.*

had been further weakened by having been disorganized into the "People's Guard"...By 2010 the Libyan Army numbered some 50,000 men, including 25,000 draftees. It also possesse[d] some 40,000 reserves organized into a People's Militia.[417]

So, Libya was a good country to attack and invade, using NATO warplanes, spooks, and the Arab-Afghan Legion.

Syria was, too.

In 2010, the IMF estimated the Syrian population to be about 21,016,000, spread over 185,180 square kilometers, that is, 71,498 square miles (slightly larger than North Dakota; WorldAtlas. com), with roughly 112 people per square kilometer (UN Data). Indexmundi.com, citing the *CIA World Factbook*, added that there were about nineteen thousand Israeli colonists in Syria's Golan Heights. With an armed forces paper strength of one hundred ten thousand men, Syrian military strength does not really compare with that of its enemies:[418]

- 1,369,000 USA
- 633,000 Israel
- 150,000 Saudi Arabia
- 130,000 France
- 127,000 United Kingdom

Nor does it compare with the estimated one hundred thousand opposition fighters seeking the overthrow of Syria's government.[419]

The largest sector of Syria's economy has been agriculture, followed by oil, industry, and tourism, sectors not really hard to disrupt with modern weapons and strategy.[420]

---

[417] *globalsecurity.org.*

[418] Ibid..

[419] *BBC Middle East News*, December 13, 2013.

[420] US Department of State, *Background Notes* (Syria).

In sum, then, the United States of America, backed by its population of 318,500,000 (US Bureau of the Census), has waged total war on the people of Afghanistan (15,300,000 in 1980, from indexmundi.com); Yugoslavia (23,842,000 in 1990, from theodora.com); Iraq (24,683,000 in 2003, from indexmundi.com); and Syria (21,016,000 in 2010, from the IMF).

There is definitely a disparity in power and influence, especially given the resources provided to the Arab-Afghan Legion on top of American arms, weapons, and funds. In 2009, the World Bank said Afghanistan's gross national income per capita was US$460; Yugoslavia's $3,600 (from kushnirs.org); Iraq's US$4,030; Libya's US$12,930; and Syria's US$4,600 (from indexmundi.com). GDP per capita in the United States in 2009 was US$48,040 (World Bank). The story of David and Goliath has been turned round and stood on its head.

Quo vadimus? (Where Are We Going?)

In a July 23, 2014, conversation with a knowledgeable journalist, we discussed where the United States is going next. Since Afghanistan, Iraq, Libya, and Syria are finished as nation-states for the foreseeable future, the correspondent opined that there are still targets of opportunity for America, particularly Tunisia and Algeria, and, possibly, Jordan. That's right. Tunisia, where the "Arab Spring" started, has bountiful "militant Islamists". Algeria is lumbered with its problematic economy as well as absolute military and presidential political control. Henry Ensher, who helped destroy Iraq, has been US Ambassador to Algeria since 2011. Jordan, while profiting from the American war against Syria and the destruction of Iraq, has a large, discontented population of Palestinians who, now, at least, contain their intense dislike of the monarchy. In my view, while Morocco has been a staunch supporter of American policy, it does not seem to have been harmed by that and, in the event of a democratic movement, would likely be supported by the other repressive monarchies to the east. Oman's oil reserves, its main economic prop, are declining while, politically, concentration of power in the Sultan and an unwillingness to allow citizen participation or dialogue play into the hands of the opposition.[421] Additionally, Greta Holtz, American Ambassador since 2012, is there to give the Omanis what she learned in Jeddah and practiced in Iraq, where she was Minister-Counselor for Provincial Affairs and ran the Provincial Reconstruction Teams. Yemen, of course, has been successfully destabilized for years, and Egypt is firmly under the rule of the US-backed military dictatorship.

And then, there is Iran.

Isaiah has the last word:

> Derelinquit impius viam suam
> et vir iniquus cogitationes suas…
> (Let the wicked forsake his way and
> the unrighteous man his thoughts…)
> (Isaiah 55: 7. Third Responsory at
> Matins for the First Sunday in Lent in
> the Roman and Sarum Rites.)

The End

---

[421] Mark N. Katz, "Assessing the Political Stability of Oman," George Mason University, 2004.

BIBLIOGRAPHY

Ahmed, Nafeez Mosaddeq. *The War On Freedom.* Joshua Tree, CA: Tree of Life Publications, 2002.

——. *The War On Truth.* Northampton, MA: Olive Branch Press, 2005.

Armstrong, David, and Joseph Trento. *America and the Islamic Bomb.* Hanover, NH: Steerforth Press, 2007.

Bergen, Peter L. *The Osama bin Laden I Know.* New York: Free Press, 2006.

Blum, William. *Killing Hope, U.S. Military and CIA Interventions Since World War II.* Monroe, ME: Common Courage Press, 2004.

Coll, Steve. *Ghost Wars.* New York: Penguin Books, 2004.

Cooley, John. *Unholy Wars: Afghanistan, America, and International Terrorism.* London: Pluto Press, 1999.

Dreyfuss, Robert. *Devil's Game, How the U.S. Helped Unleash Fundamentalist Islam.* New York: Metropolitan Books/Henry Holt, 2005.

Forte, Maximilian C. *Slouching Towards Sirte, NATO's War on Libya and Africa.* Montreal: Baraka Books, 2012.

Global Research (Center for Research on Globalization). www.globalresearch.org

Grayling, A. C. *Among The Dead* Cities. New York: Walker & Co, 2006.

Hegghammer, Thomas. "The Risk of Muslim Foreign Fighters— Islam and the Globalization of Jihad." *International Security* 35, no. 3 (Winter 2010/11).

Hopsicker, Daniel. *Welcome to Terrorland, Mohammed Atta & the 9-11 Cover-Up in Florida.* Venice, FL: The MadCow Press, 2004.

Jacoby, Susan. *The Age of American Unreason.* New York: Pantheon Books, 2008.

Kreig, Andrew. *Presidential Puppetry, Obama, Romney, and Their Masters.* Washington, DC: Eagle View Books, 2013.

Kyle, Chris. *American Gun; A History of the U.S. in Ten Firearms.* William Morrow, NY: Publisher, 2004.

Lance, Peter. *Triple Cross.* New York: Harper Collins, 2006.

MacKenzie, Angus. *Secrets, The CIA's War At Home.* Berkeley, CA: University of California Press, 1998.

Madsen, Wayne. *The Manufacturing of a President*. LuLu.com, 2014.

Parenti, Michael. *The Sword And The Dollar, Imperialism, Revolution, and the Arms Race*. New York: St. Martin's Press, 1989.

Pope, Nick. *Encounter in Rendlesham Forest*. With John Burroughs and Jim Penniston, New York: Thomas Dunne Books, 2014.

Ryan, Kevin Robert. *Another 19, Investigating Legitimate 9/11 Suspects*. n.p.: Microbloom, 2013.

Schindler, John R. *Unholy Terror: Bosnia, Al-Qa'ida, and the Rise of Global Jihad*. St. Paul: Zenith Press, 2007.

Scott, Peter Dale. *The Road to 9/11*. Berkeley, CA: University of California Press, 2007.

Stone, Oliver, and Peter Kuznick. *The Untold History of the United States*. New York: Gallery Books, 2012.

Trento, Joseph. *Prelude to Terror*. New York: Carroll & Graf, 2005.

Unger, Craig. *House of Bush, House of Saud, The Secret Relationship Between the World's Two Most Powerful Families*. New York: Scribner, 2004.

Wayne Madsen Report. www.waynemadsenreport.com.

Webb, Gary. *Dark Alliance*. New York: Seven Stories Press, 1998.

The World Factbook 2013–14. Washington, DC: Central Intelligence Agency, 2013.

INDEX

www.ingramcontent.com/pod-product-compliance
Lightning Source LLC
Chambersburg PA
CBHW062203270326
41930CB00009B/1637